NOT
THE CENTER
OF THE
UNIVERSE

NOT
THE CENTER
OF THE
UNIVERSE

A Yearly Devotional for Those
in Christian Ministry

REV. JOHN P. WORRALL

PUBLISHING
Charleston, SC
www.PalmettoPublishing.com

Copyright © 2024 by Rev. John P. Worrall

All rights reserved.

No portion of this book may be reproduced, stored in a retrieval system, or transmitted in any form by any means–electronic, mechanical, photocopy, recording, or other–except for brief quotations in printed reviews, without prior permission of the author.

Paperback ISBN: 979-8-8229-4722-1
eBook ISBN: 979-8-8229-4723-8

INTRODUCTION

"NOT the Center of the Universe" certainly piques your interest as to what this little book may contain. Obviously, that was my purpose, but it is a phrase I use often when dealing with those who do not know me.

When waiting in a line, most people are anxious to get their time to be the one being helped. I have expressed my share of frustration over having to wait. But one day, Father reminded me that the person serving me is more than likely a person of good will. They are doing their best and deserve my understanding, not my frustration. I need to be Jesus to them. Perhaps this will lead to an opportunity to share the Gospel. At the very least my attitude can honor my Father.

I am not a know it all. I do not have an inexhaustible supply of wisdom, but Jesus does, and He asked me to share what I have been given. I said, "Yes, Lord." You will certainly have mixed feelings about what I share. I am OK with that. I pray that you may find something that helps you and something that you can freely share.

Keep Looking Up!

Your friend,

John

JANUARY 1

The Love of a Friend

PROVERBS 17:17
A friend loves at all times, and a brother is born for adversity.

PROVERBS 18:24
A man that has friends must show himself friendly: and there is a friend that sticks closer than a brother.

Do you have a good friend? Father has granted me the true friendship of several godly men. My prayer is that I would always be as true to them as Jesus is to me.

Just a short while ago, Father gave me two tremendous opportunities of joy! The first was the opportunity to lead in the ordination service of my second son. The second was to meet face to face with a friend I had not seen for 53 years. My father had become the pastor of a church in Western New York. There, I met my friend, and we soon became inseparable. We sang together, worked together on the church's radio broadcast, created a "masterpiece" of comedy, and rode our bikes everywhere! He loved the Lord Jesus as much as I and we encouraged one another!

But things were changing at the church, new people were coming in and those "in power" were afraid of losing their positions. My father was forced out of his responsibility, and the biggest loss for me was that my friend's parents told him to break off his relationship with me. We parted, with weeping and prayer.

A few years ago, we connected on FaceBook, which led to our meeting at my son's ordination service. My friend has faithfully served the King, and he and his lovely wife have raised their children to love and serve our Master.

It was such a joy to hug this man and know that the years have not removed the union we have in Christ. Jesus has held us together. He will for eternity.

JANUARY 2

Not Everyone Belongs on the Bus.

2 SAMUEL 20:4-5
Then said the king to Amasa, Assemble the men of Judah within three days, and you be here. So Amasa went to assemble the men of Judah: but he tarried longer than the set time which he had appointed him.

ACTS 15:38
But Paul thought not good to take him (John Mark) with them, who departed from them from Pamphylia, and went not with them to the work.

PROVERBS 26:6
He that sends a message by the hand of a fool cuts off the feet, and drinks damage.

You might think I am "cherry picking" verses to prove a point. Well, you are right, but that doesn't change the truth. Some people do not fit in the place where they landed. Father knows why.

Some, like Amasa, don't understand being under authority or the urgency and importance of the task given to them. Their failure is dangerous.

Others are not ready to lead. They do not grasp what it means to sacrifice for the Kingdom. Praise God, Mark finally got it, but Paul wasn't the guy to teach him. You may not be the Shepherd they need.

Then there is the time you confused someone's interest and enthusiasm for the ability to carry out the simplest of tasks. This is certainly a painful situation we all have experienced.

Everyone needs the love of Jesus and as His servant, you must love what Jesus loves. However, some need His love from a different shepherd. Caring for them is not in your skill set. I am not giving you a formula, nor an excuse, just an observation.

JANUARY 3

You Cannot Talk to Dead People

EPHESIANS 2:1
And you has *He quickened*, who were dead in trespasses and sins.

ROMANS 3:11
There is none that understands, there is none that seeks after God.

This thought is not original to me. I was a teen when I heard this illustration: "You have the best, hot, fresh pizza that you can imagine, and you bring it to a Funeral Home during the viewing of a dead friend. Gauche as it may seem, you bring the pie to the side of the coffin, wave it in your friend's face, (it was his favorite) and there is no reaction. He is dead to this world."

You probably don't like my illustration, but you may remember it. We have the greatest message for all the world, but everyone is dead to it. They cannot respond because they are dead, and God says they are not interested.

We know we are commanded to *"Go and make disciples."* We also understand that people will respond to the Gospel Message. But we seem to forget that we are just messenger boys; your skill in communication will never change a heart. It is the Holy Spirit that does all the work of Redemption. **(John 16:8)** *And when he is come, he will reprove the world of sin, and of righteousness, and of judgment.* The Holy Spirit convicts us of our sinful condition. He convinces us of our need for Christ. It is His ability that conveys people into the Kingdom of God.

My responsibility is to know Christ and His goodness and prepare my mind and my life to be a testimony of His grace. **(Acts 4:20)** *For we cannot but speak the things which we have seen and heard.*

And I must be available. **(Isa. 6:8b)** *Then said I, here am I; send me.* You may not need this reminder, but I do. I cannot talk to dead people, but Jesus does it all the time.

JANUARY 4

Who Prepared You for Service?

LEVITICUS 8:30

And Moses took of the anointing oil, and of the blood, which was upon the altar, and sprinkled it upon Aaron, and upon his garments, and upon his sons, and upon his sons' garments with him; and sanctified Aaron, and his garments, and his sons, and his sons' garments with him.

Father called me into "full time" ministry at the age of 17. My father was a pastor, and well-meaning adults would ask me, "Are you going to be a preacher, like your daddy?" I quickly replied, "No, I am going to be an architect." If my parents were nearby, they often interjected, "We want him to be whatever Father wants him to be" – and they meant that.

I did have preparation for service. My mother would often say that the family motto was, "R.F.A. – *ready for anything*." It meant that I needed to be prepared to act and react to the circumstances that might be a surprise, opportunity, or a disappointment; and respond as a Worrall.

God chose Aaron and his sons to be the representatives for the entire nation in His Tabernacle. The preparation for this ministry literally took the whole nation's free will offerings, gifted craftsmen, and Moses. Moses was charged with, instructing, cleansing, dressing, and consecrating these men for that vital service.

I am sure that your calling was as personal as mine. You came to the conclusion that God wanted you to serve Him in a special way. I want you to ponder the process that Father used to bring you to where you are today. God used lots of people, good and bad, to bring you to the day when you said, "Yes, Lord." There might have been a Moses on the way, but your preparation was far more than the formal education you depend upon. I am glad my parents supported me but never controlled my choices. Who is your Moses? Are you a Moses for someone else?

JANUARY 5

Made an Asa Out of Me

2 CHRONICLES 16:7-9

… Hanani the seer came to Asa king of Judah, and said unto him, Because you have relied on the king of Syria, and not relied on the LORD your God, therefore is the host of the king of Syria escaped out of your hand. Were not the Ethiopians and the Lubims a huge host, with very many chariots and horsemen? yet, because you relied on the LORD, he delivered them into your hand. For the eyes of the LORD run to and fro throughout the whole earth, to show himself strong in the behalf of them whose heart is perfect toward him. Herein you have done foolishly: therefore, from henceforth you shall have wars.

No one ever does everything right all the time, but there are some things that can turn us into fools. "Fool" is a strong word. David gave us an understanding of the word in – **(Ps. 14:1a)** *The fool has said in his heart, there is no God.* You may respond, *"I am a child of God, I am not a fool."* However, we have all have played the fool when we choose to ignore or deny God's full control. I have been foolish, but I didn't stay that way!

Asa was a good man, a good king, but he allowed the circumstances to control his thinking, and fear to direct his actions. He had experienced the character of God in previous circumstances and saw God keep His word in a supernatural way that protected Judah. But when he faced a minor threat, it turned faith into fear, and he sought his own way out. There are always consequences when we ignore God. What Asa should have done was repent, but he "doubles down" **(v10)**, throws the Prophet into jail and turns nasty toward the people he was to protect. They probably expressed their opinion about the king's poor choices.

This is a cautionary tale. Don't let fear take the lead. You know your Father is faithful and His word is true. Do not allow pride to rule. You make mistakes!

Use *(1 John 1:9)* and don't be an Asa.

JANUARY 6

When You Cut Down, Be Ready to Plant

LUKE 11:24-26

When the unclean spirit is gone out of a man, he walks through dry places, seeking rest; and finding none, he says, I will return unto my house where I came out. And when he returns, he finds it swept and garnished. Then he goes in and takes with him seven other spirits more wicked than himself; and they enter in, and dwell there: and the last state of that man is worse than the first.

If it is foggy in the pulpit, it comes over as pure mud in the pews. You may be stirred up about wrong and failure, but if you are not prepared to offer an answer or solution – keep your mouth shut.

We never do anyone a favor in exposing their need and failure if we do not give them help and hope. On the Day of Pentecost, the Holy Spirit took a brief sermon and brought great conviction. The people cried out, *"Men and Brethren, what shall we do?"* Peter gave them the answer and they responded to life!

Our message is not one of reformation to a lost world, for they are dead in their sin! As Jesus tells us, a "rit-up" house (Western PA, for a house cleaning!) only invites greater spiritual loss. The house needs a new owner! I have observed many a religious transformation that produced an individual bound by legalism and religious activity. They replaced socially unacceptable behavior for ritualistic bondage. We all need the liberty found only in Jesus ***(John 8:36.)***

We know that the "Goodness of God leads us to repentance" ***(Romans 2:4.)*** Let us preach repentance toward God and faith toward our Lord Jesus Christ. We must be prepared to give men hope and a way out of the pit. Do not warn about the pit without bringing the right ladder to help them out. Do not attack their failure and not have a way to lead them to success. Do not cut things down, and not be ready to plant! Yes, it is a process, but do the work - or keep your mouth shut!

JANUARY 7

Son of Man

DANIEL 7:13-14

*I saw in the night visions, and behold, one like the **Son of man** came with the clouds of heaven, and came to the Ancient of days, and they brought Him near before Him. And there was given Him dominion, and glory, and a kingdom, that all people, nations, and languages, should serve Him: His dominion is an everlasting dominion, which shall not pass away, and His kingdom that which shall not be destroyed.*

This is the first time the title, *Son of Man*, is presented in prophetic scripture. Context will always determine the meaning. When the context refers to Jesus, it is as *The Anointed One*. He is the King who shall reign forever. Those familiar with the Prophets recognized this title and what it meant.

Jesus uses this title in all four Gospels when He is referring to His role. It is not an accident, and the meaning of this term is not lost on His enemies. Every time He uses it, He makes the point of His supremacy and the power to do what He purposes. He will challenge all that would oppose Him.

This truth is clearly presented in the key verse of (**Luke 19:10**) *For the Son of man is come to seek and to save that which was lost.*

Jesus will reign. Be sure to proclaim it.

JANUARY 8

Messiah, In "A Nutshell"

LUKE 4:17-19

And there was delivered unto Him the book of the prophet Isaiah. And when He had opened the book, He found the place where it was written, The Spirit of the Lord is upon Me, because He has anointed Me to preach the gospel to the poor; He has sent Me to heal the brokenhearted, to preach deliverance to the captives, and recovering of sight to the blind, to set at liberty them that are bruised, to preach the acceptable year of the Lord.

In the town where He grew up, Jesus was going to tell these folk what they did not want to hear. The rumors had gotten back to Nazareth of miracles and strange speeches but to read from the Scriptures what He read and then claim out loud, *"This day is the scripture fulfilled in your ears,"* that was too much!

The interesting thing about this passage was it was the "John 3:16" of that day. Those familiar with the text understood that the subject was the Messiah. Those who examined the Prophets and the Writings saw this passage from **(Isa. 61:1-3)** as a condensed presentation of all the information about *the Anointed One*. God had neatly put into "a nutshell!"

What is also interesting is where Jesus stops His reading. We would say it is in the middle of **(Isa. 61:2,)** before referring to the *Day of Vengeance*. This is because the rest of the passage speaks to His second coming as King. At that moment, as He sat in the synagogue, He was Prophet, speaking of His coming role as Priest.

As co-laborers with the Messiah, we are to be His reflection as Prophet, Priest, and King. Like Jesus, **(Luke 4:14,)** we need to be led by the Holy Spirit to know when to minister in these roles to those in our care.

JANUARY 9

Filing for Chapter 11

NUMBERS 11

[v1] And when the people complained, it displeased the LORD: ... [v11] And Moses said unto the LORD, why have you afflicted Your servant? .... [v15] (Moses) And if You deal this way with me, kill me, ... [v23] And the LORD said unto Moses, is the LORD'S hand waxed short? You will see now whether My word shall come to pass unto you or not.

Complaining always leads to spiritual and emotional bankruptcy. Israel complained and paid a stiff penalty. They didn't learn from the hard lesson and continued to complain about God's miraculous provision. This also didn't end too well.

Those you minister to can behave in the same way. They have *"the spiritual gift of grousing,"* and you will always be their target because you represent the Master.

Like Moses, your spiritual savings can become drained. The attack becomes heavy and happens so often that you want out and want out NOW! Your bankruptcy is around the corner.

You are not their Savior. The provision your people need is not in your limited reserve. Sometimes the drain on your spirit is just what you need. We trust in the promise that, *"I can do all things through Christ,"* but you cannot run from Pittsburgh to Dallas in two minutes. Father is working His plan and He has others to help. Your discovery of the help that Father will provide is a process. (Number 11:16 – the *gathering of 70 leaders to help.*) You must seek Father's will and ask for that help from others who love the Kingdom.

Admit your discouragement, be open to the process of seeking and accepting help and expect God to be GOD. He will do the miraculous, even to the removal of the spiritually gifted grousers.

Don't ask for the grouser to disappear, just trust His plan. He makes no mistake.

JANUARY 10

Do Not Give Up

LUKE 18:1
And He spoke a parable unto them to this end, that men ought always to pray, and not to faint.

The idea of a parable tells me that something is veiled in Jesus' message, but I take comfort in the fact that I am His own therefore, I have the inside track on His meaning.

Luke makes it clear, *unto this end.* This is the meaning!

1. I must continue in prayer. It is vital that I exercise my heart and mind in this purposeful process. I need to hear and know I am being heard. That is what the parable hammers into my heart. Prayer moves us past the circumstances into the reality of our Father's character and the content of His promises.

2. I must not give up. Give up what? Give up believing. Give up asking. Give up doing what I know is right. It is true, *"The only way evil will triumph is when enough good men do nothing."*

Many a fellow servant is ready to give up because the way is hard, and the disappointments are many. But we must listen to Jesus. He stated the absolute, and He tells me the life of faith is a life of prayer that rests not on positive thinking but what He declares is true.

Pray the Scriptures for they are true, and the God of truth will not break His Word.

*(**Titus 1:2**) In hope of eternal life, which God, **that cannot lie**, promised before the world began.*

JANUARY 11

Looks Good from Downtown!

PSALM 103:14
For He knows our frame: He remembers that we are dust.

In my second church, I met a man that became a father to me. His name was Tom Kerns. I was 25 when I was accepted as Pastor of the United Church and I *"took to Tom like a duck to water."*

He loved the Lord Jesus, and he chose to love me. He had been a carpenter by trade and part owner of a lumberyard. He could be described as a "Jack of all trades." There wasn't anything he wouldn't do for me and if I asked him to make or fix something, "he did it yesterday." He taught me how to think outside the box and gave me the basic understanding of how to build something that would last.

The stories I have of those wonderful years as his Pastor would fill many pages in this devotional, but one phrase he would use was, *"It looks good from downtown!"* For those not familiar with Western Pennsylvanian nomenclature this means, "that will do the job." It is not perfect, but it works.

Father knows me and loves me just the way I am. He is not done with me yet. Tom loved me as his Pastor, a VERY young Pastor! He willingly shared his life with me. He accepted what was my "best" at the time and valued it.

If you obsess over perfection, this is a message to you. Father isn't done with you yet. Yes, strive for the *"Good, better, best; never let it rest; till the good is better and the better best."* BUT please, since Father is so patient, try some patience on yourself and those around you. It is God's Grace that perfects, not personal effort.

JANUARY 12

Bookcase Elephants

PHILEMON 1:7
*For we have great joy and consolation in your love, because
the bowels of the saints are refreshed by you, brother.*

On one of my bookcases, serving me faithfully, are a pair of green marbled elephants. Presently they hold up my NISBE (if I must define it, you don't have one) and a few random files I have failed to return to their rightful place. These elephants remind me of the love and faithfulness of a dear sister, Joann Adams. She liked elephants!

When I met Joann, she and her husband Dave were faithful members of my new church family. I learned how faithful she was through observation. three times a day, Joann took a "meal-full" of pills, but she was in church every time the doors were open. Seeking privacy for her shots, she asked to use my office between Sunday School and worship, to which I willingly agreed.

She would pray for me regularly and encouraged me in my ministry. She and Dave would often take Alice and I out to dinner and she loved on my wife!

Finally, Father wanted her home, and she was ready. I needed something to comfort and remind me of my friend, so I asked Dave for an "elephant" and I got a pair.

I pray that Father provides you an "elephant lady," at least one. I do not ask for you to know the loss of parting but that you will know someone who will show you what a faithful friend looks like.

JANUARY 13

You Didn't Hold Your Tongue Right.

ECCLESIASTES 9:11
I returned, and saw under the sun, that the race is not to the swift, nor the battle to the strong, neither yet bread to the wise, nor yet riches to men of understanding, nor yet favor to men of skill; but time and chance happens to them all.

PROVERBS 16:33
The dice are cast into the lap; but the whole disposing thereof is of the LORD.

This is another "Tom Kerns" saying. It means that you don't know what went wrong, you can't explain it, or you are confused by the outcome. You have done this "ministry thing" many times but – this time the reaction or the results are not what you wanted!

The legalist would tell you that the fault is ultimately found in you. Either you disobeyed, or you were trusting in your experience, *"looking to their supplies,"* instead of trusting the Lord (See Joshua 9:14.) As far as I am concerned, an explanation like that is judgmental and would make me a *"miserable comforter."*

How does it help to say, I told you so? The Holy Spirit does a better job of correcting you and I will not join the enemy in condemning you. No, I want you to think about this; since Father is able to make bad things turn out for good, I would encourage you to trust His perfect love and providence.

One of my sons was in two auto accidents within six months of each other. He was not at fault in either accident. The first occurred through icy road conditions. He was not driving. The second was caused by a drunk driver and he came within inches of death. The point is not fatalism but a sovereign God, Who had a purpose that He keeps to Himself.

It is not all about you. Stop trying to control everything and next time, hold your tongue right.

JANUARY 14

The God Who Wants to be Known

ISAIAH 45:19

I have not spoken in secret, in a dark place of the earth: I said not unto the seed of Jacob, Seek me in vain: I the LORD speak righteousness, I declare things that are right.

I believe this is the textbook summation: *God is the only source of information about Himself.*

Logic makes it clear. None of us were there at the beginning. There is no other source of information except the one who has always been. This is already past my understanding. Without His testimony there is only speculation, theory, or imagination; there is no other eyewitness except God.

I have faith in God. That means that I believe His character; specifically, that He never lies. Because I hold this as true, I can believe in the content of His Word; that it is always true.

As a minister of the Gospel, the statement that God declares in [v19] is foundational to my service to all. The God I represent wants to be known. The things He says that are not hidden; they are purposed for those He chooses – *the seed of Jacob*.

God's choice of the name *Jacob* instead of *Israel* in this verse is amazing! He does not call then the noble title of *Prince of God*, but the humble label of *Supplanter!* It reminds us that our understanding of God is not based on any merit of our own but on His choice to reveal!

I the LORD – the self-existent One. He tells us that He speaks what is right, He tells the truth. We rely on the God of all truth to speak the truth into our ministry. This is your authority. This is the only way you can dare to stand before men and speak into their lives.

My God wants to be known.

JANUARY 15

Running From Here to Dallas, Texas

PHILIPPIANS 4:13
I can do all things through Christ, Who strengthens me.

This is one of those verses I learned as a kid. It wasn't hard because it wasn't long. But I don't remember anyone ever explaining it to me.

Now I don't think the verse is that hard to understand. I recall learning a chorus based on the verse. The verse is used to inspire and motivate young believers with a "can do" attitude.

Faith is the essential. It is not trying to develop a positive attitude toward life but trusting Jesus to teach us the right way and also give us the ability to serve Him! He can and will do just that. We have a wonderful Captain of our Salvation who is always by our side. Praise His Name!

But it finally occurred to me, I can't do everything. Though Jesus is always helping me, I run like a duck (Now there is a picture for you!) I have never been the fastest at anything. I know that I cannot run from Central Pennsylvania to Dallas, Texas, in two minutes.

Let us get some context to this very wonderful promise. Within the parameters of how the Creator made me (in every area) I can rely upon His unlimited power to do what He asks me to do. He knows my frame; He remembers that I am dust and promises to use me as He intended.

He is a skilled craftsman with amazing abilities. He creates people with supernatural potential to do wonderful things. He never uses a hammer to turn a screw.

JANUARY 16

Evil Beasts

TITUS 1:12-13

One of themselves, even a prophet of their own, said, The Cretians are always liars, evil beasts, slow bellies. This witness is true. Wherefore rebuke them sharply, that they may be sound in the faith

This is a passage that presents a real challenge to the western mind. To seemingly insult a whole culture while providing advice to a young pastor appears very wrong. Is Paul a bigot? Has he had a stroke?

My wife started her formal education in a parochial school. The discipline was very strict. When she started 5th grade, she attended the local public school. The teacher called her name on that first day and she immediately stood next to her desk because the teacher had addressed her. The teacher was impressed and decided to have all the students follow suit. She was not popular in her class!

My point? Culture and behavioral patterns (even in a church) must be understood and dealt with by a patient process of Biblical instruction -*rebuke them sharply that they be sound in the faith*. Every church has an established culture. It may be good or bad, but it must be understood by you so that you may lead your people into the pattern of looking unto Jesus.

I have observed church cultures of ignorance, apathy, fear, bitterness, and complaint. You must remember: *in meekness instruct those that oppose themselves* and be patient. Remember, the Holy Spirit is not finished forming Jesus in you as well.

JANUARY 17

No David Without a Goliath

1 SAMUEL 17:45
Then said David to the Philistine, You come to me with a sword, and with a spear, and with a shield: but I come to you in the name of the LORD of hosts, the God of the armies of Israel, whom you have defied.

I have learned much about life in Christ by studying the story of David. We are encouraged by the shepherd boy who became: *a man after God's own heart.* There must have been something about little brother that made his brothers give him a hard time and Dad isolate him with the sheep.

Killing that lion and bear **(1 Sam. 17:35)** were life changing events that taught him to believe in God's ability to strengthen and protect. But Goliath was something different and by this new danger, God put David front and center before everyone in Israel.

The magnitude of the adversity was what God used to change the course of history. Asaph would later pen, **(Ps. 76:10)** *Surely the wrath of man shall praise You: the remainder of wrath shall You restrain.*

Father uses everything and everyone to accomplish His purpose in your life. Even your adversaries are intended to form Christ in you. It is not always their defeat that is the primary goal in this divine confrontation. You may not see it or be able to express praise for it, but there will be no YOU without this challenge.

JANUARY 18

A Diligent Man

PROVERBS 22:29
Do you see a man diligent in his business? He shall stand before kings; he shall not stand before obscure men.

I am blessed to be the father of six wonderful children. All are gifted and bring blessing to any table. Because of my text, I call upon the experience of my eldest. He is a genius, a man of many skills and a gifted leader. (Yes, at times his siblings might have other words to describe him – but it is hard for them to deny their grudged appreciation of him.) He has worked for many big named software companies and been a valued member of their leadership. If he felt led by God, he could get another job with them with just a word. But at this season he has chosen, again, to work for a faith based, non-profit organization. I say again because this is the second time he has chosen this path.

So, I am a proud papa. It is not the paycheck he earned but the spiritual maturity and influence I have observed. He has looked at each responsibility as an opportunity to help others and grow who he is in Christ. I am not speaking about perfection but a path to maturity. Father has taught him through some hard things that he is not in charge of life, but he can make a change in many lives if he would give his giftedness over to the Savior.

A few years ago, he had the opportunity to live out my text. While he was serving God in the first non-profit organization, he was part of an official audience with a Minister of the government of the U.A.E., a prince of the royal family. I am thankful the family name was well represented. However, I am truly grateful that he loves Jesus, loves his family, is active in the Kingdom work of his church and is committed to be more than he is today. **(Phil. 3:14)** *I press toward the mark for the prize of the high calling of God in Christ Jesus.*

No apologies. I love him.

JANUARY 19

A Thought About the Future

LUKE 18:8
I tell you that He will avenge them speedily. Nevertheless, when the Son of Man comes, shall He find faith on the earth?

Jesus speaks these words at the end of a parable about being faithful in prayer. He directs us to be persistent to the point of seemly being annoying! (*This refers to the old woman in the parable.*) But the words of Jesus do not present a victorious image, at least from our perspective.

My dear friends, I do not hold to Amillennialism.

I remember the warning of Paul – **(2 Tim. 4:3-4)**

For the time will come when they will not endure sound doctrine; but after their own lusts shall they heap to themselves teachers, having itching ears; and they shall turn away their ears from the truth, and shall be turned unto fables.

I am not a date setter, but it sure does feel like the faithful are thinning out and ministry certainly is not like "the good old days." I could go on to *"bang the drum"* about the old days but I just want to remind you that the results of faithful ministry are not in your hands. You are just to work the process. Not one of you signed up for an "Isaiah" tour of duty, but then, you are not in charge of assignments.

(Isa. 6:11) *Then said I, Lord, how long? And He answered, Until the cities be wasted without inhabitant, and the houses without man, and the land be utterly desolate.*

Be faithful. Jesus knows you. He loves you. He does not put a square peg in a round hole. He will be glorified. That is sure and that is your goal.

JANUARY 20

Keep the Main Thing The Main Thing

MARK 1:37-38

And when they had found Him, they said unto Him, All men seek for You. And He said unto them, Let us go into the next towns, that I may preach there also: for therefore came I forth.

Mark, in his immediate, right away style, begins his Gospel with action. After healing Peter's mother-in-law, Jesus had a full evening of healing and casting out demons. I am sure it was taxing.

But Jesus also sets an example for us that we can duplicate. He recharges Himself through quiet conversation with His Father. When the community begins to shake and move, Jesus is still in demand for what they want Him to do. There is nothing wrong in their need, but there is an important lesson here that Jesus will also model.

The disciples get wrapped up in the urgency of the agenda of others and passive/aggressively present their solution. Jesus has other plans.

Jesus tells them that we are not doing what everyone else wants us to do. I came to proclaim the truth, not fix your problems. All need to hear, all need to be told. Healing is a blessing but not the purpose of His coming. Hanging up a shingle is not the primary objective, hanging on a tree is!

You may be very gifted. Perhaps you can do many things very well, but you must not major on minors. Keep the main thing, THE MAIN THING. Know who you are and what you have been given. Do that and get help from others for all the other things that being in ministry means.

Oh, and don't forget to pray.

JANUARY 21

Even a Child is Known

PROVERBS 20:11
*Even a child is known by his doings, whether his
work be pure, and whether it be right.*

As an adult, I learned this verse from a Sunday School song. It was often used in the opening program, though I had never heard it before. It started my mind to ponder.

If a child is known by their behavior, then adults could certainly be recognized by their habits. I was a young pastor. Even though I had grown up in a parsonage, I had never considered that people could be identified by their behavioral patterns. I guess I am just slow.

Was this an important guide to help me navigate the challenges of leadership? Duh.

Could I recognize potential problems and the needs of my people by understanding what their behavior revealed? Duh.

If I studied behavior, would I recognize my own strengths and weaknesses and find how Father would use me? Could be.

Well, it sounds like this is going to take time. Maybe it is a process? Perhaps it is more than just pigeonholing people into groups of behavior? There might be other factors that affect or stimulate their actions. I think I am going to need the Holy Spirit to help me understand this. I think that I will especially need His help to not think less of others after I have *"figured them out."* I am not sure if knowing them is the same as loving them despite of what they do.

What do you think?

JANUARY 22

Do Right

GENESIS 18:25
That be far from You to do after this manner, to slay the righteous with the wicked: and that the righteous should be as the wicked, that be far from You: Shall not the Judge of all the earth do right?

The context of this verse is a powerful conversation between Abraham and God over the destruction of Sodom. Abraham is pleading for the mercy of God toward this city. It is amazing that God would choose to have this conversation! But the conversation shows how far God will go to connect with those on whom He chooses to set His affection. Abraham shows that it is alright to question God, if you really want to hear His answer.

Abraham expresses an absolute; *shall not the Judge of the whole earth do right?* It is not a question of God's ability to do right. He is not asking if God will do right or wrong. It means that because He is God, the one who defines what is right, that He will do right!

That may have been obvious to you. As a young pastor of twenty-two, I thought I clearly understood this truth but, Wow! On this day, it jumped off the page into my heart!

Everything that God has done or ever will do is right! Even if I don't understand what is going on or what has happened, it is still right. In every situation or circumstance, He is right. This has become a basis for everything I know or think I understand about my God.

He is right and never makes a mistake.

JANUARY 23

More String

TITUS 3:8-9

This is a faithful saying, and these things I will that you affirm constantly, that they which have believed in God might be careful to maintain good works. These things are good and profitable unto men. But avoid foolish questions, and genealogies, and contentions, and strivings about the law; for they are unprofitable and vain.

I have always been a "straightener": "A place for everything and everything in its place." I showed this compulsive pattern as a child.

Packages use to come in the mail wrapped by twine. Adhesive tape is a modern miracle. My dad would get packages but never throw away the string. He tossed this into an old briefcase to be used later. As a child, I would investigate the case and see this tangled mess of twine, and the urge would come over me to make it into a neat ball. That would be a good thing and a blessing to my daddy! I set myself to the task but found the bits and pieces so knotted that it would put me to tears. In frustration, I would throw my attempt at order back into the briefcase and pout. Days later I would see the briefcase again, start to bring order to this universe and fail in frustration and tears.

Then I realized that the apparent chaos of the twine universe did not bother my father, only me. The twine was there, under his control, to be used as he needed.

Not everything needs fixing. Life does not have to be done your way. Yes, holiness and compassion are absolutes for your life *(James 1:27.)* Some things are a waste of your time, energy, and resources. You are not responsible to fix everyone and everything.

Please major on your "majors." You are not God.

JANUARY 24

Act On What Jesus Says is Real

MATTHEW 16:18
And I say also unto you, that you are Peter, and upon this rock **I will build my church; and the gates of hell shall not prevail against it.**

It is obvious. Jesus is stating absolutes:

1. He will build His group of *"called out ones."* Building speaks to me about Process. Process means there is a plan and that it is God's plan. Isaiah says it this way, *(Isaiah 53:11) He shall see of the travail of His soul and shall be satisfied: by His knowledge shall my righteous servant justify many; for He shall bear their iniquities.*

Peter states it in this manner. *(1 Peter 1:20) Who verily was foreordained before the foundation of the world but was manifest in these last times for you.*

Going back to the Matthew passage, the second thing I see is that nothing will cause it to fall or fail. Though I think about the phrase, *"the gates of hell"* as poetic, I do not consider it unrealistic. I have usually thought about the phrase in connection with Satan. I don't think I am wrong, but despite what Dante' states, Satan has never been to hell. Paul calls him this, *(Eph. 2:2) Wherein in time past you walked according to the course of this world, according to the prince of the power of the air, the spirit that now works in the children of disobedience:*

Jesus is saying, no matter what the opposition, His Divine Process will succeed. It is simple, obvious - BUT we have all looked at the post-Covid reality and considered that the church was dying. **Jesus said that it is not.** Rest in this for your comfort. Commit to this in courage.

Hope in this – it is real.

JANUARY 25

God's Great Gift

PROVERBS 18:22
Whoever finds a wife finds good and obtains favor of the LORD.

I had the typical viewpoint about women and marriage. I thought my viewpoint was "Christian." I recognized that men and women are not inferior to each other, not equal, but compatible to one another. My parents' example was of two dynamic, motivated people who complemented each other in ministry.

My mother's motto was "R.F.A." which means, ready for anything! So, subconsciously, I wanted a girl, just like the girl that married dear old dad. Then Father brought Alice Tee into my life.

She didn't grow up in a Bible believing church. My life experience was totally different from hers. Then she fell in love with Jesus. What He did in her life changed everything for me. Her devotion challenged my life, made me uncomfortable, made me want to change. She understood the call of God to be my wife.

Our life's journey together now has past the 50th year. Our love for one another has changed, and that is all good. Our commitment to Christ is stronger than ever and she still practices the advice she has shared when others sought her advice on a successful marriage. *"If you think he is wrong and you can't get him to see that, then bring it before the Throne of Grace and make Father do the work. After all, He knows best and when He changes your husband's mind, it is done the right way."*

That is advice that is hard to dispute. Father gave me a great gift.

JANUARY 26

Angry With God – Disappointment

The truth about unrealistic expectations.
(read 1 Kings 19)

Controlling people are proud, fearful, and not connected to the heart of God. They are angry with God because they can't control Him. But people become angry with God for other reasons. What they expect God to do, doesn't happen.

James calls Elijah a man of "like passions, as we are." As we read about him, we see him as brave and obedient to God. He wins a fantastic victory but experiences a tremendous crash. He is threatened and is on the run. Depression comes in (all of us can experience this) and he wants to die. Basically, he is saying I am a failure. Some would say he is just worn out, but I believe it is more than that.

He is disappointed with God. When God finally confronts him, his explanation for running is based in his experience. "*I believed in you, obeyed you, stood for you but nothing has changed; I am all alone and hated.*" That is disappointment. Elijah's expectation was, since there was a "big showdown" and we won, evil would turn on its tail and righteousness would reign. The three and a half years of waiting in the wilderness for wickedness to be defeated would be over.

Did God promise that? We don't have a recorded promised outcome for anything Elijah was commanded to do. He was just told to do it.

Do we have any promise that what we do will bring in the Kingdom? We have read the end of the story and know who wins, but God did not promise we would be the ones to score the winning goal! Jesus is the one who wins.

(Isaiah 53:11) *He shall see of the travail of his soul and shall be satisfied....*

Elijah knew that God is Sovereign, but we can read into God's victory and arrive at expectations that do not match reality. God is not obligated to do anything but glorify Himself. What have you read into your assignment that has caused you to be angry with God?

JANUARY 27

Angry With God – Confusion

I don't understand the way He works.
Read Habakkuk Chapter 1

We view a good man with a hard name to pronounce, but his name means *To embrace;* and that is what he does, embrace the life of faith. [1:1] He calls his message a *burden* – it is a message of God's coming judgment on Judah. [1:2] Habakkuk understands the problem and deplores the wickedness of the people. They deserve the punishment they will receive, BUT it is God's method of punishment that Habakkuk chokes on. [1:6] God chooses the Chaldeans. [1:12] He does not lose sight of God's Character or the Content of His Word - *we shall not die – you have established them for correction.* [1:13] His problem is this: You are God, and you always do what is right, but how can you use wicked men to judge just people who have made bad choices?

He is asking the question that you can guarantee you will hear more than once: *Why do bad things happen to good people and the bad get away with it? I don't understand why God does what He does!*

We may have asked these kinds of questions, but have we looked to God for the answer? That is what I like about Habakkuk. [2:1] *What He shall say – what I shall answer when I am reproved.*

The answer is [2:4b] The answer is always trust in the Character of God! **(Psalms 46:10)** *Be still and know that I am God: I will be exalted among the heathen, I will be exalted in the earth.* Dealing with disappointment and confusion is part of maturing. Life is not meant to be fair or understandable. **(Job 5:7-8)** *Yet man is born unto trouble, as the sparks fly upward....*

But we can trust the Character of God.

(Malachi 3:6) *For I am the LORD, I change not; therefore, ye sons of Jacob are not consumed.* We can depend on what He has promised. Living by faith will keep us from the foolishness of anger with God.

JANUARY 28

Angry With God – Control

JONAH 3:10 - 4:1

And God saw their works (people of Nineveh), that they turned from their evil way; and God repented of the evil, that he had said that he would do unto them; and he did it not. But it displeased Jonah exceedingly, **and he was very angry.**

The very title disturbs some of you. *God is God, how can I be angry with God? That makes no sense, and besides, what will my anger change?* But every one of us has been angry with God at some point in time because ….

You were or are angry with God because there is a problem with your heart. God is always the same in His love toward you, but you can be confused because you want to be in control.

Let us define: Anger – *A strong feeling of displeasure and belligerence aroused by a real or supposed wrong.* Jonah was angry because things did not turn out the way He wanted! He wanted vengeance on his enemies. In (***Jonah 4:2-3,***) we get true confessions. [v2] He knew the character of God and still wanted His own way (***Ps.103:3-4.***) [v3] He acts like the ultimate controlling person, *"Kill me!" If life can't be the way I plan it then I won't be involved in life."* Sorry, this is God's prerogative (***Job 12:10.***) [v4] God asks a question and Jonah refuses to answer. The silent treatment! This is another way you control others. Because God didn't work things the way you planned, you won't speak to Him anymore! In [**4:9,**] Jonah paints himself as shallow.

"Everything must be perfect." The anger of controlling people is never rational and always out of perspective. To them, things are more important than people. My plan is the only plan and it must work!

Signs of Controllers: *You just want your own way. You think others will hurt you. You have no compassion.*

Will you surrender? Give up your anger. Jonah did.

Give up your plan – God's is better. Admit your failure – You'll feel better. Say *"Yes, Lord,"* and mean it.

JANUARY 29

Read Out Loud

COLOSSIANS 4:16

And when this epistle is read among you, cause that it be read also in the church of the Laodiceans; and that you likewise read the epistle from Laodicea.

This perhaps is not so much a devotional thought as a bit of good advice.

I have never been an early riser. Because of this, my wife was the one to get our children up most mornings and ready for school. Because it is important to share in the responsibilities of parenting, I tried, when my ministry schedule allowed me, to be home to put the children to bed. This routine included the singing of songs, prayer and reading a story.

It was a very eclectic reading selection and as they got older, the chapters got longer with fewer pictures and deeper plots. Being theatrical in nature, I would create character voices and even make up scores for musical references. I got quite good at it.

But something else was happening. My public speaking became better. The verbal catchphrases and the "ums and ahs" began to disappear from my presentation of Biblical truth. I was able to read what was written on the page of scripture without faltering. I have been slightly dyslexic (turning numbers around.) This usually happened when I was mentally hurried, but the frequency of these mistakes became less.

Even if you do not have children, the practice of reading aloud will stimulate another area of memory and you will retain more. It takes 21 days to establish a good habit.

Obviously, I recommend it!

JANUARY 30

Backdraft

HOSEA 13:3-4

*Therefore they shall be as the morning cloud, and as the early dew that passes away, as the chaff that is driven with the whirlwind out of the floor, **and as the smoke out of the chimney.** Yet I am the LORD your God from the land of Egypt, and you shalt know no god but Me: **for there is no savior beside Me.***

When we moved into the parsonage at Naples, I was 10. It was an old house with a coal furnace in the basement. Dad tried to teach me how to get the fire started in the furnace and I wanted to learn – but I wasn't very good at it. My parents ran a Christian Bookstore in Geneva, about 20 miles away, and there were days when I would come home from school and the fire was out. I was supposed to start it – but like I said, I wasn't very good at it.

The secret was to get a kindling fire hot enough to get a good draft up the chimney. If you didn't, the backdraft would force the smoke into the vents and through the house. I lost count on how many times I had to open all the doors and fan the smoke out of the house with the front storm door.

Without help from the Holy Spirit, we will never get it right. We may be instructed in the right things to do and say, but only the Holy Spirit can heat the hearts of those we seek to warm. Our attempts to fan the flame will fail; all smoke and mirrors, till we make Jesus the one who kindles the fire that keeps all in the house safe and warm.

I never burnt the house down, but the Trustees took pity on me and put in an oil-fired burner before the next winter.

JANUARY 31

I Will Come Again

JOHN 14:3
And if I go and prepare a place for you, I will come again, and receive you unto Myself; that where I am, there you may be also.

What a wonderful promise from the Great Promise Keeper! Let us meditate on this!

I go to prepare a place for you – I am informed that the meaning is not a small cubby but a broad and open space. Jesus refers to this as mansion like.

I will come again – this is connected to the personal. Since I am preparing an area specifically for you, I will come and get you! No matter what your eschatology, we cannot ignore the certainty of Jesus' promise!

Receive you unto myself – This means a glad welcome. There is no intolerance or negative reaction to your inclusion. Jesus will receive you with open arms – *I am so glad you are here with me!*

That where I am – The book of Hebrews tells us that Jesus is seated in the presence of our Heavenly Father. In God's Home you are wanted and welcome because Jesus is our elder brother.

There you may be also – I love the emphasis of this additional affirmation. It is like saying, *"me casa, su casa."* This is my home, and it belongs to me because Jesus paid for it in full!

I want to go home!

FEBRUARY 1

I'm Flying!

PROVERBS 16:18
Pride goes before destruction, and a haughty spirit before a fall.

1 CORINTHIANS 10:12
Wherefore let him that thinks he stands take heed lest he fall.

I was back on my bike again. I had learned to ride several months before and was reveling in my new skill. I went everywhere on *Freedom Flyer!* I have never been very fast on my feet, but I thought I was like greased lightening on my bike!

I was with a friend who was walking, and I challenged him to a race back to my house. He was off like a flash, and I was pouring it on! Around the corner we came. I was standing on my pedals, pumping with all I had, **but** I did not see the rock in the road. I hit that rock and flew over my handlebars at least 10 feet! The asphalt was not kind. I limped home in tears with my friend dragging my twisted bike. (They don't make them like that anymore! A day later I straightened the handlebars and was back on the street.)

I would like to say that I learned my lesson that day – but I didn't. Still, I have thought of that experience of flying many times. It was exhilarating but the painful memory of the landing is gone. I have no scars and I can't remember who tended my wounds.

My spiritual take from this is that we lose the lesson if we forget the consequences. Without the instruction from the Holy Spirit, the circumstances of life will never provide the wisdom we need to survive the rocks in our way. We are doomed to repeat our falls without our humble dependence upon His patient care and instruction. I wasn't meant to fly.

FEBRUARY 2

Grasshoppers – Naysayers

NUMBERS 13:33
And there we saw the giants, the sons of Anak, which came from the giants: and we were in our own sight as grasshoppers, and so we were in their sight.

There are some that declare that decision by committee will always be hindered by the short-sighted and narrow minded. They affirm that decisions must be made by those, called of God to lead! But I remind you that the committee to search out the land was, *"by commandment of the Lord"* (Numbers13:3.)

We understand that God was in all this. This tremendous lesson is presented to us in **(Heb. 3:19)** *So we see that they could not enter in because of unbelief.*

As faithful servant/leaders, we wait upon God and seek to provide wise and bold leadership for the family of God. We wonder why others would question our decisions or the direction we declare to be the way of faith for our ministry. The reasons for their unbelief are too many to enumerate – **most of those reasons have nothing to do with you.**

The naysayer will always point to "the facts" and the balance sheet. The mandate or promise of God will never be their bottom line. Whatever the issue, there is something important that has been revealed about their spiritual condition. This is not honest doubt, but a heart of unbelief. What can you do about this?

Trust the Word of God and the Holy Spirit to do what Father wants. Follow this injunction: *(**2 Tim. 2:24-26**) And the servant of the Lord must not strive; but be gentle unto all men, apt to teach, patient, In meekness instructing those that oppose themselves; if God peradventure will give them repentance to the acknowledging of the truth; And that they may recover themselves out of the snare of the devil, who are taken captive by him at his will.*

Say, "Yes, Lord," and do your job.

FEBRUARY 3

The Process of Righteousness – Compassion

PSALMS 51:1-2

Have mercy upon me, O God, according to Your lovingkindness: according unto the multitude of Your tender mercies blot out my transgressions. Wash me thoroughly from mine iniquity and cleanse me from my sin.

There is an old English rhyme, *"If wishes were horses, then beggars would ride."* You might say, wishing doesn't make it so. We must resolve to follow Jesus, but without the Holy Spirit, our resolve is just noise.

There is a process for our righteous resolve. David shares it in this penitent Psalm. To get full value out of this public exposure of David's heart, a working knowledge of 2 Samuel 11 and 12 is important. We see a man in transition who forgets his responsibility to his people and his God. This forgetfulness leads David into lust, adultery, lies, compromise, and murder. We certainly can be like David in our moral failure, but are we like him in our desire for God's mercy? **(Prov.28:13.)**

We must seek God's compassion. Space does not allow me to define or explain this specific request – *mercy, loving kindness, multitude of mercy*. These are not platitudes but a genuine recognition that God is Compassionate!

Why does David need this Compassionate God?

Transgression – I am willfully disobedient to revealed command. *Iniquity* - Lack of righteousness –twistedness. All I do is convoluted. On my own, I am selfish and seek only what is my will. *Sin* - Missing the mark, sins of commission & omission.

He exposes himself in a song, and seemingly asks for the impossible *(Jer.32:27.) Blot out, wash, cleanse* – Only the Compassionate God can do this. This is the first step in Righteousness – God is compassionate. He alone can make me clean.

FEBRUARY 4

The Process of Righteousness – Confession

PSALMS 51:3-6

For I acknowledge my transgressions: and my sin is ever before me. Against You, You only, have I sinned, and done this evil in Your sight: ... Behold, I was shaped in iniquity; and in sin did my mother conceive me. Behold, You desire truth in the inward parts: and in the hidden part You shall make me know wisdom.

If I am not willing to acknowledge who and what I am, I will never be different, never be righteous. I must *confess* – say the same thing God says about my condition because I know that He is compassionate.

[v3] David has asked of God what only God can do – deal with the **consequences** of sin, **cleanse** the life, and **change** the desire of the heart. David does this through confession. If we are ever going to be clean, we must first recognize that we are dirty, and this dirt will kill us!

[v3] *My sin is ever before me* – Bathsheba and the results of that union were in front of his face. There are consequences to your actions. God can remove the hurt and heal the heart, but the history remains. God does not turn back time, He does something better – He makes us new.

[v4] *Against You* – Our sin hurts others, but it is against God. He determines right and wrong. [v5] *Shaped in iniquity – to writhe in pain.* Sin left a terrible mark on us. We are sinners by nature and by choice.

[v6] With an understanding of our old nature, it might be like an excuse (***Rom. 6:1-2.***) God requires more - *Truth in the inward parts*. God has done more than require truth, He enables it ***(1 Pet. 1:15.)*** [v6] *He makes me know wisdom.* The truth sets us free ***(John 8:32,34,36.)***

Acknowledging of the truth about our God, ourselves, and our sin, delivers us from our Enemy ***(2 Tim. 2:25-26.)*** Confession is not ritual but reality. Through it, a compassionate Father shows mercy and gives us wisdom.

FEBRUARY 5

The Process of Righteousness – Cleansing

PSALMS 51:7,10 (CONTEXT: PS. 51:7-12)

Purge me with hyssop, and I shall be clean: wash me, and I shall be whiter than snow. [v10] Create in me a clean heart, O God; and renew a right spirit within me.

The heat and grime of the day have left us feeling less than human. Oh, the wonderful feeling to be clean once more! Multiply this feeling when it comes to the cleansing that God provides. The guilty weight of sin no longer hangs on us. The smell of death is gone and once more we love the company of the redeemed. To be clean brings us joy!

[v7] *Purge me with hyssop* – A small coarse aromatic plant to which a sponge could be easily attached. It was used in ceremonial cleansing, but **ritual does not cleanse**. It is symbolic of God using little things, unrelated things, to bring about our cleansing. But cleansing is ALWAYS a process that starts with understanding God's Compassion, which leads us to our Confession of sin.

[v7] *Whiter than snow* – What could be whiter than snow? The center of every snowflake is dirt. A crystal forms around it to remove it from the air. The snow does not last but it does the job God intends, cleanse the air. That is what Father does for us!

[v8] *joy & gladness*- Walking close to the God of the Universe is not dull. God is the best at parties and joy! [v8] *That the bones You have broken may rejoice* - Yes, God puts the big hurt on your rebellion, but it brings so much joy when you are clean **(Ps. 30:5!)**

[v9] *Hide Your face from – blot out all my iniquity* - Is this farfetched? No, David is asking God to be God - the only one who can show mercy, deal with the consequences of sin, cleanse the life, and change the heart's desire. [v10] *Create a right spirit – Bara*- This is not the "wash me up till the next time"; it is, "make something new in me" *(2 Cor.5:17!)*

Only the Holy Spirit can do this (*Jude 1:24.*)

FEBRUARY 6

The Process of Righteousness - Commitment

PSALMS 51:13,17 [CONTEXT PS. 51:13-19]

Then will I teach transgressors Your ways; and sinners shall be converted unto You. [v17] The sacrifices of God are a broken spirit: a broken and a contrite heart, O God, You will not despise.

Let's get real. You claim you were called of God to the ministry. However, ministry is not an opportunity to serve the King, but a job. Either something has changed, or the truth has finally caught up with you.

When sin has been allowed to fester in your life, your spiritual experience has been what David describes in *(Ps. 32:4) For day and night Your hand was heavy upon me: my moisture is turned into the drought of summer. Selah*

Psalm 51 has given us clear instruction and abundant hope to deal with our sin. Our Father is **Compassionate** – He understands us. When we **Confess**, God alone can deal with the **Consequences** of sin, **Cleanse** the life, **Change** the desire of our heart.

[v13] *Teach/ convert* - A vessel that is cleansed can be used – *(2 Tim.2:21)*. David has been given the mercy of God and knows that what we experience from God's gracious hand, we must share (***Matt. 5:7.***)

[v14] *Deliver me from blood guilt* – He is speaking about the bitterness of memory, the shame of sin. Only God can remove this, and He does it with one simple lifelong practice, being thankful ***(1 Thes.5:18.)***

It is only by the process of giving thanks to God can we ever be free from the bondage of memory and bitterness.

[v17] *The sacrifice of a broken spirit* – God wants this, not a personally repaired one. Have you reached the end of you ***(James4:10?)*** It is hard not to make it all about you, but you know that the *collapsed, crouching heart,* is what Father will use.

Be committed to brokenness and Father will use you to *build up the walls of Jerusalem* [v18].

FEBRUARY 7

You Must Give Up, To Go Up

MATTHEW 19:29

And every one that has forsaken houses, or brothers, or sisters, or father, or mother, or wife, or children, or lands, for My name's sake, shall receive a hundredfold, and shall inherit everlasting life.

Because this indicates difficult sacrifice and does not provide a list of circumstances or an explanation for this behavior, I can say this is not one of my favorite passages. I know there are cults that have used these verses to defend their extreme control on their victims. That troubles me.

But I believe this to be true. I know Jesus loves me and loves those that I love. He is not unreasonable or unfeeling. He is challenging this: *Who is first in my life?*

As my King, He deserves my complete allegiance. Am I willing to sacrifice the comfort of family, home, and position to advance the Kingdom and proclaim the truth? I have always thought that "Yes, Lord," was a given in my life, but as I age and know my frailties, I have wondered if safety means more to me?

I understand the responsibilities of leadership. I have experienced the scrutiny that comes with the buck stopping here. What I must not forget is what the King promises to those who will sacrifice for Him. He knows my works, understands my heart, and hears my confession of dependency upon Him alone.

I want my crown. I long for the *"Well done."*

It will be worth it all when we see Jesus.

FEBRUARY 8

Problems Ignored Become Bigger Problems

JUDGES 2:2B-3

… but you have not obeyed My voice: why have you done this? Wherefore I also said, I will not drive them out from before you; but they shall be as thorns in your sides, and their gods shall be a snare unto you.

In our own strength, obeying God is not easy. That is not new to any of us. We seem to ignore the truth that the consequences of disobedience do not change just because we are "sorry." We do not get a pass because we are called by God to ministry.

The people of Israel discover this for themselves when God called them out for their failure, and they are overcome with grief. They cried so much they called the place, Weepers.

A friend taught me this short verse. I hope it will help you.

Experience is the Master Teacher,
His way is hard and rough.
Wisdom stood back
and watched the procession,
And said,
"To observe is experience enough."

Father makes certain demands on our character and performance as His servants. Though none of our missed responsibilities will separate us from His eternal love, there is the potential for loss.

My original thought when presenting this concept was what I have experienced as a Pastor when I "kicked the can" of church discipline down the road. I did not want to deal with hurt feelings or upset those I loved. It always bit me you know where, later.

How about you?

FEBRUARY 9

Set the World in Their Heart

ECCLESIASTES 3:11
He has made everything beautiful in his time: also he has set the world in their heart, so that no man can find out the work that God makes from the beginning to the end.

You might be old enough to remember The Byrds, turning the first eight verses of the chapter into a hit song. I can hear it in my head as I write! Through my years of ministry, I have enjoyed the stimulation of teaching this collection from Solomon.

This verse always stirs my thoughts. Though I don't consider it complicated, I enjoy the Divine perspective of intentional confusion. Bear with me. I ask you to take the time to examine [vv9-15] This devotion does not allow me to do more than [v11].

1. Our Creator always makes beauty, but it is through process – *in his time*. Our time is limited; therefore, so is our ability to create as He does.
2. We are made in His image, and that is seen in our ability to think and reason. To dream is the spark of the divine. We can imagine and examine all that is in the known universe - *He set the world in our heart*. I am interested in many things. "*Shoes and ships and sealing wax.*" I present a good challenge in trivia, but I would fail on "Jeopardy."
3. My curiosity makes me an expert at nothing. Though the world may declare you an expert in comparison to others, none of us can focus on one thing to the exclusion of all others nor do we have the length of days to do so - *no man can find out the work that God makes from the beginning to the end*. Our very nature is purposed to reveal our limitations and God's Omniscience.

Checkmate, God wins again.

FEBRUARY 10

What You are Doing is No Good!

EXODUS 18:17-18
And Moses' father-in-law said unto him, the thing that you do is not good. You will surely wear away, both you, and this people that is with you: for this thing is too heavy for you; you are not able to perform it by yourself.

Now, here is some advice that no one wants to hear, especially from your Father-in-law! Yet, Moses knows something very special about the one giving him the advice!

This man took Moses in, gave him the necessities of life, made him part of the family, and for 40 years, "shared life around the fire." When God called Moses, Jethro supported him. This is not an "outlaw," this is a friend. This is a man of "good will."

Moses has been given a big responsibility. God chose him for the task and part of that task is judging the people of Israel based on God's Law. This Law goes beyond the moral law of Conscience and presents "the fences" that make good neighbors. Part of your ministry might be very similar, but you feel like there is not enough of you to go around!

Jethro's advice is not about what you do but how you do it! The great thing about this observation is that Jethro provides a solution (something that all good advice includes!) If you can't offer a solution, keep your mouth shut. Without a solution , you are just a critic.

The proof of a good solution is demonstrated in a good night's sleep for everyone.

So, if someone offers a suggestion to improve things, consider the source. Is there a solution in that opinion? It is ok to prayerfully consider the results. You might get a good night's sleep out of it.

FEBRUARY 11

Everyone Needs Help

GALATIANS 6:1-2

Brethren, if a man be overtaken in a fault, you who are spiritual, restore such a one in the spirit of meekness; considering yourself, lest you also be tempted. Bear one another's burdens, and so fulfil the law of Christ.

What is the problem? I am sure that you will agree with me! We are "in ministry." I know how we think about personal problems. *"Everybody needs help - but me. I'm OK. I know how to get out or over this by myself."*

The focus of the passage is on the helper not the one who is in need of help. If we realize we are the one in need, what do we do? What if you let your guard down to someone who can't handle ministry burdens? What if you unburden yourself to someone who's besetting sin is gossip! To be "In charge" means to be in control and you don't want others to know that you are not in control and these circumstances are beyond managing!

Father has intended the family of God to be interconnected. My counselor friend, Richard George, says, *"God made us with missing parts, and He put those parts in other people."*

How do you find that spiritual helper? *Are you willing to find them?* Yes, it might be in a self-help book, but it isn't always that easy. My experience as a child of God is that Father will bring those helpers into your life. They won't be perfect, nor will they always have a list of letters after their name, but Father will give you a sense of trust. *There is no David, without a Jonathan.*

You will be "overtaken," until you get the loving help with that problem that is literally eating you up before you can do anything about it!

This is not something you can hide forever.

(**Num. 32:23b**) *... and be sure your sin will find you out.*

FEBRUARY 12

Good Instruction

PROVERBS 1:8-9

My son, hear the instruction of your father, and forsake not the law of your mother: For they shall be an ornament of grace unto your head, and chains about your neck.

I tried my hand at backyard mechanics. The most success I can claim is a few brake jobs and oil changes. I have accumulated an impressive collection of tools, mostly for woodworking, but I have my share of sockets and wrenches.

Here is my good Instruction moment. I was underneath my car, ready to undo the oil plug, but I had the wrong wrench. Steven, my ever ready to help seven year-old, was satisfying his curiosity, watching daddy work. I grumbled about my mistake and how I would have to crawl out from under to get the right size. "I'll get it for you daddy!" I accepted his offer, told him the size I needed and where it might be found – and waited, and waited.

I concluded that my helper had disappeared. Grumbling as I shimmied out from under the car, I came into my shop. There I found a little boy in tears and his mother trying to help him find a tool he couldn't describe. It quickly became a teachable moment - **for me**. Steven did not know what a box wrench was, let alone the meaning of the size I wanted. I had failed because I had unrealistic expectations for the one whom I loved but had failed to teach. My frustration with my helper was unreasonable and his concern over disappointing his daddy had been avoidable. I have **never** forgotten this lesson.

Your task is to make fully devoted followers of Christ. Do they understand the tools the Holy Spirit uses and where to find them? Show them, use them to together, and watch over them as they learn to use them. That is what a good Father does.

FEBRUARY 13

Wisdom Cries Without

PROVERBS 1:20-21

Wisdom cries without; she utters her voice in the streets: she cries in the chief place of concourse, in the openings of the gates: in the city she utters her words,

God created and established this world in wisdom. I have often said, the only way that anything succeeds, to any degree, is when Biblical principles are applied. The principles for a successful life are found in the pages of God's Word.

But the wisdom of God is not restricted to the written Word of God. The Psalmist sang, *(Ps. 19:1) The heavens declare the glory of God; and the firmament shows His handywork.*

The wisdom, creativity, and order of God are revealed in the cosmic wonder of the universe. This is not news, but His wisdom is also found in the streets, the marketplace, and in the communities where we live. Father's wisdom is found in traffic signs, for sale signs, and the do not enter signs. These things were developed by people that may not acknowledge God the way you do, yet God has used them to provide order, meet our needs, and preserve life.

Again, the Psalmist focuses our attention on the way God works in His creation with this thought. *(Ps. 76:10) Surely the wrath of man shall praise You: the remainder of wrath shall You restrain.*

Even through war, conflict, and deadly tragedy, Father's wisdom will be revealed. It is up to the child of God to observe His Father's heart and hand. It is also valuable to remember that Father's wisdom is declared in the consequences of ignorance or willful ignorance. *(Prov. 1:31) Therefore shall they eat of the fruit of their own way and be filled with their own devices.*

The wise person will recognize and follow the wisdom of God, even when it is revealed through the base or common source. Are you listening? Your unsaved neighbor might have the answer you need.

FEBRUARY 14

Candle Jesus

PHILIPPIANS 1:18
What then? notwithstanding, every way, whether in pretense, or in truth, Christ is preached; and I therein do rejoice, yes, and will rejoice.

I have an item on my bookshelf that I never thought I would possess. It is a wax candle in the shape of a bust of Jesus. It is not garish. Someone took a great deal of care with the original to present an image of the suffering Savior.

I did not purchase this item. It was a gift from an older couple in my church. While on a vacation trip they saw this in a gift shop and thought of me. There is the challenge - they thought of me. I would have never selected this for any reason but – they thought of me. It will sit on my shelf for many years because they thought of me.

You may have been, or you will be, in circumstances similar to mine. How you deal with the sentiment shown you says volumes about the grace of God in your life. Some might call me dishonest because I hold no great appreciation or affection for this gift. Say what you will, I will never remove that candle from my office. This is not like turning down beets from someone's garden (we don't like beets.)

You will have to make a judgment call about things like this. You need wisdom and grace to make the right decision. People can be very fragile. You must handle them with prayer.

They thought about you.

FEBRUARY 15

Has Not God Spoken to Us?

NUMBERS 12: 1-2

*And Miriam and Aaron spoke against Moses because ... [v2]
And they said, has the LORD indeed spoken only by Moses?
Has He not spoken also to us? And the LORD heard it.*

You have an ego. You are in the ministry because you believe God wants to use you and you enjoy it! Yes, it is possible you identify with Moses [v3] or you are like my Pastor friend who has been professionally diagnosed as an introvert. Yet, Father uses him in a wonderful way to minister to his church family and inspire me.

There are others in your sphere of influence that have also sensed the calling of God. They are perhaps multi-talented and have been used by Father to bring success in ministry and joy to others, BUT envy has taken over ego.

It can happen to you as well. Can you listen to someone else preach and not critique them? Miriam and Aaron don't like what Moses was doing in his personal life. His older siblings (always a problem working with family!) think they can correct him and try to claim equality to justify their opinion. Father does not see it their way and it is "*off to the woodshed*" with Miriam. You are God's servant; He will justify you.

So, you have someone challenging your authority/position. Is this outright rebellion or just ego controlled by envy? Be careful. Do not seek to do what only the Master can do. Listen deeper to their "frustration." Perhaps they need encouragement to trust God and reach for greater opportunities – elsewhere. Remember, you are their Pastor; intercede for them. Real leaders help others succeed.

Try not to take it personally and breathe!

FEBRUARY 16

Stick Your Head Above the Foxhole

2 CORINTHIANS 12:15
And I will very gladly spend and be spent for you; though the more abundantly I love you, the less I be loved.

Every year I am told that thousands of us (those called into ministry) drop out. The reasons are varied and complex. Perhaps you are or you have been among that number. I do not approach these few minutes as your judge. I am just sharing a thought; we cannot approach ministry as a means of fulfillment for our inner being.

When you are called by the Master to be a leader in His Kingdom it is important to acknowledge certain things (this is not an exhaustive list):

- You are wired to do this. God made you to lead. It might have taken you a while to understand this about yourself, but there it is! Remember, your strengths can be your weakness.
- You are not in business, nor is your ministry a game. You are at war and the enemy you fight is sin, self, and Satan. You are under attack. This is a given. Your King expects you to use the protection He provides. Ignore this protection and you are a casualty.
- Not everyone appreciates your efforts. That is what Paul is saying. The sheep's understanding or appreciation is not the measure of your duty assignment. (**Col. 3:23-24**) *And whatsoever you do, do it heartily, as to the Lord, and not unto men; Knowing that of the Lord you shall receive the reward of the inheritance: for you serve the Lord Christ.*

Perhaps this isn't very comforting, but it is what has helped me for 50 years.

FEBRUARY 17

You Have to Love What Jesus Loves

JOHN 13:34-35
A new commandment I give unto you, that you love one another; as I have loved you, that you also love one another. By this shall all men know that you are My disciples, if you have love one to another.

1 JOHN 4:7-8
Beloved, let us love one another: for love is of God; and everyone that loves is born of God, and knows God. He that loves not knows not God; for God is love.

The Great Commandment and the Great Commission define the church. It is significant that the Commandment came before the Commission. But what does it mean to "love one another?" Jesus uses *agape,* and this particular Greek word for love means a sacrificial, unconditional love. I am commanded to love as God loves me. That is a huge directive, but how do I do this?

Moses was commanded by God to lead Israel. After his puny arguments, God asks Moses, *"What is in your hand?"* This question caused me to think about love in a different way. I have learned to explain Biblical, agape love as, *"Using who I am and what I have been given to bless others."*

Love is behavior, it is an action, and Father revealed His love for us by giving His Son. I understand the Great Commandment as an imperative, I have no choice but to love the unlovable. This is beyond me, especially if I think of love as the world defines it, with the warm fuzzies!

However, when I understand it to be an action of who I am, then I can allow the Holy Spirit to use how Jesus made me and what He has given me to show His love.

This brings the Commandment within reach. With divine help it is possible to show love to people I do not like. It starts with the truth that Jesus loved them first.

So, what do you have in your hand?

FEBRUARY 18

He That Would Be ...

REVELATION 22:11-12

He that is unjust, let him be unjust still: and he which is filthy, let him be filthy still: and he that is righteous, let him be righteous still: and he that is holy, let him be holy still. And behold, I come quickly; and My reward is with Me, to give every man according as his work shall be.

This passage fascinates me. Here is my King saying things that make my eyes pop! It confirms to me that we are responsible for our own behavior and that the consequences cannot be avoided.

As a Pastor, it challenges me to realize that some people will not change. In 1 Corinthians Paul tells me that there are carnal Christians and that some are not going to get much of a reward at the Bema Seat – BUT I forget that these people are in my church!

Have you ever had to conduct a funeral service for a carnal Christian? I have, and it is a real problem. You have a saved soul but what *appears* to be a wasted life! Verse 12 of my text confirms that Jesus is not into giving out participation trophies. We are accountable and He will reward according to our faithfulness.

I have always loved **(Phil. 1:6)** *Being confident of this very thing, that he which has begun a good work in you will perform it until the day of Jesus Christ:*

So, I tell my people, it is not how you start but how you finish.

Jesus is telling us some do not finish well.

I am not sure if this is inspirational, but it does make you think!

FEBRUARY 19

Whatever He Pleases

PSALMS 115:1-3

Not unto us, O LORD, not unto us, but unto Your name give glory, for Your mercy, and for Your truth's sake. Wherefore should the heathen say, where is now their God? But our God is in the heavens: He has done whatsoever He has pleased.

Here is one of those thoughts that I consider a "duh!" I have discovered that this apparent simplicity is not so simple. The Holy Spirit confronts me through it and applies it to my "every day." I begin to see that the thought is deep, and it causes me to walk by faith.

Not unto us - It is a great morning when I awake to recognize that it is not all about me. I am in a better state of mind because I find comfort in acknowledging that I am not the center of the universe.

Your name, mercy, truth – Here are aspects of God that are unchangeable and unshakeable. God glorifies Himself. Who else can? It is not egotistical; it is logical. There is no one greater and no one to impress. He is the source of mercy. He is the truth. He shows mercy because He is merciful. He is always right; therefore, truth comes from Him.

Where is their God? – We know that Satan blinds *(2 Cor.4:4)* and those without Christ are dead in sin *(Eph.2:1.)* Those without light and life cannot receive the love of God in Christ. Isn't it amazing that God can give sight to the blind and life to the dead? He does this because it brings Him glory, reveals His mercy, and tells the truth, through the Cross. (**Isa. 53:11**) *He shall see of the travail of his soul and shall be satisfied: by His knowledge shall My righteous servant justify many; for He shall bear their iniquities.*

Our God is in heaven – *He does what He pleases* – He is above my confusion and limited perspective. He is not limited by my sin or those that hate me. He will do what He has planned, and I will rejoice and find comfort in this. My future is sure.

FEBRUARY 20

What Does it Take?

PSALMS 39:4
LORD, make me to know mine end, and the measure of my days, what it is; that I may know how frail I am.

Conflict and personal attacks in David's life have raised questions about his worth. He is forced to ask some hard questions. Perhaps you have been there with David?

1. [39:4] **Why am I here and where am I going?**
   Here is a prayer that goes deeper than knowing the day of your death. It is more to this idea: *Where am I going and what have I accomplished with the time I have been given?* You must always remember that there is a Divine purpose for your life *(Jer.29:11.)*
2. [39:4] *know how frail I am* – **Do I understand my limits?** Your time on earth is short *(James4:14.)*
   You are dust, but Father knows your value *(Ps.103:14-16.)*
   [39:5] *handbreadth* – from the extended thumb to the extended little finger, on average 9 inches.
   [39:5] *Age is as nothing before You* – Age is often used as a determining factor for nobility and wisdom, but it is an imperfect indicator of either. Will anyone know that you were here?
   [39:5] *Altogether vanity* – Nothing about man is sure or true *(Ecc.9:11.)*
3. [39:6] **Am I doing anything with eternal value?**
   The things the world values or occupies itself with are empty. When the troubles of life come, and Jesus is not your default position, you will feel deluded, duped, deceived, and soon filled with disappointment and despair.
   I remind you of a great old saying:
   Only one life, Will soon be past, Only what's done for Christ will last.
   Jesus is the only one that can give you positive responses to these questions. *(Phil.1:21) For to me to live is Christ, and to die is gain.*

FEBRUARY 21

The Sin of Korah

NUMBERS 16:3-4

And they gathered themselves together against Moses and against Aaron, and said unto them, you take too much upon you, seeing all the congregation are holy, every one of them, and the LORD is among them: why do you lift up yourselves above the congregation of the LORD? And when Moses heard it, he fell upon his face:

Do you understand the source of your authority? I could ask the question a different way; do you know who you are? For brevity, I will tell you the truth. Father gave you your authority. You are a child of the King; you are a servant of the Living God. In every letter Paul wrote, he stated either his authority from God or the truth of whom he served, which meant his authority.

We know that the ground is level at the foot of the Cross and that we are all part of one Lord, one faith, one baptism. But God's choice sets some apart because of their responsibility to God and man *(Heb. 13:17.)*

Western Christianity wants to either ignore this distinction or turn the pastor into a dictator position. Peter says we must look at it this way.*(1 Peter 5:3) Neither as being lords over God's heritage but being ensamples* (living example) *to the flock.*

Korah and his cronies wanted to be in charge. They rejected God's leaders and sought to make it a popularity contest. Judging by the rest of the chapter, they were popular until God made that support deadly. Rejecting Moses and Aaron was a rejection of God.

It is your responsibility to teach your people the truth about Biblical Leadership. Acting against the "Lord's Anointed" is a dangerous thing to do. If you teach with the Biblical pattern from the Old and New Testament, you are not "blowing your own horn," but doing them a favor and saving yourself heartache.

FEBRUARY 22

The Power of the Lord was Present

LUKE 5:17

And it came to pass on a certain day, as he was teaching, that there were Pharisees and doctors of the law sitting by, which were come out of every town of Galilee, and Judaea, and Jerusalem: **and the power of the Lord was present to heal them.**

Here is an interesting thought. Most would take it as an introduction to the healing of the man with paralysis. But this man's healing was only a means to an end. I believe the intention of the Holy Spirit is to focus our thoughts on this **(Luke 5:32)** *I came not to call the righteous, but sinners to repentance.*

Luke opens this account with information about the audience. They were men that should have known and recognized the Messiah, but they didn't. But Luke says, **"The power of the Lord was present to heal them."** Jesus was in that home for redemption, not confrontation. He had nothing to prove. He was not there to shame anyone but to heal everyone.

You are a messenger that has been given a powerful message. **(2 Cor. 5:20)** *Now then we are ambassadors for Christ, as though God did beseech you by us: we pray you in Christ's stead, be reconciled to God.* The Power of the Lord is present every time you share the truth. It is not up to you to choose your audience. You are responsible for the preparation *(study to show yourself approved.)*

It tells us that Jesus *perceived their thoughts.* I am not Jesus, but Father provides wisdom to those that ask, so I will ask! Recently, I have been praying for wisdom that is beyond my experience. I have 50 years of pastoral experience which shows me what I do not know.

You are a messenger boy and though you prepare to share, without the Holy Spirit's help, the gaps between your ability and understanding of how to clearly communicate to your audience may seem impossible but, **the power of the Lord is present.**

FEBRUARY 23

Not Just the Words!

JOHN 8:7-9

So when they continued asking Him, He lifted up Himself, and said unto them, He that is without sin among you, let him first cast a stone at her. And again, He stooped down, and wrote on the ground. And they which heard it, being convicted by their own conscience, went out one by one, beginning at the eldest, even unto the last: and Jesus was left alone, and the woman standing in the midst.

It is a wonderful story! I rejoice in its message of hope and forgiveness. A plot meant to catch the Savior is used to convict the hearts of all these deceitful men. A woman, guilty of sin, experiences the power of Divine forgiveness. These are powerful words: *he that is without sin.* Yet the real power is not in the words but in the one who spoke the words. (**John 3:34**) *For he whom God has sent speaks the words of God: for God gives not **the Spirit by measure unto him.***

All that Jesus said and did, He did by the power of the Holy Spirit. Jesus is our captain, leading the way. He is our pattern, demonstrating how to live and serve Him. Without the Holy Spirit empowering these words, they are just words.

Jesus promised us that the Holy Spirit would work through us *(John 16:8.)* The Holy Spirit **convicts** the world of sin, **convinces** them of their need for Christ, and **conveys** them into the Kingdom.

If it were just the words, then the educated, logical, and eloquent would be the most successful in the Kingdom. But God chooses the foolish, weak, and base to be used by the Holy Spirit to speak His Word to a world full of dead people. They will be made alive through the power of the Holy Spirit *(Eph. 2:1.)*

The Holy Spirit does the work. Humbly, open your mouth and He will fill it.

FEBRUARY 24

Wisdom is Justified of Her Children

LUKE 7:35
But wisdom is justified of all her children.

This is a verse that grabs my attention!

Matthew 11:19 tells the same story. Jesus had been attacked for His choices and conduct. Jesus was criticized for the company He kept and where they met. Both were considered contrary to a righteous man's behavior.

Jesus' proverb can be stated, "the truth will win out," or "the facts will prove otherwise." We know that Jesus never did anything against the Word of God, but He constantly attacked the self-righteous traditions of His day. He was true to His mission and His actions all agreed to this fact. **(Luke 5:31-32)** *And Jesus answering said unto them, they that are whole need not a physician; but they that are sick. I came not to call the righteous, but sinners to repentance.*

So, this is a great "put down," and I want to use it to justify my choices when others criticize them and belittle my behavior. Can I get away with this? Perhaps.

I must check my motivation. Does it match Jesus' expressed purpose? **(John 6:38)** *For I came down from heaven, not to do mine own will, but the will of him that sent me.* Do I want to do Father's will?

Do my actions/choices go against revealed truth?

(1 John 3:5) *And you know that he was manifested to take away our sins; and in him is no sin.*

Am I using this as a cloak for my sin? Am I just trying to prove I am right, and they are ignorant? **(1 Cor. 8:1b)** *Knowledge puffs up, but charity edifies.*

Do I always have to be right to be righteous? There are a lot of ignorant, self-righteous people sitting in the pews. They believe they are the Holy Spirit in judging the conduct of others, and if they can criticize the preacher, that makes them feel superior! Jesus says the lies will fail and the truth will set you free, BUT will you trust Father to protect His servant?

FEBRUARY 25

Where Do I Find Bitterness?

HEBREWS 12:14-15

Follow peace with all men, and holiness, without which no man shall see the Lord: looking diligently lest any man fail of the grace of God; lest any root of bitterness springing up trouble you, and thereby many be defiled.

I am not much of a Boy Scout, but I remember you usually find moss on the north side of a tree, the side away from the sun. Where have I found bitterness in my life? I have found it in the way others have treated or disappointed me, a part of me hidden from the Son.

I am going to go out on a limb and say that perhaps you felt disappointed by God. That sounds dangerous, and why would you ever admit that?

Just because you are "in ministry" doesn't mean you became a completely mature person. Father chose you and the Holy Spirit continues to form Christ in you. **(Phil. 1:6)** *Being confident of this very thing, that he who began a good work in you will perform it until the day of Jesus Christ.* Is He working on your hidden side?

So, my search for information about bitterness comes from a *"how to respond to Father's correction"* warning. Chastening is not easy, and it doesn't always appear like a spanking. My experience shows me that Father's correction often is revealed in conflict with others. I think He is using it to, "kill two birds with one stone." I am not sure I understand this, but He makes it work. **(Rom. 8:18)** *For I reckon that the sufferings of this present time are not worthy to be compared with the glory which shall be revealed in us.*

One more thing to provoke you – *fail, bitterness, trouble, defiled* – these are words that speak of weakness. This is not the fruit of the Holy Spirit, nor His purpose in you. You may be bitter and believe you have a right to be so. All I must do is look at the fruit of your life to know who owns the farm. The Godly process is found in the text; "*Follow peace and holiness.*" This is the pattern of your King. Is it yours?

FEBRUARY 26

What Keeps You Going?

PSALMS 39:7-9

*And now, Lord, what wait I for? my hope is in You.
Deliver me from all my transgressions: make me not the reproach of the
foolish. I was dumb, I opened not my mouth because You did it.*

Does everything seem to be falling apart? The God who loves you is behind it all – **this is the truth.**

[39:7] *My hope is in You* - This is a wake up. The answer to the critic and the questions that plague the mind are found in Christ. **Jesus is not the answer man, but the answer to man.**

Your focus must be on your living relationship with Christ and not the regulation of life. It is not obligation that defines you but your opportunity to live in Christ! [39:8] David is no longer feeling sorry for himself. The truth has made him concerned about his sin.

[39:8] *the reproach (joke) of the foolish* – Do not fret over your sorrows! Stop wasting your energy! Fear the poison of your sin. Your sin will always make you a fool (**Num.32:23b.**)

[39:9] *You did it* - David is silent once more but it is not in resentment but in reliance upon God's chastening. The difficulty of the consequences is in the hand of God. (**Isa.1:25**) *And I will turn my hand upon you, and wash away your dross, and take away all your tin.* [39:10-11] When God corrects, life is never the same. That which the world may consider the testimony to beauty will appear moth eaten (**Isa.64:5-6.**)

[39:12-13] David prays one more time. His thoughts are not about the attacks or how empty he felt, but how much he wants Father to be his everything. David knows he is not alone. Note how He phrases the truth of God's unbreakable commitment to him - *stranger with God* - **not** *a stranger to God*. You are not alone. Jesus cannot lie! (**Heb.13:5b**) *for he has said, I will never leave you, nor forsake you.*

FEBRUARY 27

Under Attack

PSALMS 39:1-3

[v1] I said, I will take heed to my ways, that I sin not with my tongue: I will keep my mouth with a bridle, while the wicked is before me.

Someone has questioned your character and motives. It does not seem that they want an answer; they only want to direct their anger at you. It is a difficult thing to be the target of others complaint. You know that the matter has nothing to do with correction of a mistake or the restoration from a sin, but the intent is your condemnation (**Phil.1:15-16.**)

David was moved to silence. He thought it the safest course of action. The wicked will take the smallest mistake, plunge it like a knife into your soul and turn it. Jesus warned His followers that trouble will come without seeking it (**John15:20.**)

You must remember that your tongues can do you great harm (**James3:6,8.**) David says he put on a muzzle. If your silence is controlled by prayer, then you will yield to Father's justice (**Deut.32:35a.**)

[39:2] *even from good* - David's confusion brought him to silence even about the good. Many medicines are in the form of bitter pills; it is better for you to swallow it whole than to chew it. Foolishness leads you to chew on the bitter things of life instead of trusting the Great Physician to work all things for your good.

[39:3] *My heart was hot* - The distress and doubt churned and boiled his insides. His focus was on his personal problem (a natural reaction.) When He let it out the right way, in prayer to the Father, **then the answer came.** Too often you fixate on the problem or the symptom and not the solution or the reason.

[39:3] *I was musing* - Meditation is valuable if its focus is Christ. He gives the proper perspective to all your thoughts. How long does a cold man need to sit by the fire? - **Until he is warm.** When you are confused, Jesus is the one who will bring you light and warmth. The longer you focus upon Him, the better you will be.

FEBRUARY 28

The Process of Sin

JOSHUA 7:20-21

*And Achan answered Joshua, and said, Indeed I have sinned against the LORD God of Israel, and thus and thus have I done: When I **saw** among the spoils a goodly Babylonish garment, and two hundred shekels of silver, and a wedge of gold of fifty shekels weight, then I **coveted** them, and **took** them; and, behold, they are **hid** in the earth in the midst of my tent, and the silver under it.*

We have all tried to tell this lie. We convinced ourselves that it was inevitable, or it just happened, that I didn't mean to do it, and perhaps the worst of all, it is not my fault. So, the last step in the process of sin is revealed, **the coverup**.

If we compare Achan's "confession" with the information about the original sin in Genesis 3, we begin to see that it has always been the same process.

I saw, I coveted, I took, I hid. Sin is a process. Sin does not come into your life like a huge hole in the street that you failed to see. Down you fall and you swear that you never saw the danger! No, no matter what area it falls under, *lust of the flesh, lust of the eyes, the pride of life*; our first parents and Achan lay it out for us.

We know Achan had to be singled out before he confessed. I am just like him. I keep on trying to get away with *"My besetting sin."* You and I think perhaps God is being merciful (which He is) and I don't have to let it go - yet. Come on, you have preached about this! (**Numbers 32:23**) *Your sin will find you out.*

- Let's be active in the fight – (**Psalms 101:3a**)
  I will set no wicked thing before my eyes.
- Use the soap Father has provided – (**1 John 1:9**)
  If we confess our sins, He is faithful and just to forgive us our sins, and to cleanse us from all unrighteousness.
- You can't cover it up – (**Prov. 28:13**)
  He that covers his sins shall not prosper: but whoso confesses and forsakes them shall have mercy.

FEBRUARY 29

Something To Touch

NUMBERS 15:38-39

Speak unto the children of Israel, and bid them that they make them fringes in the borders of their garments throughout their generations, and that they put upon the fringe of the borders a ribbon of blue: And it shall be unto you for a fringe, that you may look upon it, and remember all the commandments of the LORD, and do them; and that you seek not after your own heart and your own eyes, after which you use to go a whoring.

I believe what Paul says in (**2 Cor. 5:17**) *Therefore if any man be in Christ, he is a new creature: old things are passed away; behold, all things are become new.* But I also know that men have not changed; we need reminders. That is why, no matter what form it takes, a calendar is vital.

As a believer, I have the Holy Spirit to speak into the every day, but I still need an alarm clock. The Holy Spirit takes the Word of God and makes it live in my heart and mind – but I still wear a ring on my left hand. We married the day after my birthday, so I would remember! You need reminders of your living relationship with the God of the Universe. Father understands this, which is why we celebrate communion: *"remember His death, till He comes."*

I have been deliberate in choosing my alarm clock. It has features and failsafes that help me be on time. I use my phone calendar and the alarms it provides because I can be easily delayed. I also use traditional methods of remembrance such as photos, paintings, poems on posters, and regular experiences like a Pastor's Breakfast that helps me connect and give me accountability.

Have I driven the point into the ground yet?

You must be intentional to create personal as well as traditional experiences and reminders AND then commit to them! Father knows you need them and from our text, I would say that we need them every day.

MARCH 1

If You Cut Down – Be Ready to Plant

JEREMIAH 1:10
See, I have this day set you over the nations and over the kingdoms, to root out, and to pull down, and to destroy, and to throw down, **to build, and to plant.**

2 TIMOTHY 4:2
Preach the word; *be instant in season, out of season; reprove, rebuke, exhort with all longsuffering and doctrine.*

Perhaps this is common sense. It is in farm country. You don't clear a field unless you plan to plant. You rob the land of protection and are presented with the possibility of soil erosion.

I believe the same is true with the souls of men. To attack or seek to remove the covering of a person's psyche, culture, or personal experience, (no matter how sinful,) without the preparation to commit to the process of planting the truth and nurturing it is irresponsible. Don't cut if you are not ready to heal.

Jesus refers to the results of this abusive spiritual behavior in (**Luke 11:24-26.**) [v26] *Then he goes (the demon) and takes to him seven other spirits more wicked than himself; and they enter in, and dwell there: and the last state of that man is worse than the first.*

The Gospel is the only thing that changes lives. We are directed to preach repentance and faith toward the Lord Jesus. We must be ready to do both.

We are privileged to speak the truth "in love." The love aspect means we must be ready to commit to the process of being disciple makers. With the Holy Spirit's enablement and our willing hearts, let us prepare the ground, plant the seed of the Gospel, and encourage the harvest.

MARCH 2

It's About the Economy, Stupid!

2 CHRONICLES 10:7-8

And they spoke unto him, saying, If you are kind to this people, and please them, and speak good words to them, they will be your servants forever. But he forsook the counsel which the old men gave him and took counsel with the young men that were brought up with him, that stood before him.

When we examine the leadership mistakes of Rehoboam, we understand that this was God performing His Word *(2 Chron. 10:15,)* but there is much to be gained in not leading as he did. He followed the advice of inexperienced men who thought that ruling was a given because you have the Position. They thought leadership was by testosterone.

Leading by Position or a title (like Pastor) is the lowest form of leadership. God understands the soul of man. I believe that the basic need of everyone is to feel safe. Even in the matter of redemption, John states this basic need of people: *(1 John 4:19) We love him, **because** he first loved us.* Your church needs to feel safe under your leadership, not oppressed.

You became a Pastor/Elder by Permission. No matter what the process, you are leading because someone wants you to succeed. If you want your people to keep following you, you must (by the help of the Holy Spirit) begin to lead by Performance. This is accomplished by the process of following the example of Jesus in the ministries of Prophet – proclaiming the truth, Priest – applying the truth, and King – mirroring the truth: *"love as I love you."*

Peter warned us that shepherding calls for compassion, not compulsion *(1 Peter 5:2.)* Jesus told us His ministry rule of service *(Mark 10:45.)*

Forced leadership ends in fracture and pain for all. It is not about making your people feel comfortable but in them believing that you understand their need.

MARCH 3

Of Course!

PROVERBS 3:9-10

Honor the LORD with your substance, and with the first fruits of all your increase: so shall your barns be filled with plenty, and your presses shall burst out with new wine.

Shall we give the "Sunday School" response to this direction? *"Of course, this is the right thing to do!"* Most would consider it a promise. Others would call it a positive observation on a righteous life. You might have used this text when preaching on giving. Nothing wrong with any of this. But how does your practice line up with the instruction?

Honor the LORD – I understand this to mean that I must express a right attitude toward the God of all creation and that this attitude must be connected to my actions. I will commit to the process of recognizing and identifying the success of my efforts to prosper, in every area of life, as God's blessing.

As I express and demonstrate God's blessing in every facet of my labors, God will multiply my blessings to the point that I cannot contain them, and they will overflow to others.

Honor - is also understood to mean, *in the way God has prescribed.* The use of this blessing must be as He directs. **(Isa. 58:7)** *Is it not to deal your bread to the hungry, and that you bring the poor that are cast out to your house? When you see the naked, that you cover him; and that you hide not thyself from your own flesh?*

Real religion is Compassion and Personal Purity (**James 1:27.**) Honoring God is more than my tithe, it is my intentional attitude and actions toward ANYONE who is in need. *"I cannot do everything, but I can do something."*

I feel that I am often selfish with the blessing God has given me and therefore have missed out on greater blessing. My purpose: to make you think about how you *Honor the LORD,* to the point you pray and act in obedience. *"If the shoe doesn't fit...."*

MARCH 4

Moses or Joshua?

JOSHUA 1:5

There shall not any man be able to stand before you all the days of your life: as I was with Moses, so I will be with you: I will not fail you, nor forsake you.

Well, what are you? Are you Moses or Joshua? I was at a BRN *Accelerate* meeting and listened to a revitalization speaker use Joshua as an example of building ministry. He made a great presentation and was genuinely interested in helping and encouraging pastors in their work for the Kingdom.

But his remarks sent my mind in a slightly different direction. So, I approached him with my thanks and gave him this observation. *"Everyone here wants to be Joshua, but most of us are Moses. Everyone wants glory but most are designed for the grind."*

Are you a Moses or a Joshua? It is great to be the guy who leads a group of believers into God's promised land, but you might be the fella that helps them believe and understand those promises. It is exciting to lead committed soldiers of the Cross into battle, but you might be the Drill Sargent that prepared those soldiers for battle.

To me, this is the difference between Moses and Joshua. One patiently prepared; the other skillfully led.

Yes, by God's grace, you might be able to do both (a freak of nature) but the Scripture is full of examples that prove my point. **(1 Cor. 3:6)** *I have planted, Apollos watered; but God gave the increase.*

Jesus is Prophet, Priest, and King. It is also understood that every pastor needs to model the same ministry of being a teacher, a caregiver, and a leader to his church. BUT the truth is, you may be great at one, good at another, and will probably stink at the third.

You should major on your "Major," and, as is with all areas, rely on the Holy Spirit to provide you help with your deficit, that will be found in other leaders.

So, you may not like it, but are you Moses or Joshua?

MARCH 5

Might Does Not Make Right

2 CHRONICLES 11:4

Thus says the LORD, you shall not go up, nor fight against your brethren: return every man to his house: for this thing is done of me. And they obeyed the words of the LORD and returned from going against Jeroboam.

Most of the time, I would say that you are right. After all, you are the Pastor. You are God's chosen man. Father placed you in this sacred office for a reason. Paul backs up this in **(Hebrews 13:17)** *Obey them that have the rule over you and submit yourselves: for they watch for your souls, as they that must give account, that they may do it with joy, and not with grief: for that is unprofitable for you.*

I have been where you are. It makes no sense for you to be opposed in this manner. You are not leading people into immorality but this intentional resistance to your leadership, well,… I think the enemy is working overtime! I know the enemy seeks to divide and conqueror. Perhaps this is God revealing those that "don't belong on the bus."

But you should consider this next thought as vital. Don't feed the demons through your malice. Conflict is the door to intimacy. This is your opportunity to love what Jesus loves. The words that sustain me in this kind of hurtful time are found in **(2 Tim. 2:24)** *And the servant of the Lord must not strive; but be gentle unto all men, apt to teach, patient, ….*

Rehoboam was King. They were in rebellion, but God had other plans. You don't have to be a "doormat," but it can be hard to lead when Father does something that does not fit your five year plan.

You are still the Pastor - at least for today.

Be the pastor, even if this, fits you to a "T." **(2 Cor. 12:15)** *And I will very gladly spend and be spent for you; though the more abundantly I love you, the less I be loved.*

MARCH 6

Keep Your Vows

ECCLESIASTES 5:1-7

Keep your foot when you go to the house of God, and be more ready to hear, than to give the sacrifice of fools: for they consider not that they do evil. Be not rash with your mouth and let not your heart be hasty to utter anything before God: for God is in heaven, and you upon earth: therefore, let your words be few. For a dream comes through the multitude of business; and a fool's voice is known by the multitude of words. When you vow a vow unto God, defer not to pay it; for he has no pleasure in fools: pay that which you have vowed. Better is it that you should not vow, than that you should vow and not pay. Suffer not your mouth to cause your flesh to sin; neither say before the angel, that it was an error: wherefore should God be angry at your voice, and destroy the work of your hands? For in the multitude of dreams and many words there are also divers vanities: but you, fear God.

Isn't it wonderful that Father understands us and deals with us in mercy. I know I must follow my Father's example and keep my word. My Father speaks the truth. My Father keeps His promises.

What are vows? They are promises you make before God or to God. You call upon God to give witness and take part in this agreement. Is this a cultural matter only for the Old Testament?

I took a marriage vow. I made a promise when ordained to ministry. Some of you made a vow as you were inducted into military service.

As a child of God, I am to let my "yes and no" stand by itself, but this does not mean that vows are unscriptural. Hebrews tells us that God made a vow (**Hebrews 6:17.**) Solomon gives us a powerful warning that I believe we must accept as valid for today. Watch your words. Keep your promises. Do not be as the fools. Father is listening. There are consequences for idle words.

MARCH 7

A Pencil Can

3 JOHN 1:4
I have no greater joy than to hear that my children walk in truth.

(I admit it. When I share these personal insights, I do some cherry picking for the related scripture.)

In a place of honor on my desk is an old frozen juice can. Of course, the can is open, containing writing instruments, a letter opener, and a pair of scissors. Wrapped around the can is a faded and tattered label. It bares some blue crayon squiggles and this imprint, "I love my Daddy." A loving Junior Church teacher wrote the name of the giver, "John."

It replaced a leather-bound cup that was created to handsomely hold the tools of immediate need. That cup went the way of all flesh, but this cherished gift will remain.

Yes, I am sentimental. Does my son remember this gift? I am not sure that he was old enough to understand that he was making a Father's Day gift. But I remember his smiling face when he ran up to give it to me. He still has the same smile.

I hope you have or that you will have these kinds of items and memories in your life. Father has a way of using them to soften us when we are so sure we are right and comfort us when we know we have been so wrong. The days pass so quickly. You need these little things to remind you of what is truly important.

MARCH 8

The Principles of Christian Liberty - Expediency

1 CORINTHIANS 6:12A
All things are lawful unto me, but all things are not expedient:

Does it help me in my Christian walk?

Can a Christian truly say that he is better than an unbeliever? We are just sinners saved by grace, yet there is something dramatically different between the believer and an unbeliever; it is the power of the Cross. Are you the image of perfection? No, but you are the reflection of He who is perfect. There is someone better in us and nothing to match His perfection **(Gal. 2:20.)**

Paul taught the truth. Salvation is by grace alone through faith alone. There is no warfare between Law and Grace. They have the same author. The conflict is between our works and God's Grace. The works of the flesh condemn us, and the works of the Law convict us, but the ministry of Grace frees us to live in Christ's righteousness.

All things are lawful – those things which the Moral Law does not condemn. As a believer, God's Word is now a sanctifying force in your life through the power of the Holy Spirit using the Word of God. *(John 17:17) Sanctify them through Thy truth: Thy word is truth.*

We must therefore ask the hard questions.

But not all things are expedient – **expedient,** *it means to bear together, to contribute.* Can we ask and answer the question - **Does this aid me in my Christian life?** *(Hebrews 12:1-2)* To give an example; a boat may float, but does that boat get me where I need to go?

To answer that question requires focus. *Do you know where you are going? What is God's calling on your life?* To quote God's question to Moses,

"What is in your hand?"

MARCH 9

Principles of Christian Liberty - Self-Control

1 CORINTHIANS 6:12B
all things are lawful for me, but I will not be brought under the power of any.

Do I control it, or does it control me?

All of us can be under the control of something. Some of us fall victim more easily than others. Substances can control us but so can activities or relationships. I heard of a pastor who lost his pulpit over the game of croquet. He started playing at the community court next to the Fire Hall to develop relationships with others in the community. He discovered that he was good at it and became known as a player who was eager to win. He used the spiteful, but legal rules of the game to win and became hated for it. Soon, he was playing as often as he could, to the neglect of his responsibilities to his family and his church. The sadness in the matter was that he was unaware that he had a problem.

(***1 Cor. 9: 27***) *But I keep under my body and bring it into subjection: lest that by any means, when I have preached to others, I myself should be a castaway.*

The Greeks could allow interests and activities to define them, but we do the same. We call them fanatics and ourselves fans. Those with problems we call addicts. Christ must make a difference and provide us balance, or He is no different from an addiction. We must seek Christ and the even balance. We must ask and answer the hard question:

Am I willing to seek the Holy Spirit's power and insight to reveal and remove that which binds me?

Are you willing to pray this way? (***Psalm 19:12-13***) *Who can understand his errors? cleanse me from secret faults. {13} Keep back Your servant also from presumptuous sins; let them not have dominion over me: then shall I be upright, and I shall be innocent from the great transgression.*

MARCH 10

Principles of Christian Liberty - Glorification

1 CORINTHIANS 6:19-20

What? Do you not know that your body is the temple of the Holy Spirit which is in you, which you have of God, and you are not your own? For you are bought with a price: therefore, glorify God in your body, and in your spirit, which are God's.

Will it bring glory to God?

In **1 Cor. 6:13-14**, Paul quotes a common phrase the Greeks used in expressing their love for food - Food for the stomach. (It is like Baptists and casseroles.) God designed our bodies in a wonderful way, but it is not for self-indulgence. This physical aspect of life has a determined end.

(**Heb. 9:27**) *And as it is appointed unto men once to die, but after this the judgment:* The body is a vehicle but not an end in itself. The "Reverse", on a car is great but not at 65mph!

The body is not for fornication –The Greeks considered sex to be like eating; but Father says that fornication is a perversion of God's purpose **(Hebrews 13:4.)**

But for the Lord -You are a sexual being, but sex is not the singular purpose of your body. Your body is designed to enable you to glorify God. God's plan of salvation is the total redemption of your entire being - Spirit, Soul, and Body. That is part of the reason for the bodily resurrection of Christ **(Rom. 6:5.)** We have a better vehicle awaiting us **(Phil. 3:20-21.)**

Can we believe and do the hard thing?

We must claim the power of God over our bodies that we might glorify Christ, for He has bought us with His Blood.

MARCH 11

The Limits of Christian Liberty - Edification

1 CORINTHIANS 8:9-12

But take heed lest by any means this liberty of yours become a stumbling block to them that are weak. For if any man see you who has knowledge sit at meat in the idol's temple, shall not the conscience of him which is weak be emboldened to eat those things which are offered to idols; And through your knowledge shall the weak brother perish, for whom Christ died? But when you sin so against the brethren, and wound their weak conscience, you sin against Christ.

Does it help or hinder others in knowing and living for the Lord Jesus?

God will not love you any more than He does right now, and He will never love you any less than He does right now. [v9] *Take heed* – Because you are loved, you are commanded to show that love to those still confused and in fear.

[v11] *weak brother perish* – this does not mean that they lose their salvation, but your puffed-up attitude could enslave a weaker soul. (**Romans 14:23**) *And he that doubts is damned if he eat, because he eats not of faith: for whatsoever is not of faith is sin.*

This is a Life Principle of the Christian.

Paul is not defending legalism or ignorance. He is insisting that your motivation for your actions must not be your rights or your knowledge. Compassion on the weak and enslaved must be demonstrated from a heart ruled by King's love.

For whom Christ died – Are you glad for His sacrifice? Then honor Him by caring for the weak and the hurting.

[v12] *their weak conscience* – **As a man thinks so is he** – The thought life, the conscience is a powerful tool (**2 Cor. 10:5.**)

If you are not willing or able to consider your weaker brother, then you are not living in the liberty that Christ has provided; a liberty to do what is right.

MARCH 12

The Limits of Christian Liberty - Consecration

1 CORINTHIANS 10:20-21

But I say that the things which the Gentiles sacrifice, they sacrifice to devils, and not to God: and I would not that you should have fellowship with devils. You cannot drink the cup of the Lord, and the cup of devils: you cannot be partakers of the Lord's table, and of the table of devils.

Does it hide my testimony or show that my faith in Christ makes a difference?

[v20] *They sacrifice to demons, not to God* – No matter how sincere, no matter what they say it represents; God said, "No physical representations of me!"

(**Exodus 20:4**) *You shall not make unto yourself any graven image, or any likeness of anything that is in heaven above, or that is in the earth beneath, or that is in the water under the earth:*

Behind each icon, each statue, each false representation of God, is a demon leading lost souls away from the truth (*2 Cor. 4:3-4.*)

[v21] *You cannot drink the cup of demons and the Lord's Table* – We may not worship at the feet of icons or saints. We may not pray to ancestors or the spirits of trees. If it takes the place of God or makes a claim to represent God, it is an idol. It could be a job, sports, family, recreation, hobby – anything or anyone that removes God from first place in your heart (*Matt. 6:24!*) It doesn't say, "You should not, **it says you cannot!**" There is room for only one on the Throne!

How do we usurp God?
- Put other things in place of His worship.
- Put other tasks before His service.
- Follow other commands before His precepts.
- Love someone more than Him. (*Matt. 10:37-39*)

**If you are a devoted follower of Jesus Christ,
your habits must include intentional worship.**

MARCH 13

And Such Where Some of You

1 CORINTHIANS 6:11
And such were some of you: but you are washed, but you are sanctified, but you are justified in the name of the Lord Jesus, and by the Spirit of our God.

I grew up in a pastor's home. What I saw in the pulpit, I experienced at the dinner table. I heard the name of Jesus used as the theme of our song and lived in His love and mercy as it was extended to me.

What was a shock to my being was that not everyone knew what I knew as a way of life. Even in the homes of other believers, Jesus was not the head of the house. I was learning a lesson, but it took me a long time to learn what the Holy Spirit was imparting.

Paul reminds the Corinthians of their past and how that was a sign of their separation from God. All these wicked life patterns controlled and condemned them BUT – now everything is changing. This is what Jesus has done for all:

Washed – to be cleansed fully. The blood of Christ has removed your sin **(Col. 1:14.)**

Sanctified – you have been called by a loving God to be set aside for His use.

Justified – Confirmed to be righteous or, *"just as if I'd never sinned."*

All through the finished work of the Lord Jesus upon Calvary and the continuing work of the Holy Spirit within us.

Back to my life lesson: I came to Christ in an environment that proclaimed the Lordship of Christ. When I began to observe others; whether they were believers or seekers, I became judgmental. As I approached my teen years, "hypocrite," was the term that I often used to describe this observation of inconsistent behavior. Perhaps I was right, but I have also come to understand how wrong I was.

The Gospel will make a change in the heart and life of every believer. They will continually grow and show that they belong to Jesus. My life lesson was that not everyone has the blessing into which I was born, and then "born-again." My job is to help, not judge. Look for the change and help it grow.

MARCH 14

What is the Cost?

2 SAMUEL 24:24

And the king said unto Araunah, no, but I will surely buy it from you at a price: neither will I offer burnt offerings unto the LORD my God of that which costs me nothing. So, David bought the threshing floor and the oxen for fifty shekels of silver.

The account is challenging and dramatic. David's sin was numbering the people to determine political/military advantage. Seems like that shouldn't be a problem, in fact we might consider it wise, except God said the King was not to do this. His trust was to be in God for power and protection and not in a head count.

David is directed to make an offering for his sin and Araunah, as a devoted servant of the King, offers to give David everything he needs for free. But David understands that sacrifice means more than an act; it means the expression of your attitude toward God.

His words provide us a Biblical principle. Sacrifice should cost you something. If it does not, then it is worth nothing. It has no value to you or to God.

Next to this truth, I would place the thought of the great Missionary, C.T. Studd who said, *"If Christ be God, and died for me; then no sacrifice I make can be too great."* Paul presents it this way. **(Phil. 3:8)** *Yes doubtless, and I count all things but loss for the excellency of the knowledge of Christ Jesus my Lord: for whom I have suffered the loss of all things, and do count them but dung, that I may win Christ.*

In your call to ministry, you may have given up a pursuit that would have brought you many good things. I gave up a career as an architect to build lives for the Kingdom. Some might consider this a sacrifice, but I have come to know it as a greater opportunity.

David's sacrifice was for sin. Dealing with sin always costs you something. It is worth paying the price. The opportunity it gave David to speak into your life is priceless. May your sacrifice be an opportunity to bless.

MARCH 15

The Wrath of Man

PSALMS 76:9-10

When God arose to judgment, to save all the meek of the earth. Selah. Surely the wrath of man shall praise You: the remainder of wrath shall You restrain.

Here is a passage that, in other English versions, fails to provide the power found in it. God rises at the precise moment to act on behalf of those who fully depend upon Him. This is a truth so marvelous that it demands (*Selah*) to be repeated. The God of the Universe will act for me! He will save me! His arm is mighty, His hand is not short! There are no limits to what He will do on my behalf!

Truly, He will use the anger and visceral behavior of wicked men against them. Their cursing, plotting, and wicked traps will return to condemn, confuse, and entrap them. Instead of harming the child of God, the evil they intend will bring forth the praises of our Great Captain from His devoted followers. Jesus is the one who will be exalted because even the behavior of the wicked will be directed to accomplish His determined plan to protect, empower, and bring peace to His own.

The remainder of wrath shall you restrain – some versions say, *wear as a belt* – meaning to wear as a trophy of conquest. I prefer the Authorized rendering, for it reminds me that men's wickedness does not end with their failure or disappointment. They are still in rebellion as declared in **(Psalms 2:1)** *Why do the heathen rage, and the people imagine a vain thing?* They hold on to the emptiness *-vain thing* – thinking that their wickedness will finally defeat the Almighty. He will never allow any eternal harm to those He has made His own. The wicked will continue to fume and fuss, or as Shakespeare said, *"Sound and fury, signifying nothing."* Our God will ever be in control and the wicked will be reserved to everlasting punishment. Praise His Name!

MARCH 16

I Want to be Right

ROMANS 2:4
Or do you despise the riches of his goodness and forbearance and longsuffering; not knowing that the goodness of God leads you to repentance?

Sometimes it makes me feel superior to condemn others for their ignorance or the humanistic, destructive patterns they promote through every form of media that they can control. I am assured by the Scriptures that my Righteous God will bring the consequences of their foolishness upon their heads. Yes, it feels good to be right!

But then the Holy Spirit brings back to my memory the testimony of Dr. Carter. He was an extremely brilliant teacher (and a bit intimidating.) I remember this transparent statement. *"I had a full scholarship to Cambridge. While I was there, I never lost an argument – and I never led a soul to Christ."*

It is the goodness of God that leads us to repentance. I know I must be prepared to give answer for the hope within me and I must not be ashamed as I rightly divide the Word of Truth. But **John 3:16** is still the Gospel in the nutshell. God loved, God gave, and I believed. I must be a scholar that speaks the truth in love **(Eph. 4:15.)**

I have close family members that have chosen to reject the Gospel. I am not sure if they will ever repent. I pray for them, plead for them before the Throne of Grace. I have told them the truth as best I could, even if at that point, I was angry at their choices. I do not support nor defend their decisions, BUT I am seeking to be obedient to my King and love them, no matter what.

Jesus is the Judge. He said judgment is His right as Supreme Ruler. I am content that He never makes a mistake **(Gen. 18:25.)** By the help of the Holy Spirit, I will show the goodness of God to those I love and to those of whom I am not fond. I want to be right.

MARCH 17

Do You Know It When You See It?

LUKE 9:49-50

And John answered and said, Master, we saw one casting out devils in Your name; and we forbid him, because he was not with us. And Jesus said unto him, forbid him not: for he that is not against us is for us.

When I was young, I would take walks with my mother. She would sight something in a nearby tree and express her joy at the find. "Where is it?" I would ask and she would point. I would look along her point of sight – and couldn't see it. We eventually figured out that I needed glasses!

John sees something he doesn't recognize and believes he speaks in the best interests of his Master. He is wrong. He does not have Kingdom Glasses. We all need Kingdom Glasses when walking outside of our comfort zone.

When we are young in our faith, we need and hold on to patterns of behavior that help us protect and plan our life with Christ. They may be culturally driven, but they help. We are fully committed to following Jesus and convinced that the way we understand, express, and deliver on that commitment is THE WAY.

The conviction is not wrong, but it is not right. The illustration of a baseball pitcher comes to mind. The main idea is to get the batter out. That does not mean the pitcher has to throw strikes every time to accomplish his goal, he just must pitch within the rules. Personally, I throw a mean side arm curve ball.

Serving in the Kingdom calls for obedience to the King. God has had many servants acting in obedience that would not fit into my culture (walking around nude is out!) There are certain forms of polity that make me rankle but that doesn't mean that the Holy Spirit can't use them. I am not an Arminian in theology, but I have Brothers in Christ who have not seen it my way yet. They are still part of the family. Keep those glasses handy and walk in love.

MARCH 18

No, Not me!

1 KINGS 19:4 (READ, 1 KINGS 18 & 19)

But he (Elijah) himself went a day's journey into the wilderness ... and he requested for himself that he might die; and said, It is enough; now, O LORD, take away my life; for I am not better than my fathers.

We are all the same, but all different. All of us experience depression. Sometimes it is caused by circumstance, physical illness, trauma, and some have a chemical or physiological imbalance as the catalyst.

I am thankful that my "walks in darkness" have been brief, but others feel like they live there. I believe that attitude and how we feed the soul, have an influence on improving our condition, However, some face great difficultly. It is not, "all in their head."

Elijah is a textbook case for this **process**. I pray that you will see the truth. With Father's help, all can come through. Father will bring healing, but it is still a **difficult process**.

This is a depressed prophet! This didn't just happen. Think about his stressors. For over 3 years, he has been in hiding or an **Abnormal Lifestyle**.

[Chp.18], he experiences tremendous **Exertion** and then runs the race of a lifetime [v46.] Yes, this was all planned and enabled by God, but all this is outside the "normal."

In [19:1-2], he is now facing real **Conflict**. [v3] The threat is real, and this alters his **Perception of Reality**. This previously brave man is acting in fear. Some call this wise, but we will label it **Avoidance**.

In [v3-4] The next stressor is **Isolation**. He leaves his servant and hides in the wilderness. [v4] Now the strain of this ministry comes out in the expression of **Dark thoughts**.

We might think that he is exhausted, [v5] and he is. **Sleep Patterns** outside the normal are a sign of depression. A **Change in Appetite** is also a marker for this difficult time.

[vv10,14] We hear a **Looped Negative Focus.** If you see yourself in any of this, you are not alone AND Jesus understands. Tomorrow we speak about the healing.

MARCH 19

No, Not Me! – Solution

1 KINGS 19:9 (PLEASE READ 1 KINGS 19)
... behold, the word of the LORD came to him, and he said unto him, ***What doest thou here, Elijah?***

Our subject is depression. Our focus is that the God who made us is the only one who can help us. It took a process to get us into *"the dark night of the soul,"* and it will be a process to lead us out. This process will not be about you, but about Jesus.

Yesterday I covered the stressors in Elijah's life: An Abnormal Lifestyle, Extreme Exertion, Conflict, an altered Perception of Reality, Avoidance, Isolation, Dark Thoughts, altered Sleep Patterns, Change in Appetite, and a Looped Negative Focus. Have you ever visited any of these places?

The reverse trip is also a process. God says **Nourishment** is important [v5,7.] A trip to the table is essential, not to the altar. Do not deny the physical.

[v6] **Rest** means sleep but perhaps for you, a change of pace or venue.

[v8] **Exercise** is the next step, and it is a LONG journey. You need this in your routine. You will not heal without it.

Now, we move to the mind.[v9] **Purposeful Questions**. God is not confused but Elijah is. The question challenges Elijah's direction and his source of authority (**Very important.**)

[v10,14] To get better we have to dump. **Expression of Thought** – your burdens, problems, fear – you must let them out! Elijah is saying, *"I tried, but nothing really changed. I failed and YOU failed me."*

[v11,12] A fantastic display of power, or is it? **Examination of Values,** why do you limit God or believe that He will always work, only in the supernatural or spectacular? When did He give up His job and leave it to you? [v13] Do you think that since you now have the facts, everything is good? **God Re-questions**- do you *really* follow? Am I your authority?

[v15-17] **Responsibility** –No retirement, just reassignment. No satisfaction without service.

Finally, [v18] **Control,** this was never about you, do you understand? Never. Remember, God works in process.

MARCH 20

Did You Buy Your Ticket?

JONAH 2:8
They that observe lying vanities forsake their own mercy.

We know this story. It has always amazed me that Jonah told on himself. Jonah was the only one who could share such detail of his resistance to the will of God. He spent three days and nights inside this creature prepared by God before his resistance began to crumble. That is stubborn! I would have been begging for mercy before I was thrown overboard!

The shortest sermon ever recorded (**2:4**) brought the greatest expression of repentance ever seen, and the text continues to reveal a hard heart on Jonah's part (**4:1-2.**) Most evangelists would be overwhelmed with this kind of response! It shows that the Holy Spirit can use anything and anyone to accomplish the purposes of God.

I believe that my text is the heart of this account. It contains the confession of a rebellious heart beginning to yield to the unchanging will of God. I like to paraphrase it in this manner: *We run away from the place where we can get our only help.*

The stubborn heart turns away from the loving Father of Grace because we want to believe the lies we tell ourselves: *"God doesn't understand me. His plan will ruin me. I can't do what He is asking. I will never be fulfilled if I do things His way. My joy, my giftedness leads me in another direction. I can serve God better by doing things my way."*

To *observe* means to follow or hold to a specific pattern. *Lying vanities* is a doubling down on this truth; what you follow is a lie and it is completely empty.

Forsake is the opposite of observe, it means to turn away from it completely.

Mercy is the loving kindness of God. God was merciful to Jonah; he got to tell his story. Father has shown His mercy to us, for we have all paid for our ticket to Tarshish.

MARCH 21

And He Healed Them All

LUKE 6:19
And the whole multitude sought to touch him: for there went virtue out of him and healed them all.

Luke tells of multitudes of people that came to hear and to be healed. People with differences so vast came together with one purpose: to touch Jesus.

It is one thing to want to be in contact with someone so different, so special, and certainly another matter as to whether they wish to connect with you. This is the wonderful difference between our Jesus and any celebrity of any time in history.

Why did they seek Him? Because He could do what no one else could do: speak the truth, cast out oppression, heal our sickness! Luke so wonderfully and simply tells us, "*For there went virtue* (power) *out of Him and healed them all.*"

I am overwhelmed! I know I should expect nothing less from the Creator and Sustainer of the Universe but is fills me with thankful tears. *"He healed them all."* Of course He did! God so loved He gave – God the Son came to give Himself, and He did! All power belongs to Him. He does not have to work it up, store it up, make it up; all power is from and because of who He is, God.

(Matthew 28:18b) ... *All power is given unto Me in heaven and in earth.* He didn't get that power because of Calvary; He is that power. Calvary and the resurrection made Him our Savior, but He has always been the power.

I am partial to the word *virtue because* it gives me a vision of the purity God provides with His healing. No recurrence of the sickness, no partial cleansing, nothing in remission – it is gone, just like my sin.

Oh, to be His hand extended,
Reaching out to the oppressed.
Let me touch Him, let me touch Jesus,
So that others may know and be blessed!
"Let Me Touch Him" by Stuart Hamlin

MARCH 22

Am I Your Enemy?

GALATIANS 4:16
Am I therefore become your enemy, because I tell you the truth?

A couple comes to you with serious problems. You prayerfully listen and provide sound council from God's Word. It is the truth. What else can you say? You have proven this direction to be true in your own life. You have offered real help in this spiritual plan.

They respond to the truth and soon things are better. They are showing signs of healthy recovery. You are thankful that Father has demonstrated His faithfulness. No one else knows about this; just the couple, you, and Jesus.

BUT something is not right. You start to sense resistance, perhaps even resentment from the people that you sought to help. Too soon they are out the door over some unrelated matter and too late for you to make a difference – you became the enemy. *You knew too much.*

This is not an isolated incident. Other pastors have experienced this as well. Things like this make you want to "take down your shingle."

Let me share what I believe happened. Through the Word, you showed them the sin that was present. It was clear that this was the problem. They wanted the medicine to take care of the symptoms, but they never committed to the cure. They did not like the consequences of their disobedience, but they were not willing to invest in the process of obedience.

It is similar to King Rehoboam; God punished him for forsaking the Law. He repented and things got better but -

(**2 Chron. 12:14**) *And he did evil, because he **prepared** not his heart to seek the LORD.* **Prepare** – to be erect, to fix or apply – he did only what he had to, to avoid the consequences.

> **But you know what happened and they can't hide.**
> **You are the enemy.**

MARCH 23

Litigation

1 CORINTHIANS 6:7-8

Now therefore there is utterly a fault among you, because you go to law one with another. Why do you not rather take wrong? why do you not rather suffer yourselves to be defrauded? No, you do wrong, and defraud, and that your brethren.

In Western Christianity, we are always ready to *stand for our rights!* If we do not protest, go to court, we shall lose our God given rights! Please, I do not want to be misunderstood (though, I am on dangerous ground.) I believe God wants us to protect the weak, stand against injustice, and oppose the oppressor.

We might all be able to relate horror stories of church splits that were so acrimonious that they became a "byword" of false Christianity. Jesus commanded that we "love one another," and this active behavior must be continually refined. John Phillips declared that *"Love is not only the practical truth of Christianity, but it is also the practical test of Christianity."*

In 1 Corinthians 6, Paul recognizes that Christians can have severe disagreements, whether on an ecclesiastical or personal level, but taking the matter before the world betrays the truth of God's forever family. The Greek culture enjoyed litigation. Those who abide in the presence of God do not, must not descend to lower judgments.

To be cheated by a brother in Christ is shameful but Paul says taking him to court is worse! We deal with a Greater Judge. He says that discipline belongs to Him. The obedient citizen of the Kingdom is to trust and always keep his word **(Ps. 15:4b.)**

The legal system is established by God to protect the weak. You belong to a Greater Sovereign. Appeal to Him.

MARCH 24

The Numbers Game

2 CHRONICLES 14:11
And Asa cried unto the LORD his God, and said, LORD, it is nothing with You to help, whether with many, or with them that have no power: help us, O LORD our God; for we rest on You, and in Your name, we go against this multitude. O LORD, You are our God; let not man prevail against You.

I would like to tell you that numbers are not important. It is attitude that wins the day, but we have all lost a game by one point! I have helped fill out those "annual reports." I call it the "Nickels, Noses, and Kneelers" annual report. How much, how many, and what kind of decisions have been made. I would like to tell you that this isn't the true test of your effectiveness, but many a pastor has been fired over this reporting.

Your affect on the Kingdom is not strictly measured by numbers. As a pastor, you are to be a reflection of the person of Christ to your church family. Jesus is Prophet, High Priest, and coming King. You are to imitate these wonderful roles by the help of the Holy Spirit. You will not be great at all three. You might be good at one, OK at the second, and struggle at the third. However, you are making an impact for the Kingdom in the lives of the Master's sheep. When you are obeying the Great Commandment and using who you are and what you have been given to help form Christ in lives, we call that faithfulness. That is real success.

Getting past the numbers means you see people as Jesus sees them. You must love what Jesus loves and I can't remember Jesus ever asking for a numbers report. I know that numbers are tools to help guide us. People vote with their feet but if your focus is on head count instead of heart impact, then the program is driving the ministry.

The Holy Spirit did not make a mistake with your giftedness. When you place yourself in His control, (**Ps. 119:9,11,**) numbers reflect His blessing and not your burden.

MARCH 25

The Gracious Father God

LUKE 11:13

If you, being evil, know how to give good gifts unto your children: how much more shall your heavenly Father give the Holy Spirit to them that ask Him?

A recent tragedy in the sports world turned the world on its head and demonstrated that competitors can be compassionate. Life is of greater value than the score, and man is capable of acts of kindness that reflect the divine. It causes us to inquire, why isn't this goodness seen all the time? Truly, that is the point. Man is only good because of God. It takes the pressures of life to reveal the real motivation of the heart.

Our text is the conclusion of a group of illustrations Jesus uses to show that Father is good all the time. Jesus is teaching what is usually called The Lord's Prayer. His illustrations are examples of neighbors and families and how they might respond to needs. Jesus compares their constrained responses to the way that Father God positively answers all the time.

We respond to the needs of others because of constraint or through obligation. It causes me to wonder if man is ever capable of altruism. Father God is not evil. He does not need anything from us, nor does He require reciprocation. **(Matthew 5:45)** *That you may be the children of your Father which is in heaven: for he makes his sun to rise on the evil and on the good and sends rain on the just and on the unjust.*

God is the giver of every perfect gift, and He has taught us to give. Our motivation may be questionable, but your Father is more than able to give to His children the gracious gift of The Holy Spirit through the perfect sacrifice of Jesus. The Holy Spirit enables us to love as Father God loves, completely and unconditionally.

Our asking for the Holy Spirit is not about getting His presence but yielding to His control. We are safe and able to truly love because Father gives.

MARCH 26

Yet a Little Slumber

PROVERBS 6:9-11
How long will you sleep, O sluggard? when will you arise out of your sleep? Yet a little sleep, a little slumber, a little folding of the hands to sleep: So shall your poverty come as one that travails, and your want, as an armed man.

My life pattern has never been as an early riser. I had a poster that read, "The early bird catches the worm; but who wants worms?!" I can remember the summer days with my dad yelling these verses up to me. His favorite was, *"As a door turns upon its hinges, so does the slothful upon his bed!"* **(Prov. 24:16.)**

There is a great advantage in diligence. I have learned the satisfaction of getting a task done sooner than later. Don't misunderstand me; there are some of us that need the pressure of a deadline to find the motivation we need to get the task done. We enjoy the pressure of the limited time. We often feel we do our best work when we have these constraints. At least, that is what we like to think.

You cannot play the "Lone Ranger" and be a good pastor, You must plan ahead. **(Prov. 4:26)** *Ponder the path of your feet and let all your ways be established.* Not everyone can be extemporaneous.

My wife has a beautiful voice and loves to sing for her King, but I must give her at least a week to prepare before she is comfortable. I want her to succeed, so I plan.

As a pastor I must be a team player to help others succeed. That is what a good leader does. You patiently help them be prepared for success. I have found out that if I prepare, the Holy Spirit is given opportunity to lead, instead of my ego.

I knew of a young man asked to preach and he chose not to prepare saying, "I will just let the Spirit speak to me in the pulpit." The Holy Spirit did speak to him in a very clear way. He said to the young man, *"You are not prepared."*

Don't be a sluggard.

MARCH 27

Who Have You Been Talking To?

1 CORINTHIANS 15:33-34
Be not deceived: evil communications corrupt good manners. Awake to righteousness, and sin not; for some have not the knowledge of God: I speak this to your shame.

MATTHEW 16:6
Then Jesus said unto them, Take heed and beware of the leaven of the Pharisees and of the Sadducees.

I had the privilege of growing up in a godly home. Words of blame and shame were not part of our daily diet. The vulgar, coarse, and profane were not part of my parents vocabulary and I never developed the habit, even after being exposed to every "four letter word" available. When we established our own home, Alice and I worked hard at continuing this pattern of conversation. But – my children have struggled with this. It was hard to have a conversation with my adult children where the vulgarities of life did not break out in their descriptions. I tried to not be judgmental – with little success.

This is not true confessions. Paul makes a commonsense observation. What you feed your mind on affects the way you speak and act. God says your words have power *(Matthew 12:37.)* We must bring grace into every conversation intentionally *(Col. 4:3-6.)*

The "sticks and stones" nursery rhyme is a lie. Words do hurt. Paul says we need to wake up to righteousness! God wants to reach others with your words. Having a "foul mouth," hinders the work of the Holy Spirit. When our speech is full of attack, slander, and abuse, we make the Gospel sound like trash, legalism, or elitism.

As a teen, I had a sharp wit and a sharper tongue. After studying what James teaches about the tongue, I had to ask myself, "If I needed help or guidance, would I come to 'me' for what I needed?"

The answer was, "No."

MARCH 28

I Was No Prophet

AMOS 7:14-15

Then answered Amos, and said to Amaziah, I was no prophet, neither was I a prophet's son; but I was a herdsman, and a gatherer of sycamore fruit: and the LORD took me as I followed the flock, and the LORD said unto me, Go, prophesy unto my people Israel.

Amos was common man, perhaps good at his craft. He sought to do his best and meet his responsibilities. Yet, he was also a man who feared God and understood that God was sovereign. This was not a man that sought the attention of others or had a heritage of skilled communication or influence, but he did listen.

Let's talk about your calling. Over the years I have met faithful servants that sensed God's calling to "the ministry," and they were already on a different path of service to the King. We would agree that whatever the path we tread, it should always be for the King (**Col. 3:23.**)

Father spoke to you at a time and place that you could hear His voice and its clear and comforting commission. It still warms your heart to think of it. He **took you** from following the sheep and equipped you to speak in His name. Oh, you might have done the Moses thing, came up with excuses, reasons not to be used, but you found that there was no escaping His purpose for you.

You might have already been at that tipping point and were ready to say, *"Yes, Lord,"* immediately. Now, looking back, you begin to see the process that the Holy Spirit used to prepare you for this kind of service. Be certain that your calling was unique to you. Amos was a real "missionary." He was taken from the country life and placed in the big worldly city of Samaria. God made no mistake. His success was in faithfulness, not in the western calculation of "Nickels, Noses, and Kneelers."

Father made no mistake when He called you.

MARCH 29

I Don't Understand

LUKE 8:54-56

And he put them all out, and took her by the hand, and called, saying, Maid, arise. And her spirit came again, and she arose straightway: and he commanded to give her food. And her parents were astonished: **but he charged them that they should tell no man what was done.**

I heard someone sarcastically say that verse 56 is the life verse of many professing believers. They never make mention of Jesus or what He has done in their lives. Still, why did He give this charge?

This is not the only time Jesus gave this direction. What is my problem? People on the road heard the sad news about Jairus' daughter. When they got to the home, a multitude of mourners knew she was dead [verse 53.] How could her parents contain their joy at the reanimation of their only daughter? I know Jesus doesn't make mistakes, but it appears like He is ignoring human nature! How could you keep silent!

I consulted with some from my "theological brain trust," and we were challenged to come up with a definitive answer – except – **The answer is Jesus.** His earthly ministry, as we like to classify it, was not just Redemption but to express care for those He would touch and would touch Him. The anxious father, the sick woman on the road, and the dead girl - Jesus cared for each of them. He cared about how they were touched and what would happen after He reached into their lives. Each touch was different; each touch was just right.

I looked at my notes from the last time I preached this passage. The Holy Spirit gave me this: *"Jesus gives directions for their protection from haters and prevention from those that seek only the healing and not the Healer."*

What a Savior! Your Master knows the touch you need. Jesus wants to use your touch.

MARCH 30

Don't Do It

NUMBERS 14:41-42
And Moses said, wherefore now do you transgress the commandment of the LORD? But it shall not prosper. Go not up, for the LORD is not among you; that you be not smitten before your enemies.

This is a unique situation. Israel is forbidden to do that which days before they had been directed to do. Hebrews tells us the why – **(Heb. 3:19)** *So we see that they could not enter in because of unbelief.*

This is easy to preach. It is an opportunity to teach that faith is demonstrated by obedience. There are so many great thoughts that the whole chapter can become a mini-series!

But is it possible to apply this personally? I am struggling to think of a time when I said, "No" to God; then changed my mind and Father said "No" to me. What measure of unbelief is necessary for God to close the door so I would have to go through the wilderness to have this faithlessness killed in me? I want to say that I have never experienced this kind of discipline, but the more I muse, the more I wonder if portions of my journey have been in the desert, and I was too dull to notice?

(Numbers 14:36-40,) tells us that it took the death of the 10 negative spies to make Israel think they could change God's mind. They admitted they had sinned and were ready to put out human effort to make things happen. That did not work.

I am going to have to think about this for a while. Have I ever been so ignorant of the Character of God and the Content of His Word that I acted in unbelief? I know Father isn't done with me but is this a moment when I should pray **(Psalms 139:23-24)** *Search me, O God, and know my heart: try me, and know my thoughts: And see if there be any wicked way in me and lead me in the way everlasting.*

MARCH 31

Chambers, Reasons, Purposes

EZEKIEL 40:2 (SEE EZEKIEL CHAPTERS 40-48)
*In the visions God brought me into the land of Israel,
and set me upon a very high mountain, ...*

DEUTERONOMY 29:29
*The secret things belong unto the LORD our God: but those things
which are revealed belong unto us and to our children
forever, that we may do all the words of this law.*

I have read and taught this portion of Ezekiel before. It is hard to understand. It is even harder to fit into our understanding of Redemption. Though the description is clear, (I get lost in all the chambers!) it challenges our understanding of God's "clock." Where does this fit? It doesn't match the past and when he talks about the sacrifices; we think about what Paul says in **(Heb. 10:18)** *Now where remission of these is, there is no more offering for sin.*

So, it is hard. Because of this, some seek to reason it away calling it symbolic or some other metaphysical interpretation. But I believe the principle of **Deut. 29:29.** Here is a prophetic message, *a revealed message,* that seems to abide in "The secret things." Personally, the best explanation I have found was from Hobart Freeman, "An Introduction to The Old Testament Prophets" (Moody Press.) But that is not my point!

When you are confronted with difficult passages of Scripture, what is your default position? You are commanded to live by faith **(Romans 1:17.)** That means to trust in the God who wants to be known, the God who has revealed Himself. Is your scholarship objective or subjective? God reveals what you discover. Explaining away your doubts only leads you to unbelief. Study to be approved by God and trust Him when you examine the difficult.

I am still on my journey of understanding, but I am fully convinced in the promise of Christ that the Holy Spirit will guide me into all truth. It is a process.

APRIL 1

A Lying Tongue

PROVERBS 26:27-28

Whoso digs a pit shall fall therein: and he that rolls a stone, it will return upon him. A lying tongue hates those that are afflicted by it; and a flattering mouth works ruin.

"*Oh, what a tangled web we weave, when first we practice to deceive.*" The Word of God has many things to say about liars. I find these particular thoughts very intriguing. Devices intended to surprise and harm others are likely to catch and damage their creators. Those who lie will develop a hatred for those to whom they lie. Flattery (speaking lies) will ruin the deceiver.

The practice of sin is always destructive (**James 1:15.**) God says sin's wages make payment in death. This is not a "*perhaps you die,*" but you "*shall surely die.*" We know the "ins and outs" of hamartiology, but I wanted to focus in on dealing in ministry with people who lie to you.

A lie is always a means of controlling something. As an example: a situation, people, or the outcome. We have all lied. At the very least it was to make us feel safe. There is no excuse, but there is a reasoning behind it. We know that Satan is called the father of lies *(John 8:44.)* God never lies. (**Titus 1:2**) *In hope of eternal life,* **which God, that cannot lie,** *promised before the world began.*

Jesus never uses lies to tell the truth. John provides an important principle (**1 John 2:21b**) … *that no lie is of the truth.* We are directed to lie no more because that is not the way our Father or this New Life works. We still do, though hopefully it is getting less.

You are going to catch people in lies. They will get caught and lie some more. You may help them, but without the Holy Spirit's help in changing their pattern, they will hate you and begin to transfer their lies onto you. They will even lie about you. This Proverb is should not be considered as poetic license. This can get ugly. That is Satan's plan. Love them anyway and speak the truth.

APRIL 2

It's Just a Joke!

PROVERBS 26:18-19
As a mad man who casts firebrands, arrows, and death, so is the man that deceives his neighbor, and says, Am not I in sport?

Some of you are going to say that *"the preacher has gone to meddling."* Listen, I am a pastor; that means that I have a weird sense of humor. Some would say that preacher humor is dad jokes on steroids. Your funny stories are not my target for this devotional.

I confess. I caused a dorm riot at Baptist Bible College, Clarks Summit, PA in 1971. Everyone was tense. A dorm filled with freshman facing their mid-terms is a dangerous place. I "just suggested" that my roommates try to (modesty prevents me) and it went from there! It finally ended when they were trying to get the Resident Advisor out of his apartment, and someone took a fire extinguisher off the wall and started to shoot it at everyone. I can still hear Dr. Pickering at the end of chapel the next day. (In a strong southern drawl) *"You boys from Shaffer Hall will stay after chapel."*

I didn't do anything – just suggested. The Dean asked the wrong question and I only answered what I was asked. No disciplinary action taken. That day, I learned a lesson about the power of my words and also about the deceitfulness of my heart.

Some of you are jokesters. If you can pull a prank, you will. If you can get away with an insult, you say it. I am not your boss but remember **(Num. 32: 23)** *But if you will not do so, behold, you have sinned against the LORD:* **and be sure your sin will find you out.**

Can you handle the consequences? Will this act or remark dishonor your Master? Not everyone has such a refined sense of humor like yours. You are called upon to care for hurting people. Are you able to pour in oil and wine or will it be insult and injury?

I know, shut up already!

APRIL 3

A Song of Degrees
Psalms 120- Caught in Trouble

PSALMS 120:1
In my distress I cried unto the LORD, and he heard me.

Psalm of Degrees, what does that mean? Whatever the origin, the idea is a progression in worship. From Psalm 120 to 134, this collection is valuable to every pilgrim.

The Source of Deliverance – [v1-2] We are in distress, but we need not stay there. (**James 4:10**) *Humble yourselves in the sight of the Lord, and he shall lift you up.* The promise of God's ear is precious. (**Jer. 33:3**) *Call unto me, and I will answer you, and show you great and mighty things, which you do not know.*

[v2] If you seek to lead, the enemy will lie about you. Whom Satan uses to tell the lies about you can be shattering! How can we deliver ourselves from their lies? (**1 Peter 2:15**) *For so is the will of God, that with well doing you may put to silence the ignorance of foolish men.* Do the opposite and speak the truth!

The Consequences of Deceit – [v3-4] This is God's fight, not ours. *Coals of Juniper* – The Midrash tells a story about a fire of juniper wood made in the desert. A year after it had provided a cook fire for its maker, it was discovered that the coals of that fire were still burning. Whether true or not, the illustration shows the lasting consequences of lying. Vengeance belongs to God.

The Burden of the Disciple – [v5-7] *Mesech* is in the North; *Kedar*, is in the South. No matter where we go, we will face trouble. This is not going to change. (**2 Tim. 3:12**) *Yes, and all that will live godly in Christ Jesus shall suffer persecution.*

[v7] But that does not change our calling. (**Matt. 5:9**)

Blessed are the peacemakers: for they shall be called the children of God. I will not be captured by lies, God will fight for me. My eyes are open, and I will do good.

APRIL 4

A Song of Degrees
Psalm 121 - The Source of Help

PSALMS 121:1
I will lift up mine eyes unto the hills, from whence comes my help.

Today, you can find help **if** there is a cell tower nearby and your device has a charged battery. But will the help you find, really help? Imagine yourself without the ability to connect. This is never true for God's child. You are connected by the power and privilege of prayer.

Protection [1-5] [1] In a world of confusion, down in the valley of difficulty, we are forced to look up; but we must look higher than the hills, past the high ground of what might seem like safety *(Jer. 3:23.)*

[2] The one who made more than just the hills is the source of our protection. Have I asked for His help?

[3] When you climb, your footing is vital. Father will protect you without need of rest *(Prov. 3:23-24.)*

[3-5] Keeps - The Hebrew word *shamar*, means to hedge about (as with thorns). It is used three times. The song writer is building the concept of God's protection. This is the heart of God revealed toward us. He does not sleep but shows continual love and care. God provides shelter in all types of difficulty. He alone has the ability to protect from the uncontrollable.

Preservation [6-8] [6] Again, we are led to take steps that bring us to a point of total confidence *(Ps. 91:5.)*

[7] How can we know the extent or the purposes of the evil one, except that he hates us. God is greater than our enemy**(1 John 4:4.)**

[8] Here is assurance that Father is directly involved in your life. Even when we are mistaken, we are never forsaken. Every step is under the watchful care of a loving God. Are we allowed to fail? Yes, but never are we abandoned. **(Psalms 37:23)** *The steps of a good man are ordered by the LORD: and he delights in his way.*

We can cling to Father's determination; He is working for our good *(Phil. 1:6.)*

APRIL 5

A Song of Degrees
Psalms 122 – The House of The Lord

PSALMS 122:1
I was glad when they said unto me, Let us go into the house of the LORD.

What makes you glad? A State Trooper stopped an old man driving recklessly down the road. "Sir, your wife fell out of the car back about a mile." "My, am I glad!" said the old man, "I thought I had gone deaf."

For David, gladness was being with others where God said He would meet with them *(Matt. 18:19-20.)* Two things are needed. God's people and God's presence. [2] Spiritually unity is good - but physical connection is the thing *(Heb.3:13; Heb. 10:25!)*

The Place [3-5] The physical location is not the main thing. Obedience to God's direction is *(Eph.4:3-6.)* We must focus on what unites us, not on what divides us. Obedience to loving what Jesus loves is our priority *(Eph.4:15-16.)*

[4] *The tribes go up* – A command from God for gathering three times a year *(Ex.23:17.)* Think about evaluating the following areas of your life three times a year as a measure of your spiritual growth:

1. Your part in the body of Christ.
2. Your testimony for Christ.
3. Your attitude of gratitude.

[5] What kind of accountability do you have? You supposedly know the truth, but it does not remove your need to submit to authority *(Heb.13:17.)* If we do not submit, we war with God *(Rom.13:1-2.)*

The Prayer [6-9] [6] Let's go to application. Pray for your people by name. Pray for your community *(John 17:9.)*

[7,8] Do you want to prosper? Then you must pray for the prosperity and labor for the maturity and spirituality of your church *(John13:35.)*

[v9] *I will seek your good* - Because of what Jesus Christ has done for you, you can do no less than seek to bless the family of God *(Eph.2:19.)*

APRIL 6

A Song of Degrees
Psalms 123 – The Cry for Mercy

PSALMS 123:3
*Have mercy upon us, O LORD, have mercy upon us:
for we are exceedingly filled with contempt.*

We define mercy as not getting what I do deserve, but our passage is fixed upon the treasure of God's shelter and help. *Can you recall the last time you called for the mercy of God and did not receive it? Do you remember the last time you were merciful?*

The Right Perspective [1-2] What is your view of God? Does that view come from the view of your own Father? Here are just a few of the things Father says about His nature:

He is greater than your problems **(Isa.55: 6-9.)**

He is not untouched by your problems **(Matt.10: 29-31.)**

He is not limited by your problems **(Jer.32: 27.)**

[2] The Master/servant idea might be difficult for you to grasp, but the truth of this picture is total dependency. We must admit that we cannot determine anything. All we must do is ask and then wait. But there is such a blessing in the waiting **(Isaiah 40:31.)**

The Right Petition [3-4] What do you want God to do? That by itself, may not be the right question; for it indicates some type of control on our part. David says *"until."* God is not bound by our request, but He must keep His Word and act in accordance with His nature.

He cannot break His word **(Num.23: 19.)** He will always deal with us as His beloved children **(Ps. 103: 13.)**

David waits upon the mercy of God. There are those who seek your destruction, but Father is not one of them. Those that oppose you would fill your soul with their negativity, gainsaying, insults, and lies. Your Father's thoughts toward you are positive **(Jer. 29: 11.)** His love toward you is continual **(Ps.139: 17-18.)**

In a world of darkness, walk in His promise. Do you need mercy?

You need only to ask!

APRIL 7

A Song of Degrees
Psalms 124 – If the Lord had not Been on our Side

PSALMS 124:1
If it had not been the LORD who was on our side, now may Israel say.

Ever been in a fight and your friend or brother came at the right moment to help you? That is the idea of this song! We are encouraged to celebrate that our great God will come to our aid!

The Danger Faced – This song might have had a quick meter that would cause the blood to run swiftly and the spirit to rise. We need our focus on truths such as this. We are not promised an easy path. Our enemy is real (**1 Peter 5:8.**)

He is our accuser (***Rev.12:10-11.***) But our confidence is in this (**1 John 4:4**) *You are of God, little children, and have overcome them: because greater is He that is in you, than he that is in the world.*

Do you have the assurance that God is with you? Are you so confident in the one who promised to never leave you that you can say with Paul *that nothing will separate you from His love?*

An army, a whale (beast), a fire, a flood – are all things that could easily take us down, but our God was there with His chosen ones, and is with us as well! He is with us in every conflict, even the kind of affliction that would drown the soul (***John 14:27.***)

The Delivery Found – Think of Daniel in the lion's den: not even teeth marks, says the Psalmist, and why not? Because he breaks the teeth of the wicked (***Ps. 3:7.***) Our God does not just bring about great rescues but works in a way that sets the spirit free. He not only delivers but can break the trap so it will never snare us again (***Heb. 7:25***; ***Rom.8:2.***)

How is this possible? It is because our God has promised it and the Creator has no limitations.

But you must call upon the Lord (***Ps.18:3.***)

APRIL 8

A Song of Degrees
Psalms 125 – A Safe Place

PSALMS 125:1
They that trust in the LORD shall be as Mount Zion, which cannot be removed, but abides forever.

Does that which surrounds you inspire you? Are your senses stimulated by where you live? You must remember that nothing you say this day will teach you anything. If you are going to learn, you must take things in. Tomorrow morning you may see wonders that will turn to memories and others will have memories return that give you pause to wonder. In all of this, will you see God? We need to remember the focus of these Psalms of *Degrees* – (Degrees means elevation.) The purpose is to journey to a higher place. The Psalmist wants to lift our eyes and fix our gaze on the unmovable God.

A Place Of Security [1-3] *Trust in the Lord* - Our confidence in God is not based on our ability to understand Him but in His changelessness *(Mal. 3:6; Heb.13:8.)*

The Psalmist says that Mount Zion shall never be moved, and that God is like the mountain. For the lifetime of the Psalmist, the mountain is unchanging.

Round about His people - Our God has assured us He will always be with us *(Heb.13:5.)*

[2-3] God understands our limitations and will not allow us to exceed the breaking point *(1 Cor.10:13.)*

A Prayer of Sanctification [4-5] *Do good, O Lord* [4] This is spoken about the source of blessing; yet it focuses on the truth of *(Matt. 7:7-8.)* We must seek and express our dependence upon the source of all blessing. We need to act upon the truth of *(James1:17.)*

Peace upon Israel - [5] The challenge for us to not tempt God is plain – *their crooked ways.* The God who searches our hearts also rewards our lives *(Jer. 17:10.)* We must have confidence in God's ability to keep and complete us *(Phil. 1:6.)*

Our concern must be **Process** not **Product.**

APRIL 9

A Song of Degrees
Psalms 126 – Released from Captivity

PSALMS 126:1
When the LORD turned again the captivity of Zion, we were like them that dream.

To be released from bondage is a wonderful experience. I have dealt with many a prisoner and they all count the days till they are set free. Not all these *Songs* were written at the same time, but they all lead the worshiper into the presence of God.

The Dream [1] Who did this wonderful thing? The sovereign of the Universe! Mount Zion is the Temple area, but it poetically speaks to us about the family of God *(Eph. 2:19-22.)* Our Savior has broken every chain, every fetter – He opened every door that was barred *(Luke 4:18.)*

Our Delight [2-3] If you were surprised with the release of a debt or presented with an abundant provision, what would be your response? But this is your wonderful lot! Christ has set you free and in Him and given you all you will ever need **(2 Pet.1:3-4!)** This is reason to rejoice!

Our Desire [4-6] [4] Why ask for deliverance when it is already done? Because we need Jesus not only to deliver but also to provide us direction out of the prison house. If not, then we sit like Peter **(Acts 12:11.)**

[5-6] It is not an easy matter to change a life or a community, but it is worth the effort! The Holy Spirit is doing this every moment and will use you. Spiritual development is always worth the cost and the wait to gather the harvest *(Gal.6:4,8-9.)* Sharing the truth and living out the truth is always worth it!

[6] This is all about Process. God calls you to proclaim liberty. Focus your attention on the process of sowing the seed, and leave the Product to God.

APRIL 10

A Song of Degrees
127 – Building a Life

PSALMS 127:1

Except the LORD build the house, they labor in vain that build it: except the LORD keep the city, the watchman wakes but in vain.

What is the one thing you must know in order to build? To protect your home, is there one thing that is absolutely necessary? What is the one essential needed in building a life?

Dependence [1-2] (**Proverbs 1:7**) *The fear of the LORD is the beginning of knowledge: but fools despise wisdom and instruction.* What has that got to do with building? Certainly everything! The Creator of all life is directly involved in the building of your home. David uses the picture of shelter because it is one of the basic needs of life. If we seek Him first, everything falls into place *(Matt.6:31-33.)*

There is so much we can't control, but your Father can. He sees and knows all things. Every detail of your life is in His care.

Have you ever been robbed? Eventually you come to understand that you can't prevent wicked men from being wicked, but your Father can *(**1 Pet.3:12!**)*

[2] To labor on and on without rest is foolishness and faithless *(**Mark 2:27-28.**)* Sleep is God's blessing. Fail to rest, and you will try to do the work of the Kingdom by self-will, and will act in unbelief *(**Ps. 4:8.**)*

Heritage [3-5]   [3-4] Children are God's gift and not His curse. Children in our youth are God's blessing. We continue the work of God as we strengthen and train them. Parents are primary instructors for them to follow Christ.

[5] What is a *full quiver*? Many offer numbers but the concept is the important thing. They are God's blessing (**Prov. 10:22.**) Children are a blessing even in old age if the fear of the Lord is present.

APRIL 11

A Song of Degrees
Psalms 128 – Building a Home

PSALMS 128:1
Blessed is every one that fears the LORD; that walks in his ways.

As a boy, I saw the results of a home built on quicksand. I never forgot the image. It doesn't matter if the materials used to build the house are the best if the foundation is not dependable. A Firm Foundation is identified as a life of deep respect for God and acting in obedience to the truth (***Rom.2:13.***)

[2] When we fear the Lord, the potential blessings are tremendous. *Labor* - this is not a curse! When God is honored, work accomplishes its Divine purpose (***Gen.1:26.***) God makes our work prosperous and satisfying (***Ps. 1:3.***)

[3] Out of all creation, God said that one thing was not good (***Gen. 2:18.***) To share life with the one we love is God's blessing (***Prov.18:22.***) When you fear the Lord, the marriage relationship isn't a warfare but a great opportunity to obey God and show His love through intimacy (***1 Pet.3:7.***)

The blessing of an orchard comes by tending it and giving it nourishment. What you put into your wife you will get out! Do you want to live in an ordered home? Then order your priorities:
1. Fear God.
2. Love your wife as yourself.
3. Teach your Children.

Children are pictured as olive plants; when the care is given early, they will grow, and their production will be long and full. Olive oil is a type of the Holy Spirit. Your obedience will produce children of rich blessing to all (***Prov. 10:1.***)

[4-5] There is a blessed future because we Fear the Lord (***James 1:17.***) To be in the center, *"Jerusalem,"* of God's will requires us to honestly say, **"Yes, Lord."** Obedience brings blessing. It is not easy, but it is the best for all.

[6] This blessing we can give as an inheritance to multiple generations. Your children are your means of blessing the world, but it will never happen if you do not fear the Lord.

APRIL 12

A Song of Degrees
Psalms 129 – Get Them, God!

PSALMS 129:1
Many a time have they afflicted me from my youth, may Israel now say:

Just to refresh your memory *(Matt. 5:44-45)* presents the "Golden Rule." So how can we reconcile this Psalm with the "Rule?" We know that God is not the author of confusion. He wants us to know His will, and that vengeance and mercy belong to Him. How can we use this Psalm for our benefit?

We all would like (at times) to sic God on those who irritate us or are wicked beyond our understanding. Is God at our "beck and call?" No **(Eph. 1:11b.)**

The important thing is to know what the Psalmist is saying. *This is a Song of Degrees* - that means it is part of a choral or public worship. How can this be worship? The previous song was about the blessing of family and bringing generational blessing. But this chorus seems like a bitter remembrance. How can this song lift the soul?

[1-2] Dealing with the past can remove the barriers to future blessing. Examining the trouble can cause us to triumph if we do not live in the pain but the provision of God.

[3] The pain was real. The scars are still there, but the focus is not on the Oppressor but on the Deliverer.

[4] *The LORD is righteous* - Our help does not come from God's vengeance but His Righteous One *(Matt.21:44.)*

[5] Why ask for this confusion and failure for others? They hate God's chosen *(Zech. 2:8!)*

[6-8] Those who oppress God's people will be judged. Consider your part in the process of healing and follow through:
1. Acknowledge the pain – denial is not the answer in dealing with hurt.
2. Trust in the Righteousness of Christ – Jesus is the only one who can make bad things turn out good.
3. Allow God to be the Judge – He keeps accurate records and will not in any wise acquit the guilty.

APRIL 13

A Song of Degrees
Psalms 130 – The Mercy of God

PSALMS 130:1
Out of the depths have I cried unto You, O LORD.

I am a desperate man. I need a God who is able to meet me in the "now." This Psalm is for the here and now. I need a God who understands!

[1] *Out of the depths* – What kind of depths? He doesn't say. If he did, we might think God only helps in a particular way **(Heb7:25; 1 John1:9.)** But he is specific in whom he seeks **(Ps. 65:2.)**

[2] *Lord hear my voice* – Is He trying to convince God to listen? **No (Prov. 8:17!)** Please don't be like Jonah and take three days to cry out to God.

[3] *mark iniquities* – What does that mean? To keep a record of our sin and hold it against us! BUT Father promised to do this **(Exodus 34:7.)**

[4] *But there is forgiveness – that you may be feared.* Here are two very important matters: **forgiveness and reverence.** They should never be separated **(Ps.103:12-13!)** In fearing God, we find forgiveness **(Jer. 33:8-9.)**

[5] What is our hope? It is not a transaction or an event, hope is in the person of Christ **(1 Peter 1:7-8.)** How is hope expressed?
1. You wait on the Lord.
2. You look with expectation to His Word.

[6] How long do we wait? Until that which is a certainty appears! The day will come **(Ps. 30:5!)**

What is my attitude? *As those that watch for the morning* – He gives us His promise of deliverance from fear. This is confidence in the Son Light of His Love!

[7-8] What shall we talk about while we wait?
1. Our Trust in God. **(Heb.11:6)**
2. His Mercy – **(Isa. 55:7-8)**
3. Our Redemption – **(Ps. 40:2-3; Ps. 33:19-22)**
4. Our Glorification – **(Phil1:6; Rom. 8:29)**

APRIL 14

A Song of Degrees
Psalms 131 – The Spirit of Humility

PSALMS 131:1
LORD, my heart is not haughty, nor mine eyes lofty: neither do I exercise myself in great matters, or in things too high for me.

Everything rises or falls on leadership. God uses people to do His Kingdom work in this shadow land. How one leads is as essential as the direction. Direction relates to competency but the "How" is a mirror of the heart. We call this Character. Being a leader of Character is a process. This song expresses that process.

[1] *My heart is not haughty* – to say this, David must have God's help. *Eyes not lofty* – The eyes are the windows to the soul; what do your windows reveal? A *"high look,"* God hates **(Prov. 21:4.)** *Exercise in great matters* - Remember what God has done for you. Humility is not a trait, but an attitude developed in the heart. It is a process that says that God is sovereign.

[2] *Behaved – quieted myself* -This is an act of the will, not a boast of the proud. It speaks of submission to God's total authority. Can we be quiet before the Lord **(Hab. 2:20?)** Please don't start legislating silence in your worship! Such an act would make submission a work of the flesh.

As a child weaned - This isn't an event, it is a process! A loss of interest in only one kind of food and a longing for maturity. So, it must be with you **(Heb. 5:12-14.)** You want the meat of the Word and desire to see the world from the side of your Father and not from under your mother's skirts. No longer crying to be fed, you can sit at the table and learn you are not the center of the universe. BUT many are still in the crib, using emotions to get their way.

Is that an accurate description of your soul?

[3] This is submission as an adult, a heart eager to hear. *Israel – Prince of God* – You are chosen by God to serve our King! Let us speak boldly for our King and know that the attitude of humility is maintained when Jesus is our Hope and Proclamation.

APRIL 15

A Song of Degrees
Psalms 132 – The Affliction of David
OR The Fulfillment of Promise

PSALMS 132:1
LORD, remember David, and all his afflictions.

The pilgrim has arrived in the House of the Lord! They are in the place where God has put His Name! This song reminds the pilgrim how all this place came to be. It is to remind you as well.

[1] *Lord, remember David* – God doesn't need reminding **(Ps. 139:17-18.)** Remember means *mark*. We must claim what God has promised **(Heb. 11:6.)**

[2] To lead God's people is to claim what God wants to do. David did this by making a *Vow*. This vow is based on what God had already honored **(see Gen. 28:20-22.)** God honored the vow of the "Supplanter" because God was ordering the circumstances of Jacob's life. What will this God do in your life for His glory?

[3-5] David's vision is clear. He wants to establish a center for worship. He was not acting on his own. In faith, David was "doing what God wanted to bless!" **This is what we seek as well.** We are called upon to fulfill the Great Commission and to keep the Great Commandment, and we are to do it here. We are supposed to make it hard for people to go to hell!

[6-8] *Hear* - people caught the vision; they got excited about a place where they could come before God. Heed the promise of **(John 12:32.)**

[9] *Clothed in righteousness* – You must be righteous and ready to serve. Excellence is not an option. *Let the saints shout for joy* – Teach others that worship is not "chore-full" but joyful!

[11-18] God made a promise and will never turn away from it. His commitment to this promise makes an eternal difference. It is the presentation of His Son, as David's Son. This is not wishful thinking, but the eternal promise of God **(Isa. 53:11.)**

We find fulfillment as we look to Jesus. **(Heb. 12:1-2)**

APRIL 16

A Song of Degrees
Psalms 133 – A Song of Unity

PSALMS 133:1
Behold, how good and how pleasant it is for brethren to dwell together in unity!

I was in a chapel service at Baptist Bible College as the student body sang a cappella, <u>O the Deep, Deep Love of Jesus</u>. It still stirs my soul. Music has the ability to speak to us on every level: **spiritual, intellectual, emotional** – This song reminds us of what unites. That, dear ones, is worth singing!

[1] *Behold* – What are the marks of a healthy church? Space allows me only the bullet points:
1. The REALITY OF CHRIST.
2. There are LIFE-GIVING RELATIONSHIPS.
3. There is MEANINGFUL RESPONSIBILITY.
4. PRAYER IS ITS OXYGEN.
5. EVALUATION BY THE CHURCH IS ON GOING.

Good – So how good is it? Are these things true?
Pleasant – a place of individual and collective growth.
Brethren – not our differences but what we have in common. **(Gal. 3:26-29)**
Dwell – This is commitment to someone else.
Together in unity – a unit, together. It is not uniformity. Every believer, every church is different but Christ, our common bond, is the same **(Heb. 13:8.)**

The Picture [2] *Precious ointment – (Ex.29:1-7.)*
This is a symbol of the Holy Spirit in the life of ministry.

The Promise [3] What are the results? *The dew* – Soft, gentle, it covers all, touches all, nourishes all. The love of God is wonderful and causes all things to grow. *Of Hermon* – Mount Hermon is the source for all fresh water in Israel. But, if it does not flow out, it becomes like The Dead Sea. Full of nutrients but unable to sustain life.

Your blessing flows from the Rock, Jesus. He commands us today to pass on the blessing. It must flow to be fresh. God does not want your comfort but your vitality.

APRIL 17

A Song of Degrees
Psalms 134 – Blessings in the Night

PSALMS 134:1
*Behold, bless the LORD, all you servants of the LORD,
which by night, stand in the house of the LORD.*

The purpose of this "Degree" collection is to train the heart to worship. Imagine yourself to be one of the pilgrims who have come to Jerusalem for the High Holy Day. Now it is time to pack up your things and go home. A man that everyone loves and admires begins to sing a simple song that ties the whole experience together. Heads nod in agreement to these deep thoughts. You look around and see eyes filled with knowing and wonder - and soon, everyone is singing with him.

[1] This is a song of departure, for the gathering is over and it is time to think about what God has done in your life *(Ps. 4:4-5; Ps. 63:5-7.)* Do you set aside time to consider God's work in you? Night can be a great time to be quiet before God. Think about those who labor in the night to keep the fire on the altar burning or the doors open – consider their faithfulness to the mundane and realize they do it to worship the King *(Col. 3:23-24.)*

[2] The night is an easy time to slack-off. Paul tells us we are approaching the night and encourages our faithfulness *(1 Thess. 5:1-10.)* If we remember what we have been taught, we can keep on keeping on *(1 Cor. 15:58.)*

[3] Here is a simple statement; *The Lord that made Heaven and earth bless you out of Zion.* What does it mean? This is passing on the blessing. It is a simple benediction that recognizes the source of blessing *(James 1:17.)*

The one who made and sustains all, may He bless you out of the center of His will – **Zion.** May your life be found in and centered on His purposes in this earth. It is a prayer that says**,**

"May you do what He is blessing!"

Only then can you pass on the blessing *(Matt. 5:44-48.)*

APRIL 18

A Congregation or a Mob?

NUMBERS 16:41, 46, 48
But on the morning all the congregation of the children of Israel murmured against Moses and against Aaron, saying, you have killed the people of the LORD. [46] And Moses said unto Aaron, take a censer, and put fire therein from off the altar, and put on incense, and go quickly unto the congregation, and make an atonement for them.... [48] And he stood between the dead and the living; and the plague was stayed.

I hope you have never had this kind of rancor directed at you. But when the Enemy stirs up the demons that have snared believers by their hard heart and unconfessed sin, anything can happen!

The people of Israel were murmuring against God because He had killed these "friends of the people," but Moses and Aaron were the targets. Korah and his cohorts had rebelled against God's choice of leadership (*sounds familiar!*) It is always dangerous when you seek to "Touch the Lord's Anointed."

The problem went deeper than the ring leaders. The people did not want to follow God. Neither do we, until the Holy Spirit begins to rule our lives. He has taught us that Father's way is perfect, and He did that through the process of the Word of God ***(Ps. 119:11.)***

We know that God's purpose for 40 years of wandering was to eliminate the unbelieving. This event was just one of those big chunks. When the *"incense cleared,"* it was close to 15,000 dead.

How does Moses respond? In intercession. He can't save everyone, but Aaron's good running (not bad for and octogenarian) saved the rest of the people! My point is, how do you respond when your church rebels against revealed direction/truth? If you don't make the decision now to be a shepherd and not a herder, the enemy will make the decision for you. You do not work for yourself; you serve the King, and you MUST love what Jesus loves. Trust your God and do good.

APRIL 19

Seeing People, the Right Way

1 CORINTHIANS 10:31-32
Whether therefore you eat, or drink, or whatsoever you do, do all to the glory of God. Give no offence, neither to the Jews, nor to the Gentiles, nor to the church of God:

I enjoy sorting my parts and fasteners. I have storage bins and trays for all my nuts and bolts. When time and circumstances permit, I remind myself of what is in "the can." This knowledge helps me complete my projects and it saves me money and trips to the store!

Using groupings and classification of people and behaviors is Biblical, if done God's way –

(**Prov. 20:11**) *Even a child is known by his doings, whether his work be pure, and whether it be right.*

(**Matthew 7:20**) *Wherefore by their fruits you shall know them.*

We can appreciate this bit of wisdom if it helps us see the spiritual need of others. Our passage is not a discrimination of people but a recognition of their need for Christ. The text is part of a conclusion on the Principles of Christian Liberty. Verse 32 jumps off the page with a presentation of how God looks at people.

The Jews refers to the physical descendants of Abraham. A people that God chose to receive specific promises and demonstrate His glory. But they failed **(Rom. 10:3-4.)** *The Gentiles* are every human who is not a physical descendants of Abraham. Paul describes them in **(Eph. 2:12)** *That at that time you were without Christ, being aliens from the commonwealth of Israel, and strangers from the covenants of promise, having no hope, and without God in the world.*

To be without hope is a miserable classification! *The church of God,* here is the wonderful mystery of Grace; that Jew and Gentile are not just in the same class but are made one family through the finished work of Christ **(Eph. 2:19.)** We must abandon every other grouping of people that does not have Christ at the center. To look at people in any other way is a mistake you must correct.

APRIL 20

Pray for your Help

LUKE 10:2

Therefore said He unto them, the harvest truly is great, but the laborers are few: pray therefore the Lord of the harvest, that he would send forth laborers into his harvest.

This command was part of the "fourth step" in the Discipleship process: 1. I do it. 2. You watch me do it. 3. We do it together. 4. You do it. There is a fifth step – 5. You teach someone else to do it.

Jesus made disciples. He wants us to do the same. I do not believe it is "mishandling" the passage to insist that it is not only written for us, but its interpretation is to us. Yes, this text provides a great tool to remind us as spiritual leaders that we are to duplicate ourselves, BUT I do not want to lose sight of what the King says is the essential step of prayer.

1. The Work/harvest is bigger than you can imagine or handle. It is also the greatest opportunity ever given.
2. The "80/20" principle is real. If you are blessed to be in a ministry with a greater percentage, the Holy Spirit was working through someone before you arrived. We must commit to duplicating ourselves. We must see the harvest and begin to understand the process.
3. Prayer is always a confession of dependence. You must look to the One to whom all ministry, all glory belongs. Salvation is His work. Kingdom building is His plan. I will pray and submit to His Leadership. He will not fail.
4. Ask for help! We accomplish more in synergy, *"two are better than one."* Solomon was smart. We are not chosen to lead because we are "Lone Rangers." Asking for help does not mean that the result is a bigger staff or a greater ministry. Our prayer is for *"Thy Kingdom come; Thy will be done."*

The words that follow in the chapter confirm the commitment of the King to us and our opportunity to honor Him. I like the small print! This is a great job!

APRIL 21

Open Your Mouth Wide

PSALMS 81:10
I am the LORD your God, which brought you out of the land of Egypt: open your mouth wide, and I will fill it.

2 CORINTHIANS 1:20
For all the promises of God in him are yes, and in him Amen, unto the glory of God by us.

I understand that not everything is written to me, but all things are written for me. I know that the definition of Biblical Faith is believing in the Character of God and the Content of His Word. I face a challenge to my faith. The regular means of Father's gracious provision for me is no longer available. My question is not, "What shall I do?" but "How shall He provide?"

Our text clearly presents the Character and Content of faith. *I am the LORD your God* – I behold an intimate expression of power and possession. The all-powerful, self-existent One, declares Himself connected with me and personally responsible for me. He says that He is *your God*. In the phrase, *Brought you out of Egypt* – tells me that the intimate God did not just cause me to be delivered from my place of bondage but carried me Himself **(1 Peter 2:24.)**

I have received a command that connects me to His promise. I must act upon my belief in the Character of the LORD. *Open your mouth wide* – I picture the fledgling sitting in the nest prepared for its care and the parent ready to deliver the life sustaining nourishment. It is accepted with mouth open wide. There is no doubt in the open mouth, no mistrust or questioning of the self-sacrificing parent. What will be provided is good and this baby bird – *will be filled*. Oh, Father may I be open in this way!

Am I presumptuous in my claim upon this promise? The Apostle says "No." The just shall live by faith. It is a command. I must act in faith, with mouth open wide! Whether fed by the ravens, the widow, or the sweat of my brow, I will trust Him and His gracious promises for by it, He will be glorified.

APRIL 22

I Will See You Soon, Mom

2 CORINTHIANS 5:4
For we that are in this tabernacle do groan, being burdened: not for that we would be unclothed, but clothed upon, that mortality might be swallowed up of life.

As I held my dear mother in my arms and leaned in close to her ear, these were the last words I spoke to her, "I will see you soon, Mom." She gently nodded her head and went home.

This dear one, was my primary instructor in the way of righteousness. She was adopted into a loving family, and through their love and prayers, Maisie had been adopted into God's forever family.

Oh, how she loved Jesus! As a teenager she asked God to let her be a missionary or a pastor's wife. She was a pastor's wife for forty years and then Father gave her the first choice of being a missionary in Haiti for ten years.

"Amazing Maisie," is what they called her in Port-au-Prince, Haiti. They gave her work that no one wanted to do or could do. Even if she had never done it before, she did it by the grace of God. They moved her from place to place, filling in for those on furlough, even doing minor medical care. The family motto had been, R.F.A. – *ready for anything,* and Jesus helped her do it.

She got malaria, dengue fever, and amebic dysentery, which eventually made her come home and be my secretary for several years. As the days grew shorter, her thankfulness became greater. This was my mother. So glad Father gave her to me.

One day, my last words to her will be true.
Even so come, Lord Jesus.

APRIL 23

An Original?

1 CORINTHIANS 4:7

For who makes you to be different from someone else? What have you that you did not receive? Now, if you received it, why do you glory, as if you had not received it?

My son Philip is perhaps the only natural athlete in my family. Everyone else must work at it. He was a 1,000 - point player in basketball during high school. I taught him the basics of shooting and he took it from there. I never played on a school team. I learned the fundamentals from my observation of successful shooters and practiced what I learned over twenty years of playing basketball in Monday night pick-up games. I learned to shoot from those who were willing to share. I taught someone who was eager to learn.

My father was a pastor for forty years. He learned by observation, preaching in the park and in the air-raid shelters. His form of training others was, *"John, I want you to preach next Sunday night." "Alice, I want you to teach a Sunday School class. Here is a quarterly, go out and get some students."* Perhaps not the best form of instruction but being "thrown into the deep end of the pool" was a great way to make me look to the Holy Spirit for help!

Paul informs us that we learn, in one way or another, from the instruction or example of others. We take that instruction and build upon it. We are commanded to make disciples of others, to pour our lives and experience into them. There are many men and women who unknowingly have been my teachers. I have built upon their instruction, experience, and my observation of God working in their lives. Spurgeon said, *"If you never read, you will never be read. If you never quote, you will never be quoted."*

Father has given you many instructors in Christ. You did not discover the truth on your own. The Holy Spirit gives us wisdom through willing hearts. It is a great thrill to know that the Holy Spirit will use you to point others to follow the King.

APRIL 24

The Value of Life - You Are Valuable - Psalm 139:1-6

PSALMS 139:1
O LORD, You have searched me, and know me.

How does God rate your value? David does not say how handsome, intelligent, talented, nor anything about your brilliant personality – no, not once! He does speak about your inner being, and clearly, you need help! David speaks about who God is. This is a song of Theology. Everyone needs to see themselves through God's glory. Only then can you know your value.

Comprehension - God Knows Me [1]

God's view is the only one we can trust. God is Omniscient but He is constantly asking men questions! He does so, that we will discover the truth about ourselves and our accountability to Him.

Searched – God is not static in His interest in you.

Know – God's comprehension of you is not, "one among billions" but, "I can count how many hairs you have on your head, TODAY!"

Custom - God Knows my Patterns [2]

You know when I sit, how I sit and when I stand - Father understands the way you think – which for some of us is a miracle all by itself! God knows, by His intellect and observation, your physical patterns and mental tracking.

Communication - God Knows my Thoughts. [4]

He recognizes your speech patterns, understands your colloquial expressions, and knows the next word out of your mouth before you do *(Ex. 4:11!)*

Control - God Sets my Limits [5]

Father creates the maze we call our daily existence, and He directly intervenes in your affairs.

Confusion - God has a better view of me [6]

How is this possible? He works everything in such a wondrous way and all for my good *(Rom. 8:28.)* His attention is always, **His attention** *(Job 12:10.)*

I didn't earn it, I don't deserve it, but He gives His love to me *(Tit.3:5; Rom. 8:31.)* God values you.

APRIL 25

The Value of Life - You Are Known - Psalm 139:7-12

PSALMS 139:7
Where shall I go from Your Spirit? or where shall I flee from Your presence?

The Psalmist changes the way we examine life, by making us see through God's eyes. The second verse of the song is about Omnipresence *(Psalm 104:1-5.)* The Triune God created all things, but He is separate from His creation *(Heb. 1:10-12.)* To make this Omnipresence real, he phrases it in the rhetorical.

I Do Not Seek God [7]

Where can I go – where can I flee? If it sounds like we are trying to hide from God? Because that is our nature *(Gen. 3:10.)* We do not seek after God *(Ps.14:2-3.)*

I Cannot Hide From God [8]

Heaven and Hell. Certainly, two extremes and to a degree, we understand David's meaning is symbolic, but there is a deeper lesson. God pursues us all. God speaks about this through the prophet *(Amos 9:2.)*

Self-righteousness does not conceal us from God *(Jer. 17:9-10.)* Hell *– to make my bed -* David insists that no matter what the pain, grief or rebellion that occupies our hearts, God is still there.

I Do Not Follow God [9]

Wings of the morning – This touches on a means of escape. Some think that they can run away from God *(Jonah1:3.) Uttermost part – I will live beyond the familiar, change my scenery, get away from home!* (You know, the Prodigal Son.) *(Luke 15:12-13)*

I Do Not Understand God [10]

Lead me, hold me – Our conclusion about God is that since we want to move away from God, perhaps He wants to punish us for our rebellion. His love for us is not based on our correct response *(Rom. 5:8.)*

I Cannot Be Separated From God [11-12]

God is Light. He has perfect night vision. We are limited. He has no limits. The darkness will never extinguish the light. You cannot hide from God.

APRIL 26

The Value of Life – Life Is Precious – Part 1 Ps. 139:13-18

PSALMS 139:17
How precious also are Your thoughts unto me, O God! how great is the sum of them!

How do you start putting together a jigsaw puzzle? You find all the edge pieces first. You know it has an outside edge! You solve problems by what you do know, to discover what you don't know. Your value comes from God. He sought us. Ignorance of our value causes our destruction **(Hosea 4:6.)**

All Life is Precious

God placed upon man the responsibility of managing His creation **(Gen. 1:28.)** In the poetry of song, David makes the divine case that we are intentionally made. If God requires accountability for the care of the earth, how much more for those who are made in His image?

1. We are the direct act of God. **(Gen. 1:26-27)**
2. We are in the image of God. **(1 Thess. 5:23)**
3. We are not animals. **(Ps. 8:3-9)**

Possessed [13] – *possessed my reigns* – This gives us the image of creative ownership. God knows how you think. *Covered me* – to entwine or fence in. It is "to protect and not limit." *In my mother's womb* – This tells us where and when life begins, implantation!

Praised [14] – Man is the direct act of the creative God **(Gen. 1:27.)** *Wonderful, marvelous* – Set apart. The creation of man was separate from all other creatures on the fifth day. *My soul knows* – All living beings have a spirit, but Man was made a living soul **(Gen.2:7.)**

Purposeful [15] *substance not hidden* – the power of life is not confusing to the God who made it **(Heb.4:13.)** *Made in secret, lowest parts* – In the dimness of the womb all is plain for the ever-present God. *Curiously wrought* - painted as with a needle. He is directly involved in your life and death **(Isa.46:3-4.)**

The detail He has put into every person speaks of loving care. God values you.

APRIL 27

The Value of Life – Life Is Precious – Part 2 Ps. 139:13-18

PSALMS 139:17
How precious also are Your thoughts unto me, O God! how great is the sum of them!

The Psalmist has revealed to us that we are valuable. That value comes not from our abilities or accomplishments but by the choice of God, who has set His love upon us. Still, we live in a world that continually devalues life. Many Christians are ignorant of how precious life is; and this ignorance, whether through darkness or willfulness, causes our destruction.

Planned [16] *My substance* – the embryo, the wrapped unformed mass. *In thy book* – the book of DNA, unchangeable, protected, shaped by the process of life! We are not mistakes, even when there are missing parts! Abortion is murder. Euthanasia is the usurping of the authority of God. Suicide is a denial of God's ability to bring peace to troubled hearts. God does not give what belongs to Him *(Isa. 42:8.)*

Precious [17] Life is precious. Life is never a mistake. God has a wonderful plan for every life, no matter what the outward circumstances supposedly tell you *(Ps. 121:3-4.)*

Present [18] The number of His thoughts toward you are greater than you can count. A single grain of sand might seem unimportant, but you can be buried in sand! His thoughts do not destroy but are directed toward your blessing.

But think of the even greater power displayed to redeem that same life! Even if your sin seems great to you, God's Grace is GREATER *(Rom. 5:20!)*

There are many questions about life that puzzle me. I often ask why? But I have learned to go by what I do know, and not by what I don't know.

And what do I know?

Jesus loves me,
This I know,
For the Bible tells me so.

APRIL 28

The Value of Life – You Are Accountable
Psalm 139 :19-24

PSALMS 139:23
Search me, O God, and know my heart: try me, and know my thoughts:

When it comes to value systems, we live in a day of iron and clay. The clay has always been with us. It is the attitude expressed in **(Judges 21:25)** *... every man did that which was right in his own eyes.*

This subjective mentality mixes freely in your home, your church, and certainly in our government. In a world where it is so important to be "politically correct," the old saying becomes true: *"If you don't stand for something, you'll fall for anything."* Our text demands you take an active position. You must make this personal. So many deny absolutes **(2 Tim.4:1-4.)**

The God who has allowed you to find "the edges of the puzzle" by giving you a glimpse of Himself, does not promise you control of the Product. He just commands you be part of the Process. You are morally accountable to a Holy God. The God who declared your value by His divine attention to your life, says that your accountability is now, not later.

God calls for two things: Separation and Sanctification. There is a divine direction to make a clear difference between good and evil and, therefore, a division between those that practice good or evil. [19] The wicked are just that, wicked. It is revealed in their deeds and the focus of their hearts. God will punish sin **(Gal. 6:7-8.)**

[20] As we observe the world, many deny the direct hand of God in creation and reject the authority of His name. [21-22] Hate - It seems so strong a term. How can a Christian hate? To love Jesus is to hate the sin and love the sinner. As a fully devoted follower of Jesus, I must live my life *"set apart"* for His use. There is and there should be a difference in our thinking and our behavior. We must always ask,

"What would Jesus do?"

APRIL 29

The Value of Life - A Life Changing Prayer

PSALMS 139:23-24

Search me, O God, and know my heart: try me, and know my thoughts: And see if there be any wicked way in me and lead me in the way everlasting.

This is a dangerous prayer that resonates with the heart of God *(Prov. 17:3.)* What David prays for and what God does continually is examination. The Holy Spirit is helping you discover the truth about who you are. The Holy Spirit's examination leads us to humility and transparency. It is called holiness.

What is this idea behind this deep introspection? We are easily deceived. If we do not purpose self-examination, we will lose out *(2 Cor.13:5.)* I cannot emphasize this enough - It is so easy to be fooled *(Prov. 28:26.)* Paul suggests the Lord's Table is a great time to do this *(1 Cor. 11:28.)*

Most of us still think we have to do something to make ourselves acceptable to God. "*Blame and Shame*" is our favorite spiritual activity *(Gal. 3:1-3.)* The direction of the song is comforting but difficult for us to practice, yet practice it we must, for it is the path of faith *(Prov. 3:5-6.)*

Who are you really? Paul informs us that without Christ we are out of control *(Rom.8:7.)* When dealing directly with God, Abraham and Isaiah were forced to think about themselves as helpless. I think every believer needs an experience like this.

David wants us to realize that what we really need is what God alone can do! No one can really know you unless He is the Omniscient, Omnipresent, Omnipotent God *(Ps. 26:2.)* This prayer is a beautiful expression, full of poetry and power.

Wanting what God wants is the biggest part of the battle *(Ps. 19:12-14.)* If you believe that He values you, it is not that scarry. This is a process, not a magic wand. It is better to seek the examination from God than to wait for His judgment. Grace is always greater than your sin *(Rom. 5:20.)*

APRIL 30

Now I Know

1 KINGS 17:22-24

And the LORD heard the voice of Elijah; and the soul of the child came into him again, and he revived. And Elijah took the child and brought him down out of the chamber into the house and delivered him unto his mother: and Elijah said, See, your son lives. And the woman said to Elijah, now by this I know that you are a man of God, and that the word of the LORD in your mouth is truth.

1 CORINTHIANS 1:22-24

For the Jews require a sign, and the Greeks seek after wisdom: But we preach Christ crucified, unto the Jews a stumbling block, and unto the Greeks foolishness; But unto them which are called, both Jews and Greeks, Christ the power of God, and the wisdom of God.

When pressed by the circumstances of life, who among us does not long for a miracle. The widow had grown accustomed to the daily experience of the miraculous (the flour and oil). Now tragedy caused her to think of God's judgment. The circumstances defined her understanding of God.

The nature of man has not changed. Men still believe they know God by their circumstances. Does God bring good and bring trouble? Of course He does, for all things are ordered by His Word. But faith in God does not come from the reaction to circumstance but through the acceptance of His Word **(Romans 10:17.)**

It is the Gospel that is truly miraculous. Whether people seek power or wisdom, only the miracle of the sacrifice of Christ can transform the life, empower the soul, and give purpose to all who will trust in Him. It is the goodness of God that leads us to repentance. The goodness of the God, who gave His only Son so that we might have the miracle of Eternal Life.

(**1 John 5:12**) *He that has the Son has life; and he that has not the Son of God has not life.*

Now, I know.

MAY 1

My Heroes

1 CORINTHIANS 4:16
Wherefore I beseech you, be followers of me.

1 CORINTHIANS 11:1
Be followers of me, even as I also am of Christ.

I love Jesus. I am eager to define myself as a fully devoted follower of Jesus Christ, but Father has placed people in my life that have made a significant impact in the way I follow my King.

At the risk of embarrassing my friends, I call them heroes. Lindy and Carol Drake have been serving God for over 45 years in a Gospel Ministry in South America. The testimony to a transformed life was evident long before they prepared for the mission field. I was in elementary school and high school with Lindy. His love for Jesus and the Word of God was a compelling influence on this lazy preacher's kid. It forced me to do things that were way out of my comfort zone.

Lindy and Carol met at Practical Bible Training School. His four older brothers had graduated from there to go out to work for the King with Village Missions. But Lindy and Carol knew that Father had a different path for them. They went out under New Tribes Missions (Now called Ethnos 360). When they told me it might be years before they see any fruit from their labors, it once more challenged me to be faithful in my service to my Master.

Father has been good to His servants and given them a harvest! My heroes point me to Christ and make me want to be faithful to my calling.

Do you have a hero?

MAY 2

Mary or Martha?

LUKE 10:38-42

… and a certain woman named Martha received him into her house. And she had a sister called Mary, which also sat at Jesus' feet, and heard his word. But Martha was cumbered about much serving, and came to Him, and said, Lord, do you not care that my sister has left me to serve alone? Tell her to help me. And Jesus answered and said unto her, Martha, Martha, you are careful and troubled about many things: But one thing is needful: and Mary has chosen that good part, which shall not be taken away from her.

You have shared this passage. Perhaps you have used the poetic summary, *"first occupied with Jesus, then occupied for Him!"* We recognize that these women represent two types of believers. But can you spot them? And if you can identify them, can you help both types to grow in *the grace* and *the knowledge* of Jesus?

Certainly, Mary is commended by Jesus for her attention to the truth. I have had my share of "Martha's." If there is a church dinner, they are driven to make sure everything is ready to eat, following the closing "amen." It always is, and our appetites are glad for it, but ….

Your responsibility is to help people who are wired differently to first learn what it means to be rewired to the person of Christ. How do you get the spiritual sponge to be a cup overflowing with grace to others that the mercy of Christ is revealed in meeting other's needs? How do you turn the one geared to human effort to grease the gears with the oil of gladness found in the knowledge of Christ so that their engine does not burn up?

The answer is more than just, "Stop it!" It will not be found in rules or work schedules but in making both types understand the joy found in serving differently. It will become for them the excitement of, *"sharing what I know and living what I feel."* Every aspect of growth is always a process. Commit to it as their shepherd.

MAY 3

What God Speaks

1 KINGS 13:18

He said unto him, I am a prophet also as you are and an angel spoke unto me by the word of the LORD, saying, bring him back with you into your house, that he may eat bread and drink water. **But he lied unto him.**

"What God speaks in the Daylight, do not doubt in the Dark." This is a great challenge to steadfast faith. But I would like to present a similar thought, **"What God has Promised Privately, do not fail to Perform Publicly."**

This is a challenging chapter. We understand the task of the prophet, the reasoning behind it, and we enjoy the punishment inflicted upon this evil King, Jeroboam. But the directions for no lunch break are confusing and then the intentional sabotage by this other prophet – that is a head scratcher!

Certainly, this is a test of this young prophet's obedience. We are likely to consider jealousy as the motivator for the older prophet's deception. God shows the heart condition of Jeroboam following a judgment and his deliverance. He was a bad dude!

Are you convinced that Father has called you into ministry? If that is a given - are you sure that where you are and what you are doing is His revealed will for you? I do not believe that Father puts square pegs into round holes. I know that "Father equips the called, not that He calls the equipped." I have often asked others, "What is in your hand?" What has Father given you by way of experience, gifts, and a skill set that has prepared you for this opportunity? Has the Holy Spirit started a fire in you that cannot be put out?

Then don't doubt what God has "restricted" you to do, even if other skilled, mature servants have a different opinion. Do not measure your success by "nickels, noses, and kneelers." On your knees, be faithful to the vision. You won't be buried in the wrong place.

MAY 4

This is Better

ECCLESIASTES 7:8
Better is the end of a thing than the beginning of it: and the patient in spirit is better than the proud in spirit.

PROVERBS 30:5-6
Every word of God is pure: he is a shield unto them that put their trust in him. Add not unto his words, lest he reprove you, and you be found a liar.

True confession time. I am sure you have never been in this situation. It had never happened to me – until just recently. I wanted to encourage a fellow pastor and warn him against the let down that comes following a great spiritual struggle and a wonderful victory for the Kingdom. Elijah experienced this let-down and I know that I have come close to it. My friend was glad for my words; and then - I did it.

I misquoted the scripture. I not only misquoted but I also claimed it was in a different book. The passage is our text in Ecclesiastes. I reversed the order. I was trying to make the point that a let-down that affects the entire being was possible after a hard-won fight. I am right in the principle, but it was wrong.

Perhaps you think I am being too hard on myself. I will not make any excuses or take refuge in any other factors that some might offer in a defense. I was wrong. When I realized my error, I had to wait till morning to text an apology to my friend. I don't think the matter bothered him too much, but I am thankful that the Holy Spirit did not let me go on in my mistake. As the writer of Proverbs expresses, I trust in the Word of God, and I do not want to "cherry pick" proof texts to make my point. Doing so is deceitful, and I turn the Sword of the Spirit into a weapon for my own purposes.

To admit your mistake, as soon as possible, helps you to recognize your frailty and confess a dependency upon the Holy Spirit to guide you into all truth. But I am sure you have never done this, right?

MAY 5

The Prayer of an Addict

JONAH 2:2 (SEE JONAH 2)

And said, I cried by reason of my affliction unto the LORD, and he heard me; out of the belly of hell I cried, and You heard my voice.

An addict? Why call Jonah an addict? Jonah was rebellious, and rebellion is sin. Sin is manifest in addiction. The idea I want to present is the principles that are demonstrated in his prayer fit the need of an addict.

Jonah is in the middle of the consequences of his rebellion. I mean that he was literally "inside" the great fish (whale.) He knew he was disobedient, but he continued in his sin. He knew he would not be able to avoid the consequences, though God surprised him. The surprise came because he thought a watery grave would be the end of his disobedience, but God had other plans. THREE DAYS LATER, he is forced to cry out!

He admits that God is the only one who can hear him in his affliction. He is "so low that he has to reach up to touch the bottom." He acknowledges that God has controlled what no one else could – *all your billows and waves passed over me* [v3].

[vv 4-6] He understands that he is past human redemption. I believe we can codify it with this phrase, "*There is nothing in man, to redeem man in God's sight.*" In this prayer is the confession that redemption is the will and work of God. His psalm focuses on the place where God has promised He would meet with man [vv4,7]. At that moment, it was impossible for Jonah to be in the Temple. His song shows that he understood the difference between a "place" of worship and a real relationship with God which is revealed through obedience. He declares the key thought in verse 8 and says, "*Yes, Lord.*"

God's response tells us that Jonah has rejected his addiction to rebellion but now must be exercised with the process of obedience. Righteousness is always a process. Breaking addiction is a process. God is no one's fool ***(Galatians 6:7-8.)***

MAY 6

Sin No More

JOHN 5:14

Afterward Jesus found him in the temple, and said unto him, Behold, you are made whole: sin no more, lest a worse thing come unto you.

What could be worse than a 38-year physical disease? What could be worse than being so near a place of healing and never getting what you need? What would it be like to have no hope of help because everyone around you is just as desperate?

This whole scenario seems beyond belief. What would be gained by the unpredictable stirring of a pool by an angel? How was this blessing discovered? Consider the stories of hurting multitude languishing at this spot for one possible moment of release. I have no answers. I only know that at this "pool" of wretched humanity, the Great Physician approaches only one. He knows all about him. We might correctly conclude that his sickness had something to do with his sin. It is a reasonable thought. I allow myself to become distracted by the truth that Jesus could have healed everyone there and we don't know if He did. Since I am convinced that Jesus never makes a mistake and that He's always good, I will focus on His goodness, not my ignorance.

Jesus' second contact presents the man with a clear warning. Jesus knew his backstory and chose to be merciful. His present is connected to failure in his past. The One who does not lie presents this blessed man with a better life by avoiding his failure. His report to the authorities should not be considered a rejection of Jesus' direction, for it provided Jesus with an opportunity to confront hypocritical judgment and teach us who is the true Judge.

We have all been affected by the infirmity of our sin. We may seek for some kind of relief, but it seems there is no one to help. Then Jesus comes to us, knowing us and our past, and is still able to make us whole. His Word is great, and we believe. But true deliverance is a process. Will we forsake sin and obey?

MAY 7

Rejoice Not Against Me

MICAH 7:8-9

Rejoice not against me, O my enemy: when I fall, I shall arise; when I sit in darkness, the LORD shall be a light unto me. I will bear the indignation of the LORD, because I have sinned against Him, until He plead my cause, and execute judgment for me: He will bring me forth to the light, and I shall behold His righteousness.

"You never finish anything." My loving mother said these words to a boy of five years. She said them in a moment of personal distress. I have never forgotten them (obviously.) They have shaped the way I view life and what I have accomplished with my giftedness.

The last chapter of Micah is a personal reflection upon his time. Disappointment shaped the way he viewed his day. To keep from total despair, he adopted a default position based in truth and it gave him hope. Because God is Salvation, he would rise in strength; there would be light. He admits and accepts his need of Divine correction, but he declares that his Judge is also his Savior. God brings us through to the light and a blessed hope.

After remarks made about me by those that wanted to hurt me deeply, I remember a wise man saying to me, *"Be glad your enemies don't know the truth about you."* Learn the lesson: life is not fair. If we do not understand this, we can be of no help to others in distress.

Father is not your enemy. He knows all about you. He will defeat your enemies by giving you strength to stand and light to see that there is hope. Father will use your circumstances to refine you. He will defend; He will bring justice, His light will shine through you, and those around will behold His righteousness through your life.

Do not let the condemnation of others define you or be prophetic. May Micah's declaration of faith be your expression of hope.

MAY 8

People Do Change

ACTS 15:37-38
And Barnabas determined to take with them John, whose surname was Mark. But Paul thought not good to take him with them, who departed from them from Pamphylia, and went not with them to the work.

2 TIMOTHY 4:11
Only Luke is with me. Take Mark and bring him with thee: for he is profitable to me for the ministry.

"Are you the same person you were a year ago?" I have often used this as "a hook" for a New Year's message. Do we believe people can change? Mark is the best example of the work of the Holy Spirit in changing hearts and relationships.

These first missionaries had a hard journey. I confess, I would have been on my way home with Mark. Barnabas shows the grace that most of us pretend to show. He is a leader that understands that leaders help others succeed.

As a pastor, I know that I am to help set the agenda for my church. I should also instruct believers to reach toward godly goals. But do I know how to deal with people who disappoint me? Paul had a God-given direction (just like you!) It was hard work, and he didn't need to have someone let him down, again.

Mark needed a Barnabas. When we examine scripture, we give thanks for the grace of God revealed in Mark and (here is the miracle) also in Paul! He learned that we all need to mature.

We are thankful for the work of the Holy Spirit in us, and hope others see more of Jesus in us all the time. Are you looking for Jesus in others or are you focused on their past failures? Is it possible for you to be a Barnabas in someone's walk with Jesus? If you are not a Barnabas, can you connect troubled people with someone who will mentor them over the rough places?

We all need someone to help us. Be a good shepherd.

MAY 9

Oatmeal? Yum!!

PHILIPPIANS 4:12-13

I know both how to be abased, and I know how to abound: everywhere and in all things, I am instructed both to be full and to be hungry, both to abound and to suffer need. I can do all things through Christ who strengthens me.

I was 17 and eager to serve the King! Also, I was going to be with my friends on an adventure. We all "volunteered" to be counselors for three weeks at three different kids camps. It was a blast!

The first camp was held at "Camp of the Woods" in the Catskill Mountains of New York State. When I was a little boy, I had lived just a few miles from the camp. I and two of my friends were responsible for twenty boys from the ages of 7-10. We didn't know any better, so we survived!

Here is where the oatmeal comes in. Every morning the cooking staff fed us nothing but oatmeal and toast. I didn't like oatmeal. It was a texture thing with me. But Father was telling me I had to eat it. All these kids were watching me. If I didn't eat up, I would be teaching the wrong things. Milk and LOTS of brown sugar was my way through the glop! That summer I grew up (a little) and I learned to like oatmeal!

Oatmeal taught me a beginning lesson on leadership. I must become willing to do things I do not like, to reveal obedience, commitment to the greater good, and express thankfulness for the ministry of others. As John Maxwell says, *"You must be willing to give up, so that you may go up."* The higher you rise in leadership, the fewer the options you have. When I became a pastor, I needed the wisdom and courage that my "oatmeal" lesson had taught me. I also learned that Father would help me find *"the milk and brown sugar;"* I need to make what I must stomach enjoyable.

I still don't like beets.

MAY 10

No Advantage to the Enemy

2 CORINTHIANS 2:10-11

To whom you forgive anything, I forgive also: for if I forgave anything, to whom I forgave it, for your sakes forgave I it in the person of Christ; Lest Satan should get an advantage of us: for we are not ignorant of his devices.

Corinth was a troubled church. Only the poorly instructed would hold this group of believers up as a pattern of success. They were occupied with their problems and not how to fulfill the Great Commission or keep the Great Commandment. A church is not a church unless it is seeking to do these two things in its own unique way. Through the correction of Paul's letters, we find the wisdom we need to avoid a pattern of disobedience and wasted effort revealed in Corinth.

Yet these people were God's people and deserved to be led by the example of godly leaders. Paul commends them for focusing on the process of forgiveness. There were people in Corinth that did not respect Paul. They had used anything to dishonor him. Paul says to the church, "I am onboard with your process of forgiveness. I am doing this because I support you. I do it through *the person of Christ.*"

This phrase is best explained by Paul in **(Eph. 4:32)** *And be kind one to another, tenderhearted, forgiving one another, even as God for Christ's sake has forgiven you.* Jesus has forgiven us everything. We must be like Jesus. I must love what Jesus loves and that means broken people who may be led by their fallen nature.

[v 11] If as a leader, you try to grasp your honor as "The Pastor," you will end up doing the work of the enemy. Paul instructed Timothy, *"in meekness instruct those that oppose themselves."* No one wants to help the enemy. Be the more mature one in Christ. Do not overlook sin but forgive frailty. Be like your Master and do not be mastered by the stupidity of unforgiveness.

MAY 11

The Lord Will Not Hear Me

PSALMS 66:18-19
If I regard iniquity in my heart, the Lord will not hear me:
But verily God has heard me; he has attended to the voice of my prayer.

What a moment! I realized what David was setting before me! I was afraid. My fear had nothing to do with my eternal destiny, for that had been settled on the Cross of Christ. I am convinced that Jesus never lies, so when He said, "It is finished," I found rest in the truth of His promise.

But David was saying that my line of prayer was vital to my existence. I was taught at my mother's side how to pray, that I must pray, that Father was waiting to hear my prayer. To not be heard gave me thoughts of despair and desperation.

Since I am a frail man, how would my sin hinder this breath of life? *If I regard iniquity in my heart* – if I realize that my thoughts, my actions are disobedient to my God, and I continue to cling to my sin; this attitude of my heart will block the comfort and assurance that could be mine when I pour my heart out to my Abba.

God understands my words, but my *regard* for things that offend Him block the path of intimacy. Father's care is not removed but my fellowship is restricted. I will not sense what has been the "deeper than deep" care of the Holy Spirit because my grasp on sin has grieved Him.

My prayers do not change the will of God, but they do assure me that I am being heard! I need this. Father knows that I need this. That is why He tells us to ask just like my children asked me **(Luke 11:13.)**

I memorized verse 18 because of the challenge it gave, but then committed verse 19 to heart because of the comfort David knew I needed. *Verily God has heard me* – I know the heart of my Father. I trust His promise. Therefore, I can rest in the intercession of my loving Savior. I am heard.

MAY 12

A Mother in Israel

2 SAMUEL 20:19

I am one of them that are peaceable and faithful in Israel: you seek to destroy a city and a mother in Israel: why will you swallow up the inheritance of the LORD? [Read 2 Samuel 20 for a good story.]

Joab could be a hasty man. I believe he was driven by duty to David and his own ego. A man named Sheba was causing the Kingdom real problems and David declared him public enemy number one.

Joab and a large part of the army had cornered him in the city of Abel. Joab's way of capturing Sheba was to destroy the city. It seems a bit excessive.

(I am sure we are missing something.)

A wise old woman intervenes, the city is spared, and Joab comes out "a head." The question that comes to mind is, why didn't someone in responsibility come to this solution sooner? My answer is that testosterone was fully in control!.

My point - God has given your wife a valuable insight into life. It is intentionally different from yours. To ignore or discount her insight is to play the fool. You do have an ego. You would not be in ministry if you did not. Posturing never allows you to be a good shepherd.

Believe that Father did not make a mistake when he gave her to you (**Prov. 18:22**) *Whoso finds a wife finds good and obtains favor of the LORD.*

She is committed to your success. Her voice is not the Holy Spirit, but the Holy Spirit will use her to speak life into your ministry.

MAY 13

It Smells Wrong

LEVITICUS 10:1-2

And Nadab and Abihu, the sons of Aaron, took either of them his censer, and put fire therein, and put incense thereon, and offered strange fire before the LORD, which he commanded them not. And there went out fire from the LORD, and devoured them, and they died before the LORD.

Very few of us have experienced spiritual activity or emotion that relates to our olfactory nerves. That is why it is difficult for us to connect with this event. Smell has the strongest retention in our memory and Father wants our "smell" to direct others to Him. Paul said, *"to one we are the smell of death and another the smell of life."* (See 2 Corinthians 2:14-16)

Both these men were new at this task of being a spiritual representative. Up to this point, they followed as they were directed by Moses. This is the first (and last) time they acted on their own. The point is, God had given instructions about the creation of this specific incense (**Exodus 30.**) No other kind was to be offered. God directs every aspect of man's approach to His worship.

Our way may be with the best of intentions, but it is not accepted. (**Proverbs 14:12**) *There is a way which seems right unto a man, but the end thereof are the ways of death.*

Jesus made this very clear to us – (**John 14:6**) *Jesus said unto him, I am the way, the truth, and the life: no man comes unto the Father, but by me.*

You understand this vital truth, but there comes a time when we all want to "make our mark," do something that sets us apart from others who serve. You have an ego; otherwise, you would not be serving the way you do.

As you try to distinguish yourself from others, remember what is non-negotiable. Jealously guard what God says is absolute - the Great Commission and the Great Commandment. But how these are carried out and displayed is determined by the Holy Spirit and the "vessel" He chooses to use. Smell good to God.

MAY 14

Family

JOHN 7:5
For neither did his brethren believe in him.

PROVERBS 18:19
A brother offended is harder to be won than a strong city: and their contentions are like the bars of a castle.

ACTS 1:14
These all continued with one accord in prayer and supplication, with the women, ***and Mary the mother of Jesus, and with his brethren.***

I am so glad Jesus had brothers and sisters. He understood how difficult it can be to serve God and be accepted by your family. I was encouraged by my parents. But I don't know what my brothers thought. Oh, they loved me, but it was still, "little Johnny doesn't understand life."

The Gospels give insights into the family dynamic of Jesus. They caved to public pressure that said that Jesus was crazy. His actions were bad for business and made it socially awkward for the family.

What was it like for Jesus' brothers and sisters to grow up with a brother that never did anything wrong? How about the "stories" about his conception? Are your relatives embarrassed to have a "preacher" in the family? That didn't stop Jesus from loving them. You need to love your family, even if they never get it.

The goodness of God leads people to repentance. The Holy Spirit worked in Jesus' family. We know that at least two of His brothers (James and Jude) had a powerful testimony for their King.

I want you to have hope in what Jesus is going to do with your testimony and your family. You know there are no guarantees about their eternal destiny. To some we smell of life and to others of death *(2 Cor. 2:16.)* Your assignment has always been to be a light in a dark place. Love your family, especially without words. Let the Holy Spirit do His job. He is good at it.

MAY 15

Dad's Life Verse

1 CORINTHIANS 9:16
For though I preach the gospel, I have nothing to glory of: for necessity is laid upon me; yea, woe is unto me, if I preach not the gospel!

My father was a pastor for 40 years. He was raised in a godly home in Birmingham, England. My grandfather was a deacon in his church and a street preacher. He had a voice that carried and the courage to stand up to relentless heckling. Dad accepted Christ as a teenager during a communion service. His mother encouraged him to his decision by saying, "Robbie, if you love the Lord Jesus, you can share in this remembrance." The Holy Spirit used that as an invitation. "I do love the Lord Jesus." Jesus became his first love.

I don't know the circumstances that led him to become a pastor, but I am sure he learned to preach on the street. I personally think that this was a baptism by fire, but it worked. He ran a Christian book "stall," started and pastored a church, and served as an air raid warden. Dad would take every opportunity and preached the Gospel in the shelters during the blitz.

Following the war, he took his family to Canada and then got a green card to be the pastor of a Baptist Church in Upper Greenwood Lake, NY. That was when I arrived. I am the only Yankee in the family.

My father pastored churches all over New York State. He was a rolling stone. The longest he stayed in one church was six years. Why so much movement? He was far from perfect, but he would preach wherever there was an empty pulpit. Many times, the people were not Gospel minded and opposition to the truth grew, and he moved on. Our Heavenly Father always gave him an opportunity to keep true to his life verse. His greatest gift to me was a genuine love for God's Word and a love for me. I am thankful.

MAY 16

God Cannot Lie

TITUS 1:2
In hope of eternal life, which God, that cannot lie, promised before the world began;

NUMBERS 23:19
God is not a man, that he should lie; neither the son of man, that he should repent: has he said, and shall he not do it? or has he spoken, and shall he not make it good?

"Don't lie to me. What you did is disappointing but lying is worse." As we took on the opportunity of raising six children (five boys, one girl) I heard this, or something similar, directed to the offending child by my dear wife. She was never a "wait till your father comes home," type of nurturer. She dealt with opportunities to build in their lives, in that moment! She valued the truth and recognized the importance of teaching the lesson of truth-telling to these precious souls. They love their mom! That is what the truth produces.

Our God always speaks the truth. He has no purpose in lying. We lie to hide, avoid, and dodge the consequences of our actions. God has nothing to avoid because He always does what is right. As a child of God, I am to be like my Father **(Ephesians 4:25.)**

Our future is based in the promise of eternal life. Jesus is Eternal Life (***1 John 5:11-12.***) Jesus always speaks the truth (***John 14:6,***) because He is the truth. I find the greatest of comfort in God's inability to lie! I am commanded to have faith and believe in His Character and the Content of His Word, so I see this as more than common knowledge – everything hinges on this point!

In the times of woe and deepest desperation, I cling to the promise, *"I will never leave you."* If God can lie, I have no hope. He proved He is no liar by keeping His word and giving us Jesus. Jesus is true and is always there – that is no lie.

MAY 17

Eternal Confidence

JUDE 1:24-25

Now unto him that is able to keep you from falling, and to present you faultless before the presence of His glory with exceeding joy, To the only wise God our Savior, be glory and majesty, dominion and power, both now and forever. Amen.

Here is a mighty benediction! In these few words we are assured that the love of Christ goes beyond Calvary. Father has spoken these words into my heart, and they have brought me a sweet peace.

Let's consider the parts of the whole: Jesus has Prevented - *Him that is able to keep you from falling.* Jesus' one sacrifice paid the penalty for all our sin. Now our King continually intercedes for us. Jesus did more! He broke the power of sin in your life –*He is able to keep you from falling.* You know the power of the resurrected Christ. In Him we find the confidence we need when we believe as Abraham **(Romans 4:21.)**

Jesus will Present us - *Present you faultless* – The Bible teaches us that our standing in Christ is one of perfection, but our state is one that is going through a process. *Faultless* – seems an exaggeration, but we must have faith in the Provision of God. Here is a simple question – **Was Jesus' sacrifice on Calvary what God had planned to pay for our sin?**

His sacrifice was perfect.

His work was perfect.

We are not condemned because of Jesus.

We are being changed eternally because of Jesus.

We are part of God's adopted family, never to be disowned because of Jesus.

Jesus brings Praise - *The presence of His Glory* – Salvation is all about Jesus, not about you. But you will know joy **(1 Peter 1:8.)** Jude's last words to us are praise to God. How often do your prayers end this way? Praise Him and "pink elephants" (what you can't control) will never be a problem.

MAY 18

You Shall Not Oppress

LEVITICUS 25:17
You shall not therefore oppress one another; but you shall fear your God: for I am the LORD your God.

To live above with Saints in Heaven,
Will be endless bliss and glory!
But to live below with those same Saints,
Is quite another story!

I was called to build lives. Some of those lives are pretty broken. I learned very early that I was to concentrate on the process and leave the product to the Holy Spirit. I went from an Idealist to a pragmatic. I know that there are two things that make a church a church. They are the Great Commission and The Great Commandment. A church must have these two things going on, or it isn't a church. How that is "fleshed out" is always different from place to place, but it is always there.

I chose this text because it makes us think about what Jesus Commanded. **(John 13:35)** *By this shall all men know that you are my disciples, if you have love one to another.* Forgive me as I state the obvious: Jesus commanded this. It does not come naturally. We need the Holy Spirit and the Word of God to carry this out every day. Love is an action. It is my response in obeying my King. My love is revealed by using who I am and what I have been given to bless others. I have no other option as a child of God and as a Servant of the King. As a leader I must model this for those I lead.

Oppression is not Christ like. I am not in charge of anyone, not even myself. I am accountable *(1 Cor. 4:2.)* I am to encourage and instruct others in loving behavior. I am to rebuke behavior that does not match the pattern of Christ. That rebuke must be to restore, not destroy another life. Loving is hard, but Jesus does it all the time. With His help, you can model and also teach others to love what Jesus loves.

MAY 19

Who is Responsible?

DEUTERONOMY 21:6-8

And all the elders of that city, that are next unto the slain man, shall wash their hands over the heifer that is beheaded in the valley: And they shall answer and say, Our hands have not shed this blood, neither have our eyes seen it. Be merciful, O LORD, unto Your people Israel, whom You have redeemed, and lay not innocent blood unto Your people of Israel's charge. And the blood shall be forgiven them.

Why does the death of a stranger matter? Because God insists that all life is precious. This is certainly what our culture denies through abortion and placing the blame for murder on the weapon used and not the individual who commits the crime. So, this whole process found in (**Deut. 21**) is foreign to our experience.

Measuring which town is closer, slaying a certain type of animal, making the leadership participate in a ceremony and take an oath – what a process! But that is exactly what God is saying! No one is worthless. Every life must be honored, and we all must be ready to give an account. There are no spectators with our fellow man. *"He wasn't from my town! They are not my kind of people."* But he was found in your backyard! God knows who did the deed! He wants them to care! He held them accountable, and apathy **always** brings a curse!

You are a leader in the family of God. Our God is still the same. Though we are not obligated by the Mosaic Civil law, The Moral law still holds firm control.

"You shall not murder." It is your responsibility to teach, proclaim, and promote the moral code of God. You are your brother's keeper. Encourage those that govern and those that protect our communities to understand God's demand on human society is to protect all life. Life is God's gift and He holds us accountable (**Gen. 9:5-6.**) The frightening principle is found in (**James 4:17**) *To him that knows to do good, and does it not, to him it is sin.* We are all measured by this.

MAY 20

What Do Sinners Know?!

JONAH 3:9-10

Who can tell if God will turn and repent, and turn away from his fierce anger, that we perish not? And God saw their works, that they turned from their evil way; and God repented of the evil, that he had said that he would do unto them; and he did it not.

If you have never had a moment in your ministry when you have felt "Spiritually Superior" to the ungodly or rebellious, then count yourself among the few. (Don't shine your halo too much!) We know that Jonah did not want Nineveh to repent because he didn't want them to survive! They were too much of a threat to Israel. There are some people in our churches who don't want the change that will happen if strangers start coming in!

Our text gives us part of the repentance demonstrated by an entire city through a sermon that consisted (in English) of eight words! This was a change of heart that started at the "grass roots" level [3:5] and made its way to the throne room. To call it any less than miraculous would be an understatement!

They did not have the Law of Moses. They knew little of the interaction of God among His chosen people, and they did not have any historic figures to examine and consider in this call from God to repent. This sounds similar to what our culture has become!

How could they repent? Two things come to mind.

1. The Witness of Creation. *(Ps. 19:1; Rom. 1:20)*
2. The Witness of Conscience. *(Rom. 2:14-15)*

We, as His servants, are given the Great Commission (*Matthew 28:19-20.)* But Father will not be stopped by our hard-heartedness. As Mordecai told Esther, **(Esther 4:14a)** *For if you altogether hold your peace at this time, then shall there enlargement and deliverance arise to the Jews from another place.* In other words, "May we be doing what He is blessing and not ask Him to bless what we are doing."

No one can stop God. Not even our ignorance.

MAY 21

The Biblical Pattern

DEUTERONOMY 19:15

One witness shall not rise up against a man for any iniquity, or for any sin, in any sin that he sins: at the mouth of two witnesses, or at the mouth of three witnesses, shall the matter be established.
(See 1 Timothy 5:19)

I can still remember the setting. I and a few of our Deacons had been invited to a member's home to hear an accusation of immorality made against one of the Home Missionaries we supported. This accusation had been made by this man's sister and shared with her friend. Our member and her husband were upset and believed it was their responsibility to bring this matter before the church leadership so that action would be taken against this individual.

I listened to what information they had received and asked a simple question, "Is there another witness against this Brother in Christ?" They seemed troubled by my question and referred back to the blood relation as evidence enough. I took them to (*1 Timothy 5: 19.*)

In turn, they stated that this woman was their friend, and she would not lie to them. I asked again for another witness. My Deacons understood the importance of the Biblical Principle before them and supported me in this simple request. We eventually left some very dissatisfied church members. (A few months later, they arranged an ambush of me over another matter. That also ended in their embarrassment.) Nothing was ever proved or pursued about the missionary.

This principle was given because "all men are liars." The enemy wants to destroy those who lead and that means YOU *(1 Pet. 5:8!)* Your responsibility and your protection lies in teaching this truth as soon and as often as you can, from the Pulpit, in the Board Room, the Classroom, and the private conversation.

Beware, the enemy preys on ignorant people.

MAY 22

Power Struggle – Clear or Unclear

1 KINGS 1:11
Wherefore Nathan spoke unto Bathsheba the mother of Solomon, saying, Have you not heard that Adonijah the son of Haggith reigns, and David our lord knows it not?

1 Kings starts with important information, *"David was old."* Because of this, Adonijah, his fourth son, thought he should be King. Now, God had already chosen Solomon (**1 Chronicles 22:9.**) God loved Solomon, but that was not clear to everyone. When God allowed Israel to have Kings, He told them, *"I am the one who chooses." (Deut. 17:15)*

Do you understand your part in the Kingdom? If you are pastoring, do you understand your responsibility in the government of the body of Christ? If you have studied the instruction of Paul, then the answer is, Yes. But there are some who have their own ideas. They've been in this church longer than you (*just like Adonijah*). It doesn't matter what the King says, we sheep are in charge!

Now, if you took this assignment and didn't know which way the wind was blowing, shame on you! You may be leading by "permission" at this moment, but Western Christianity has this funny thing that happens to it when there is a vote. They think that means that they are in control of the local kingdom!

You must certainly follow the admonition of Peter, (**1 Peter 5:2**) *Feed the flock of God which is among you, taking the oversight thereof, not by constraint, but willingly; not for merely the pay, but of a ready mind.*

Leaders help other succeed. Your responsibility is not showing them who's boss, but leading them in the paths of righteousness for HIS Name sake! Part of your task is instructing them that faith in the Master and His choices are the best for everyone. You REALLY need the Holy Spirit's help on this one or you will be hurt and so will the sheep!

MAY 23

You Have Strengthened Me

DANIEL 10:19

And said, O man greatly beloved, fear not: peace be unto you, be strong, yes, be strong. And when he had spoken unto me, I was strengthened, and said, Let my lord speak; for you have strengthened me.

If you have been communicating the truth as the messenger of God for any length of time, there is nothing like the thrill of being that guy! I have such a sense of personal satisfaction and I have never experienced anything to match it!

Jeremiah had a different expression for it. (**Jer. 20:9**) *Then I said, I will not make mention of Him, nor speak any more in His name. But His word was in my heart as a burning fire shut up in my bones, and I was weary with forbearing, and I could not stay.* His description sounds painful. Perhaps it was. But this is how it speaks to my heart; communicating the truth is like an urge that must be met or an itch that must be scratched.

At times, the preparation for a message can be difficult and you might despair that "if it is foggy in the pulpit, it will be pure mud in the pew!" But prayer changes things. You humble yourself before the King and wait on the Holy Spirit for light. You busy yourself with something else; then the light breaks forth! The words flow; the alliteration is clear! The Holy Spirit gives you "the hook" and gives you a closing that demands a response. The deep things in the text can be seem right to the bottom but you can still "put the cookies on the lower shelf." There is no more wondering if it makes sense but you long to bring the sense to those you love.

I love to preach! Father called me to build lives. I want to die with my boots on. But don't misunderstand me, it is because I get to help some to meet Jesus and others will grow in His grace. I know that not every preacher experiences what I feel, but I identify with Daniel.

Let my lord speak; for you have strengthened me.

MAY 24

Who is a God Like You?

MICAH 7:18-19

Who is a God like unto You, that pardons iniquity, and passes by the transgression of the remnant of His heritage? He retains not His anger forever, because He delights in mercy. He will turn again, He will have compassion upon us; He will subdue our iniquities; and You will cast all their sins into the depths of the sea.

There are some who, in their ignorance, try to tell us that the God of the Old Testament is not the God of the New Testament. They have never read this passage. Our God is changeless, **(Malachi 3:6)** *For I am the LORD, I change not; therefore, you sons of Jacob are not consumed.* **(Heb. 13:8)** *Jesus Christ the same yesterday, and today, and forever.*

We can come with boldness to get the help and the mercy we always need. All of us are needy, broken, imperfect failures. But the God of Eternity pardons our sin against Him and does not gather up our intentional rebellion. He is not governed by His anger with disobedience because He delights in being directly involved with His loving kindness toward us.

He will turn again - He is the only one that will give us a new beginning. His compassion is not expressed in impossible expectations but in real time help. He is the only God that knew that we didn't need to turn over a "new leaf," for that was the definition of insanity! Instead, He gave us a New Nature by the gift of the Holy Spirit through the finished work of Christ! That nature is transforming us so that all our sin and failure will be separated from us. He is doing the process of change. He is turning death into life!

Buried in the deepest sea.
Yes, that's good enough for me!
I will live eternally,
Praise God!
My sins are gone!

MAY 25

Transfer of Guilt

1 CHRONICLES 19:4
Wherefore Hanun took David's servants, and shaved them, and cut off their garments in the middle hard by their buttocks and sent them away.

David had sent his servants as ambassadors to the Kingdom of Ammon to express sorrow in the death of the King, his friend. The new King listened to fools who accused David of spying and greatly dishonored these men and David as King.

What were they thinking? Did they think at all? Instead of a prank, it was an act of humiliation. It was understood as an act of war. We know God used it to clear out the fools that would oppose Israel, but talk about stupid!

I call it, the transfer of guilt. They assumed that others were as hateful and cynical as themselves. They considered their insults to be acts of wisdom. No one would ever just be kind, to be kind! No one ever really means what they say!

You will deal with people just like this. The sin in their life colors everything they say and do. They have lived so long in disobedience to the law of love, that they believe everyone thinks and acts as they do. They transfer their guilt on to everyone they meet. Do you think you are going to set them straight?

Please, do yourself a favor and don't try to do what only the Holy Spirit can do. (**Rev. 22:11**) *He that is unjust, let him be unjust still: and he which is filthy, let him be filthy still: and he that is righteous, let him be righteous still: and he that is holy, let him be holy still.*

Some of you cannot stand still for this kind of foolishness. Perhaps you shouldn't, but even though King David had been grievously insulted, he did not make the first move. King Hanun could have humbled himself, but instead he armed himself, to his destruction. Father is working on your behalf, removing those that oppose Him!

Remember, it is not about you.

MAY 26

Prepared For Our Failures

DEUTERONOMY 19:3-4
You shall prepare a way, and divide the coasts of your land, which the LORD your God gives you to inherit, into three parts, that every slayer may flee there. And this is the case of the slayer, which shall flee there, that he may live: Whoever kills his neighbor ignorantly, whom he hated not in time past.

God provided Cities of Refuge. There were six in total, three on either side of the Jordan River. I can't say that I am in full understanding on the "Avenger of Blood," but it seems that every family had that designated uncle that dealt with such tragedies. There was no Homicide Division to take care of murder or any other reason for the loss of life in the extended family. It is very foreign to our way of thinking, but God provided a way to protect the innocent, *"while his heart is hot"* **(See Deut. 19:6.)**

Interesting history, but it demonstrates that God understands our culture, our circumstances, and our failures. We know that the sin question is under control **(1 John 1:9.)** Our mistakes are not out of His interest or beyond His ability to mend and heal. We know that not all sickness is because of personal sin. We must also realize that not all that breaks, fails, or blows up in our faces is because we are being punished. That would be a theology of fatalism – that is not Biblical faith.

God knows everything and we certainly do not. The Cities of Refuge testify to God's ability to provide for us in things that Solomon described in **(Eccles. 9:11b)** *... but time and chance happens to all.*

Instead of wringing our hands and wailing about our confusion and the tragedy of it all, find your default position and flee to the God of Refuge. The confusion of this moment is in the hands of our loving Father, who has provided a way to protect you. But we must flee and get His help! The accidental slayer had to stay in the safe place until the danger had past. So do you.

MAY 27

Poured Out Before the Lord

1 CHRONICLES 11:18-19

And the three broke through the host of the Philistines, and drew water out of the well of Bethlehem, that was by the gate, and took it, and brought it to David: but David would not drink of it, but poured it out to the LORD, And said, My God forbid it me, that I should do this thing: shall I drink the blood of these men that have put their lives in jeopardy? for with the jeopardy of their lives they brought it. Therefore, he would not drink it. These things did these three mightiest.

In a moment of nostalgia, David remembers the joy found in the refreshing water from the town well. Three of his bravest followers overhear his lament and do the crazy! David is so overwhelmed by this act of devotion that he does a sacred thing, pours the water out in thanks to God.

Why not drink it? That is why they did it, so their leader, their hero would be blessed! David sees it differently. It makes me ask: would I have responded the same way?

I want to see this from the point of view of these men that ran into Bethlehem with their swords drawn. It must have shocked them to hear David's prayer. I would have wandered off to think about what my friend had just said about my deed. It wasn't contempt, no. He was thankful for me. He thanked God - for me!

Do the people with whom you serve know that you appreciate them? Thanks is powerful when it goes beyond what they do for you in ministry and reaches to who they are. Your relationship is not based on their activities but your attitude. This requires you to sacrifice your wants (the water of the well.) See their motivation and determination and hold it as precious as your own. Help them see that what they do is for God and what they do is more than just routine.

I am not sure that I have done this kind of honoring to the best of my ability, but I want to try.

MAY 28

Open Your Hand Wide

DEUTERONOMY 15:7-8
If there be among you a poor man of one of your brethren within any of your gates in your land which the LORD your God gives you, you shall not harden your heart, nor shut your hand from your poor brother: But you shall open your hand wide unto him, and shall surely lend him sufficient for his need, in that which he needs.

DEUTERONOMY 15:11
For the poor shall never cease out of the land: therefore, I command you, saying, you shall open your hand wide unto your brother, to your poor, and to your needy, in your land.

Abraham Lincoln is quoted as saying, "God must love the poor, He made so many of them." When I was beginning in ministry there was a foolish debate engaged about the "social versus the saving Gospel." Which was more important? What does either one mean and which comes first? The confusion came from the enemy, and not the King! What foolishness!

Peter said this about Jesus' ministry: **(Acts 10:38)** ... *who went about doing good, and healing all that were oppressed of the devil; for God was with Him.* James tells us if we know to do good and do it not, it is sin. Whether it is the need of the soul or the belly, we are required to do what we can, where we are. All modern Missionary work is based on the method of caring for physical need and sharing the Gospel. This is the will of God and the pattern of Christ. Feeding the hungry or tending the sick are all acts of a loving God. We must do so because this is the will of God for us, to show compassion, and not a way to manipulate the receiver into agreement. To do so is to assume the responsibility of the Holy Spirit, who alone Convicts, Convinces, and Conveys souls into the body of Christ *(John 16:8-11.)*

Trust the Lord, share your faith, and do good.

MAY 29

"Monday, Monday..."

MARK 6:31
And he said unto them, Come apart into a desert place, and rest a while: for there were many coming and going, and they had no leisure so much as to eat.

The context of this passage is the first time the disciples are sent out in teams of two, their successful return to Jesus to share their report, and the execution of John the Baptist. Is that busy enough for you?! I consider this a major stressor!

The advice from Jesus is, "Let's take a break." Yes, I know the ministry does not stop (feeding the 5,000 +,) but the principle is still there! We need to plan for rest. (**Prov. 4:26**) *Ponder the path of your feet and let all your ways be established.*

I tried to take Monday off from the regular ministry routine. I was not always successful, but the last half of Mark 6 gives me encouragement. Why Monday? When I was at "full throttle" in ministry, I had four different preps on a Sunday. On Monday, I was in need of a variation of responsibility.

Not everyone agrees with my choice of a day off, but don't lose the point. If Jesus saw the need, you should too. Some people in ministry are big into Sabbath rest and even insist you need to take it from Friday evening to Saturday evening. This is too legalistic for me. The principle is far more important than the day of the week (**Col. 2:16-17.**)

Your rest or change of pace is not a mark of your spirituality. The sabbath was made for man. Jesus said so! Ignoring regular planned rest is foolish, for we hurt ourselves and tell God we know better than He. I imagine you have never considered your failure to rest as an act of disobedience. Your disobedience is not in breaking the Moral law but in ignoring the pattern of the Creation cycle. The question is, what will you do about this?

Do this: (**Prov. 4:26**) *Ponder the path of your feet, and let all your ways be established.*

MAY 30

I Shall Rise

MICAH 7:8-9

Rejoice not against me, O mine enemy: when I fall, I shall arise; when I sit in darkness, the LORD shall be a light unto me. I will bear the indignation of the LORD, because I have sinned against Him, until He plead my cause, and execute judgment for me: He will bring me forth to the light, and I shall behold His righteousness.

Oh, the burden of being human and being in ministry! Stop your whining! You aren't any different than anyone else. But the consequences of your sin do seem to reach further than someone else's failure **(James 3:1.)**

Father does not abandon you when you sin. Before any other title you may bear, you are first and foremost a child of God! Father made a promise; Jesus confirmed that promise, "I will never leave you!" He may take you to the "woodshed" and you may be there a while, but no longer than you need! His sovereign will is to make you into the image of Christ ***(Phil. 1:6!)***

This wonderful, personal expression of trust by Micah makes me weep. What I have done may have brought shame and loss, and the enemy may have gloated over the crash of my façade. Yet the light of His love is still shining on me!

I MUST bear the chastening from my loving Master because I sinned against Him. There are consequences to my sin. I may bear the scars all the rest of this earthly existence. I may have to share the story many times before the pain of my failure is no longer "as hurtful." But Jesus promised that it was all for my good and eventually for His greater glory!

That is where the "light" comes in! I understand the truth. I am becoming a greater witness to the wisdom of His Word and the Grace and Mercy of my one and only Master! I had to fail (not all must) to be a trophy of His Grace! I love Him because He has forgiven SO much!

MAY 31

Go, Again!

1 KINGS 18:43-44

And [Elijah] said to his servant, Go up now, look toward the sea. And he went up, and looked, and said, There is nothing. And he said, Go again seven times. And it came to pass at the seventh time, that he said, Behold, there arises a little cloud out of the sea, like a man's hand. And he said, Go up, say unto Ahab, Prepare your chariot, and get down, that the rain does not stop you.

JAMES 5:16B-18

The effectual fervent prayer of a righteous man avails much. Elijah was a man subject to like passions as we are, and he prayed earnestly that it might not rain: and it rained not on the earth by the space of three years and six months. And he prayed again, and the heaven gave rain, and the earth brought forth her fruit.

I am inspired by Elijah's story! This is a demonstration of faith and obedience. James calls Elijah, "*a man subject to like passions.*" He was just like us. I want you to remember this drought thing was not his idea **(*1 Kings 17:1.*)** God told him to speak and hide, and he did! There are many great sermons on this fellow, but above all he believed and obeyed.

I also think it was important to emphasize that he grasped the importance of his part in the display of God's sovereignty over Baal. Baal represented the collection of the region's gods of ecology/fertility. (Thinking about it – in comparison to our present culture, it shows that nothing has changed!)

Our text relates his obedience in bringing back the rain as God directed. He did this by praying. That's what we must do! God wants to demonstrate His glory through your obedience. In your case, It may take longer than three years, but if you believe and obey, your prayer is just as effective in bringing honor to His name!

You must encourage those with you in ministry to "keep on keeping on" (*Elijah said, seven times.*) Keep on praying! The atmospheric river of God's purpose (note: I did not say blessing) will come.

JUNE 1

Thoughts On the Dead

LUKE 16:22-23 - (SEE LUKE 16:19-31)

And it came to pass, that the beggar died, and was carried by the angels into Abraham's bosom: the rich man also died and was buried; and in hell he lifted up his eyes, being in torments, and saw Abraham afar off, and Lazarus in his bosom.

Our focus is the account by Jesus in Luke 16. The theme is accountability. This event is before the resurrection of Christ. I believe it to be personal information that the Son of God shares with us, proving that God, the final judge, knows all men's hearts. If you believe this a parable, let us agree on certain things:

1. Jesus' illustrations were familiar with the people.
2. He never lied or exaggerated when He spoke.
3. Jesus did not communicate spiritual truths with imaginary or facetious illustrations.

- There is a difference between the physical and spiritual existence.
- There is a place of existence that is recognizable.
- Transport (at least for the righteous) is by angels.
- The rich man had senses.
- The rich man was tormented. **(Mark 9:43-48)**
- The rich man could understand his circumstances.
- The rich man could recognize others.
- Jesus calls hell a place of torment, not the grave.
- The rich man has conscious thought.
- The ability to communicate is available to all.
- Pain is real and experienced by those in hell.
- At least one torment is flame. **(Revelation 14:11)**
- There is memory in death. **(Revelation 6:9-10)**
- There is a separate place of comfort for the righteous, but it is not heaven.

JUNE 2

The Hardship of Obedience

NUMBERS 15:32-36

And while the children of Israel were in the wilderness, they found a man that gathered sticks upon the sabbath day... And they put him in ward, because it was not declared what should be done to him. And the LORD said unto Moses, the man shall be surely put to death: all the congregation shall stone him with stones without the camp. And all the congregation brought him without the camp, and stoned him with stones, and he died as the LORD commanded Moses.

Perhaps you do not agree with me. Thankfully, I have had very few times when I have had to publicly discipline a church member. I can also remember a few times when I should have done so. (That decision came back to bite me.) The timing of this event follows hard on the disobedience of Israel to take the promised land, their attempt to do it on their own, and one of their many times of murmuring.

There is no offering for sabbath breaking. This man must have reasoned that he was just making good use of idle time. His actions affected everyone! As a leader in the Kingdom, you will face discipline challenges. Hard as it may seem, you should not avoid them. Others will try to rationalize the circumstances. You must ask, what does God's Word say about the issue, and stand for the truth. You do not have to rush to judgment, but you must stand for the direction of the Word, to bless all.

Today, we have the guidance of **Matthew 18** to keep us from being despotic and to use correction for restoration and not destruction. If Matthew has been followed (so rare that it is) then Paul's instruction to Timothy becomes valuable. **(1 Timothy 5:20)** *Them that sin rebuke before all, that others also may fear.*

We must understand the ability for someone's personal sin to influence others. *(See Rev. 2:20-22)*

Seek the wisdom of the Holy Spirit and do right.

JUNE 3

The Gospel

1 CORINTHIANS 15:3-4
For I delivered unto you first of all that which I also received, how that Christ died for our sins according to the scriptures; And that he was buried, and that he rose again the third day according to the scriptures:

We call **John 3:16** the Gospel in a nutshell, but our passage is the clearest presentation of the elements of the Gospel. This is the message that must be *shared* (delivered) by those that have *received* it. It is the basis of a living relationship with God and our sure release from an eternal death sentence.

Christ, the Chosen One, did the unimaginable; He died for our sins. He took our deserved punishment by dying upon a Cross. This was promised and foretold by God's Word.

To provide proof, fulfill the promise, and the symbolism found in Scripture, Christ died. His physical body was placed in a tomb for three days.

In evidence of God's power and to show the keeping of the Word of God, Christ also rose from the dead after three days of physical death. He was raised by the power of God into a physical body that will never die.

So, through Paul's statement, we are given the three elements of the Gospel account. They are the physical death, burial, and physical resurrection of Christ. They must be accepted and believed in order that anyone might be saved. Saved means delivered from eternal punishment and given Eternal Life (**1 John 5:11-12.**)

The briefest statement of the Gospel is this -

(**Romans 4:25**) *Who (Jesus) was delivered for our offences and was raised again for our justification.* We must understand and believe this message to share it. To receive it, others must hear it. Only the Holy Spirit can make this message live in the hearts of those that hear it. Trust God and keep it simple.

JUNE 4

Our Eyes Are Upon You

2 CHRONICLES 20:12

O our God, will You not judge them? for we have no might against this great company that comes against us; neither know we what to do: but our eyes are upon You.

Why has this trouble come? That is the question that, if you had an answer, (any answer) you think you could reason your way out. For Jehoshaphat, this attack was the result of poor choices **(See 2 Chronicles 19:2.)**

If you think that finding a reason for the trouble makes a difference as to whether deliverance is available for you, you need to keep reading.

The greatness of this passage is that Jehoshaphat does have an answer for the trouble. That answer is not dependent on a reason. The answer is found in the Deliverer!

O our God, – Claim your relationship to the Almighty. He is your Father, and He will not abandon you. **(Galatians 3:26)** - *For you are all the children of God by faith in Christ Jesus.*

Will You not judge them – the enemy sought to take what God has given. Believe that God's promises are unshakable. Be like Abraham in **(Romans 4:21)** *And being fully persuaded that, what he had promised, he was able also to perform.*

We have no might – Proclaim your own weakness. **(2 Corinthians 12:9)** *And He said unto me, My grace is sufficient for you: for my strength is made perfect in weakness. Most gladly therefore will I rather glory in my infirmities, that the power of Christ may rest upon me.*

But our eyes are upon You – Wait for God to do what He alone can do – bring you through. **(Luke 18:1)** *And He spoke a parable unto them to this end, that men ought always to pray, and not to faint.*

What greater answer could there be? There is no other help.

JUNE 5

No Success Without a Successor

NUMBERS 27:15-17

*And Moses spoke unto the LORD, saying,
Let the LORD, the God of the spirits of all flesh, set a man over the
congregation, Which may go out before them, and which may go in before
them, and which may lead them out, and which may bring them in; that
the congregation of the LORD be not as sheep which have no shepherd.*

How do you look at this account? Is Moses being promoted or is this forced retirement? That question is not the point of this devotion, but it does say something about the way you look at ministry.

Let's think about Moses' request. Does God need Moses' insight in this matter? Does Moses think that God has made a poor plan?

Moses has been at this job for 40 years. He **is** the job. Some of you are like Moses. You know more about the facilities that God has given you than the oldest trustee on the board. You, like Moses, care deeply for the people and want them to experience the best of what God has for them.

God chose Joshua to be the replacement, and God did not make a mistake. What this story shows us is that God is getting Moses to the point where he is willing to let go of the reins. Father knows that once we have made our mark, we don't want to let go. But this is His work. It does not belong to you. Prepare to be replaced.

To truly succeed, there must be a successor. There is a tremendous failure rate with this truth. We should be working our way out of a job as soon as we start, but few of us do. Yet, one of my friends told me that he is preparing his Associate for this transfer, and his Associate knows the plan and is preparing for it. AMAZING! Someone seems to be listening to the Holy Spirit! Make disciples, that is the command.

God will do the rest.

JUNE 6

My Conduct as a Pastor

TITUS 3:8
This is a faithful saying, and these things I will that you affirm constantly, that they which have believed in God might be careful to maintain good works. These things are good and profitable unto men.

I just got off the phone with my brother. He was speaking about a gift he received that takes the thoughts about your life and turns it into a book. We both mentioned my father. He was a pastor for 40 years. We knew him as a good man, but he sometimes used "the clergy card."

What is that? *"Don't you provide a discount for pastors?"* "Yes officer, I was driving over the speed limit, but I was urgently needed to _____." To be clear, it is using ministry to gain an advantage, to avoid unpleasant consequences, or claim a "privilege."

It is tempting to take advantage of society's confusion about ministry and use it the wrong way. Though Paul does not say this injunction is specifically for those in ministry, I say that those who lead must hold to the higher standard of Grace. We must avoid "pleading preacher" and instead should do this: **(1 Peter 2:13)** *Submit yourselves to every ordinance of man for the Lord's sake.*

As Peter goes on to say, *"this is the will of God, that by well doing you may put to silence the ignorance of foolish men"* **(1 Pet. 2:15.)** My witness is always up for attack. We know the ground is level at the foot of the cross but those who lead are the ones the enemy targets. I need to make it a smaller target.

I wish I could say that I have never done anything that could be misunderstood or was ethically wrong – *but you would have a hard time accepting that.* What I will tell you is that I need to be reminded to not cut corners or make excuses. I must exercise my faith in my Father, who promised to meet my every need. He will chasten me and enable me to walk in the light.

JUNE 7

Mercy, We Find Hard to Accept

1 KINGS 21:29
See how Ahab humbles himself before Me? because he humbles himself before me, I will not bring the evil in his days: but in his son's days will I bring the evil upon his house.

Punishment delayed. We don't quite understand it, especially after reading the summation of his life in verse 25 - *But there was none like unto Ahab, which did sell himself to work wickedness in the sight of the LORD, whom Jezebel his wife stirred up.* Yes, God never makes a mistake, but can you help me out here? This is way too generous.

So that you understand, my purpose in these few moments is to "poke the bear." I don't mean that God is the bear; I mean you. I want honesty. Some of you have thought what I said in my opening words. Perhaps some of you are so spiritual that you "used the God card" right away and focused on the sovereignty of God and that He never makes a mistake. Good for you.

If we have been in ministry for any length of time, it is possible we have had an encounter with an Ahab. Here is someone who abuses others. They are so self-absorbed that they do not care about the consequences of their actions. It never matters to them how much hurt and harm they bring to others.

Bad stuff happens to them, and we want to say, "FINALLY!" But then they do that repentance thing, and that messes up our sense of vengeance.

What have I got to learn from all this? (**Heb. 10:30**) *For we know Him that has said, Vengeance belongs unto me, I will recompense, says the Lord. And again, The Lord shall judge his people.* We want to think of ourselves as righteous and therefore capable judges of others. But examination of the soul is not our venue.

Yes, we are fruit inspectors, but at the very least we have got to remember "*It is not my zoo, and not my monkeys.*" God has this.

JUNE 8

Listening to the Spirit

ACTS 8:26, 29
And the angel of the Lord spoke unto Philip, saying, Arise, and go toward the south unto the way that goes down from Jerusalem unto Gaza, which is desert.

{29} Then the Spirit said unto Philip, go near, and join yourself to this chariot.

Have you ever heard the voice of God? I have. In fact, I would hold that every believer has heard the voice of the Holy Spirit, based on what Paul says in (**Rom. 8:16**) *The Spirit itself bears witness with our spirit, that we are the children of God.* This is blessed assurance to hear *"You belong to me; you are mine."*

I would go further than that to say that there are times that He chooses to speak in an inaudible voice. In (**Acts 13:2**) *As they ministered to the Lord, and fasted, the Holy Spirit said, separate Me Barnabas and Saul for the work whereunto I have called them.*

Our text tells of a divinely planned encounter with a stranger. The place was unlikely and to speak with a foreigner is even more outside of the comfort zone. But when the Holy Spirit speaks, fear is gone!

My call to the ministry was a special encounter. I do not hold that I am special or that your experience should be similar. I wanted to be an architect. In high school, I had the unique opportunity of having four years of Mechanical Drawing/Architecture. I graduated with a major in Mechanical Drawing. No regular high school in New York State offered this. But while at a Christian camp, the Holy Spirit said to me, *"John, I want you to build lives, not buildings."* I bowed my head and said, *"Yes, Lord."* I have never regretted those words.

He has also used my training in mechanical drawing to bless others and aid in the ministry. He does not put square pegs into round holes. Listen, He is speaking.

JUNE 9

It is Covered

ACTS 13:38-39

Be it known unto you therefore, men and brethren, that through this man is preached unto you the forgiveness of sins: And by him all that believe are justified from all things, from which you could not be justified by the law of Moses.

Justified – The act of God whereby He declares the believing sinner, righteous through the finished work of Christ. I still enjoy the simple explanation, *"Just as if I'd never sinned."* Do you recall (*Of course you do!*) what you felt in that moment you knew you were forgiven? But justification is far more than the release from the burden and consequences of our sin.

Paul shares justification in this way: (**Rom. 5:1**) *Therefore being justified by faith, we have peace with God through our Lord Jesus Christ.* Peace with God. I am accepted by God through the finished work of Christ into His glorious presence.

The sermon that Paul preached that day in Antioch of Pisidia, presented a hope that was never possible under the law. For those that were convinced they could redeem themselves through obedience, this message was hard to receive. How could mere heart belief in the Christ, justify them? When you have put so much into one idea, it is humanly impossible to cast it all aside, unless you understand that God made a greater way. (**Rom. 3:20**) *Therefore by the deeds of the law there shall no flesh be justified in his sight: for by the law is the knowledge of sin.*

We are justified freely by His grace through the finished work of Jesus. Man says we must "Do." God says in Christ that it is "Done." Dear fellow servant, may the peace of God rule your heart today. It might be a great witness starter to talk about being justified!

JUNE 10

I AM the LORD

LEVITICUS 22:31-33

Therefore shall you keep my commandments and do them: **I am the LORD***. Neither shall you profane my holy name; but I will be hallowed among the children of Israel:* **I am the LORD** *which hallow you, that brought you out of the land of Egypt, to be your God:* **I am the LORD.**

This powerful postscript was attached to many directions but this one was in connection with an offering of thanksgiving. It was not a required offering but a sacrifice made in appreciation of God's goodness.

[verse 31] Even this personal expression was directed by God. Any approach to the God of the Universe is always His way, not ours, because **I AM the LORD**.

[verse 32] The purpose of this direction was to make it clear that our way is profane. (**Prov. 14:12**) *There is a way which seems right unto a man, but the end thereof are the ways of death.* It is very important that you help your people see that the Gospel is not a broad way to God but a very narrow one. Jesus said He was the only way (**John 14:6.**)

Our way fails, but **I AM the LORD**.

[verse 33] Redemption is not man seeking God, but God paying the cost and buying us out of our bondage. He did this *to be your God.* (**John 3:16**) makes this very clear. *God so loved, God gave His Son*, God determined that faith in the finished work of Christ was the means of this complete redemption. (**Rom. 10:9-10**) *That if you shall confess with your mouth the Lord Jesus and shall believe in your heart that God has raised him from the dead, you shall be saved. For with the heart man believes unto righteousness; and with the mouth confession is made unto salvation.*

His purpose will not fail, and I am free because,

I AM the LORD.

JUNE 11

Words of Life

ACTS 5:20
Go, stand, and speak in the temple to the people all the words of this life.

PHILIPPIANS 4:8
Finally, brethren, whatsoever things are true, whatsoever things are honest, whatsoever things are just, whatsoever things are pure, whatsoever things are lovely, whatsoever things are of good report; if there be any virtue, and if there be any praise, think on these things.

I write these devotionals from my personal experience and 50 years of observation of the human condition. I say that serving the King is a joy. Yes, ministry is hard, but I am not one to dwell on the negative. I have determined to occupy my mind with the abundant blessings of life.

I consider the opportunity to speak the truth into someone's life my greatest joy. I get to see the light go on in a seeker's eyes. I share in the tears of a thankful heart when they understand what Jesus is doing in them at this moment. It is even rewarding to recognize that some decide to say, "No" to the leading of the Holy Spirit. It is sad, but it is as Paul says, *"to one we are the smell of death and to another the smell of life. Who can handle that?"* **(2 Cor. 2:16)**

You need to see your ministry to others through joyful eyes. You have the greatest message in the world: "be reconciled to God." There is sacrifice, opposition, and hardship; but none of that matters when Jesus is your focus. You must not measure your task by *nickels, noses, and kneelers.* You can and will be faithful as you keep Jesus in view. We all want His *"Well done, good and faithful servant."* Jesus knows how to motivate, direct, correct, and reward you. He is the best leader in the world, for He has done everything to help you succeed with joy! Yours is not a job or a burden; it is an opportunity!

JUNE 12

Whatever is Not of Faith

ROMANS 14:22-23

Do you have faith? Have it to yourself before God. Happy is he that does not condemn himself in that thing which he allows. And he that doubts is damned if he eats because he eats not in faith: for whatsoever is not of faith is sin.

Here is one of those great passages that gives us a **Life Principle**. Paul is using a favorite topic, food, and speaking about Christian Liberty. Since we are to live by faith (**Romans 1:17,**) your faith is an essential in coming down on the right side of liberty.

Once more, Biblical faith is based on two things; The Character of God and the Content of His Word (**Heb. 11:6.**)

Have it to yourself before God – This is the true basis for conscience: How is my heart before God in this matter? (**1 John 3:20-21**) *For if our heart condemns us, God is greater than our heart, and knows all things. Beloved, if our heart condemns us not, then have we confidence toward God.*

He that doubts is damned if he eats. Damned – a strong word usually softened by translating it *condemned*. (Not the loss of your salvation.) *Condemned* doesn't really soften it, especially when you are a spiritual leader, and your lack of faith is saying you are a hypocrite. Where is your Biblical faith or do you have "faith" that no one is going to call you out on this? Two questions make it (or break it):

1. **Does what I allow reflect the character of God?**
   Is it loving? Does it focus attention on me instead of Jesus?
2. **Does it agree with the principles of God's Word?**
   (You know, is it - illegal, immoral, fattening) Here is the why. This is a principle. A Principle is a guide your behavior or provide evaluation. It fits in every situation. If you cannot answer in confidence, **it is a sin.**

What will you do if you cannot answer the question?

JUNE 13

The Wrong Kind of Friends

2 CHRONICLES 19:2

And Jehu the son of Hanani the seer went out to meet him, and said to king Jehoshaphat, should you help the ungodly, and love them that hate the LORD? Therefore, wrath is upon you from the LORD.

A man is known by the company he keeps. You understand we are not talking about developing relationships to share the Gospel. *Contact means impact*; but to keep company with the ungodly is to join yourself to their activities that do not honor your King.

Jehoshaphat was a good King, but his understanding of coexistence was opposite from what God wanted for him. He joined in a war and almost got killed. The consequence of his disobedience was more war. He had the sense to seek God in his trouble and once more God delivered *(2 Chron. 20.)* From that great deliverance, you think he would have gotten the principle, but he repeats his political mistake with Ahab's son, Ahaziah. This time it is not real estate but gold! *(See 2 Chron, 20:35-37)* The ships are destroyed by God and God sends a prophet to make sure the point is clearly understood.

You may not appreciate this thought. You believe that you are ready to use any means or opportunity to share the Good News. To you, I am an isolationist. This doesn't apply to my life for I am never going to neglect the Gospel for compromise!

Paul warns that intimate connection with those that do not recognize the Lordship of Christ, dishonors your Master **(2 Corinthians 6:14.)** *(See also 2 Cor. 6:15-18)*

Jehoshaphat didn't worship with the enemy; he just chose sides and went into business with them. He never asked God personally about these matters. Both decisions were failures. God will not bless these choices or you.

Who is in charge of your life?

JUNE 14

The Great Enemy

1 CORINTHIANS 15:26
The last enemy that shall be destroyed is death.

HEBREWS 2:14-15
Forasmuch then as the children are partakers of flesh and blood, He also Himself likewise took part of the same; that through death He might destroy him that had the power of death, that is, the devil; And deliver them who through fear of death were all their lifetime subject to bondage.

REVELATION 20:14
And death and hell were cast into the lake of fire. This is the second death.

I could fill up the entire page with the quotation of Scripture on the concept of death. As I consider my subject, I feel that I will create more thought than conclusion. I realize there is a poetic view that must be remembered when referring to death, but I cannot shake this "personification" of the event or state of being, called death.

I have often explained death as the inability to respond to life. Since God is the giver of life, then being dead is being unable to respond to God. (The philosophers are mulling that over!) I know that Jesus is life, so to be without Him is death (***Eph. 2:1.***)

The Bible tells us that death is **not** non-existence. (***Matthew 25:46***) speaks about everlasting punishment for the unbelieving. Since we are eternal beings, eternal death (separation from God) is a reality.

But let us give thanks for the sacrifice of Christ. He died for us and destroyed Satan's power of death. Jesus now holds the keys of hell and death **(Rev. 1:18.)** The fearful power of death has been eliminated by the one perfect sacrifice of Christ upon the Cross. For us, there is no possibility of eternal separation because Jesus is Life! There is coming a day when death itself will die. Jesus did that for you. Praise His name!

JUNE 15

Pride and Going Through

1 CORINTHIANS 10:11-13

Now all these things happened unto them for ensamples: and they are written for our admonition, upon whom the ends of the world are come. Wherefore, let him that thinks he stands take heed lest he fall. There has no temptation taken you, but such as is common to man: but God is faithful, who will not suffer you to be tempted above that you are able; but will with the temptation also make a way to escape, that you may be able to bear it.

What a precious passage! What a powerful promise! The accounts of the past, with its heroes, victims, and villains are given by the Holy Spirit to be living examples (ensamples) to prepare us for the future and the expectation of God's glorious purposes.

With every account we are presented with successes and failures, each showing that God is true, and His Word is sure. If we consider that our success and a golden future is through our own effort, we will fall under the weight of our pride.

The challenges that you face are not new. Someone else has been through this same circumstances. Your joy or pain has been experienced by others before you. This experience has the potential to crush you, even when it first appears as a blessing, unless you depend upon the God of the Universe. As the Psalmist sweetly reminds us, *He knows our frame, He remembers that we are dust* (**Ps. 103:14.**)

God is good, all the time, and understands our limitations, even if we do not want to admit them. It is the hard things that make us strong, but there must be hope. Ther must be a way of release for the pressure exerted. That relief is found in the person of Christ. He is our hope, our help, and our healing. God will not remove the test. With Jesus' promise found in *(**Matthew 11:28-30**)* we will not only bear it, but we will be overcomers, telling others, *"Look to Jesus, and live!"*

JUNE 16

No Such Thing as Neutrality

LUKE 11:23
He that is not with me is against me: and he that gathers not with me scatters.

I would hold to this famous quote: *In things essential, unity; in things doubtful, liberty; but in all things, charity.* Our verse is found in an account of Jesus rebutting an attack by His enemies. They asserted that the miracles He was performing were the acts of Satan. We understand the foolishness of this attack, but Jesus is not just defending Himself, He is teaching us about His power. There is nothing equal to His power.

We must never consider tolerance to mean acceptance. We proclaim what Jesus says; He is the only way to God. We acknowledge the liberty of others to profess another way and reject the person of Christ. Even the Scriptures proclaim the right to choose a false path and the certainty of judgment for that choice. But we must not accept as equals, those that represent the false, for they are against our King.

This is not meant to justify attack, dishonor, or any hateful treatment of the unbelieving. Jesus tells us this, **(Matthew 5:44-45)** *But I say unto you, Love your enemies, bless them that curse you, do good to them that hate you, and pray for them which despitefully use you, and persecute you; That you may be the children of your Father which is in heaven: for he makes his sun to rise on the evil and on the good, and sends rain on the just and on the unjust.*

He that is not with me – here is an essential. Jesus is sovereign. All that He does is perfect. Our opinion of Christ cannot be different from what He says He is. Jesus is not just a good man, or a glorified man, He the Son of Man. He is God manifest in the flesh *(1 Timothy 3:16.)*

If we would gather for Him, we must be with Him.

JUNE 17

Mistaken Identity

2 TIMOTHY 2:15
Study to show yourself approved unto God, a workman that needs not to be ashamed, rightly dividing the word of truth.

This was the very first verse I memorized. I do not recall the reason for the memorization, but it has stuck, and it is precious. Being a preacher's kid, we moved a lot. I was a teenager, trying to fit in and still seeking to maintain a testimony for my Savior. A new friend, part of the group I gravitated to, had a unique classification. She was the last person in the county to contract polio. She was in the hospital having another surgery, and "the gang" was going to visit her and cheer her up! I went along and we did a good job at our assignment. She had a new cast and we all agreed to sign it. She didn't know me very well and I wanted to write something spiritually meaningful, but all I could remember was the reference for **(2 Timothy 2:15.)**

The months passed and I had many opportunities to share my faith, and this girl was one I tried to witness to. We were at a dinner with our group, and she asked, "What did you mean by the reference you wrote on my cast?" I had made a mistake. I had written the wrong reference.

(1 Tim. 2:15) *Notwithstanding she shall be saved in childbearing, if they continue in faith and charity and holiness with sobriety.*

So much for a meaningful witness. I was teased for this and after an embarrassing explanation, I was forgiven. This story does have a purpose. Everyone makes mistakes as they attempt to witness. Perfection is not a requirement to share the love of Christ, but a deeper knowledge of God's Word is helpful. The Holy Spirit chose to use my mistake to show my sincerity. Since then, He has helped me become a workman that is not ashamed. My friend still teases me.

JUNE 18

Look and Live

NUMBERS 21:6-9

And the LORD sent fiery serpents among the people, and they bit the people; and many people of Israel died. Therefore the people came to Moses, and said, we have sinned, for we have spoken against the LORD, and against you; pray unto the LORD, that he takes away the serpents from us. And Moses prayed for the people. And the LORD said unto Moses, you make a fiery serpent, and set it upon a pole: and it shall come to pass, that every one that is bitten, when he looks upon it, shall live. And Moses made a serpent of brass, and put it upon a pole, and it came to pass, that if a serpent had bitten any man, when he beheld the serpent of brass, he lived.

Bitterness and complaint are killers. It is not just a bad attitude; it is behavior toward the things of God and the leadership that God has placed over you. To justify yourself, you may want to enumerate the many mistakes and failures of God's servants. Perhaps you begin to share this with others because you know that change is necessary. You claim that God is not being honored and the work is suffering. People are "jumping ship" – the bleeding must stop! Perhaps you are right.

But have you prayed about it? Did you ask or tell God what to do? Did you just complain about these pitiful servants and tell God that you could do better?

OR did you pray for them? Did you ask Father to help them? Did you ask God what you could do to help them? Did you speak with them privately? Did you ask if there is any care or woe they are bearing? Do they lack materials, training, or help and can you provide this or pray for it?

"*Touch not the Lord's Anointed*". Instead of dehumanizing them so you can kick them to the curb, do what Jesus did, "*in loving them, He loved them to the end*" **(John 13:1.)** I know you are in ministry – but you are capable of this kind of hurt. Please, don't be bitter.

JUNE 19

It Never Gets Dull

HEBREWS 4:12-13

For the word of God is alive, and powerful, and sharper than any two-edged sword, piercing even to the dividing asunder of soul and spirit, and of the joints and marrow, and is a discerner of the thoughts and intents of the heart. Neither is there any creature that is not manifest in His sight: but all things are naked and opened unto the eyes of Him with whom we have to do.

I am sure that you have committed this passage to memory. We have a gift from our loving Father that does so much! The sad testimony to the spiritual condition of our age is that the majority of "Christians" do not accept the Word of God as any type of authority in their lives. The statistical report tells us that over 60% of "Evangelical" Christians reject the idea of absolutes.

Hebrews tells us that God's Word is our absolute. It speaks into every situation. When the Holy Spirit uses the Word of God (**Eph. 6:17,**) it will reveal our hearts and expose our thoughts. Through the Word, your intentions are put out for examination and possible condemnation. His Word makes the old spiritual true, *"There is no hiding place down here."* God shows us how frail and sinful we can be and how much we need God's help.

But the Holy Spirit also uses The Word to bring life, provide power, and deliver us from the one who would torture us so cruelly – ourselves. He shows us who Jesus really is and why we should love and trust the Savior.

No matter what the popular position may be, you must preach the Word. Always do this and at every possible opportunity. Faith in God is only possible when God's Word is proclaimed. (**Romans 10:17**) *So then faith comes by hearing, and hearing by the word of God.*

To change the world, preach the Word.
When necessary, use your words.

JUNE 20

I Could Not Sleep

PSALMS 77:1-3

I cried unto God with my voice, even unto God with my voice; and He gave ear unto me. In the day of my trouble, I sought the Lord: my sore ran in the night and ceased not: my soul refused to be comforted. I remembered God, and was troubled: I complained, and my spirit was overwhelmed. Selah

Since becoming an adult, I am familiar with these kinds of nights. I want to tell you that it is not because I am worrying about something – but I don't think you would believe me. I have also known (and this has only been in the last few years, really) that I am awake because I am thinking through a wood working project.

I am glad that I can identify with Asaph, *I cried, and I know God heard.* Fear and preoccupying thought are typical. It is what we do with it that makes or breaks us. Isn't it wonderful to have the comfort of, *He gave ear to me!*

[verse 2] I am thankful that Father understands how uncontrollably runny a sore in our mind can be. There are many that would say, "You prayed, but you didn't leave it with God." Asaph seems to get the intensity. I know it is not logical to fret and it doesn't seem like we are trusting, but Father knows what is going on!

[verse 3] This seems to be a contradiction! You are focused on God but you are still overwhelmed. Listen, the psalmist is working us through the steps. We are not stuck at this point. He is saying, this is how I felt, even though I knew better. Consider his thoughts later in the psalm [**vv 13-14.**] Does this sound like a man who doubts?

What is the point? Give yourself a break, God does. Let it out, that allows the process to begin. David said, *"What time I am afraid, I will trust in You."*

I will side with the man that was after God's heart.

JUNE 21

GOD, BE MERCIFUL TO ME

LUKE 18:13
And the publican, standing afar off, would not lift up so much as his eyes unto heaven, but smote upon his breast, saying, God be merciful to me a sinner.

Every time I read this story **(verses 9-14,)** I weep. Truly, no one would ever identify themselves as the pharisee. We rejoice for the wisdom that the publican demonstrated about his condition and the One who was greater than his need; the One great enough to show mercy. Thank you, Jesus!

Yet I am led to ask; have I ever played the part of the pharisee? For many years I have walked and talked on the narrow way. The road, though hazardous, has taken on the feel of the comfortable. Perhaps that isn't a bad thing, for I have been walking with Jesus. But have I looked down on others with less time on the job or frowned at those morally weak because I never fell in "that hole." Do you get my point?

I am not one to live in the past. Jesus paid for all my sin and I am a New Creature in Him. I rejoice in being "washed, sanctified, justified" by Jesus **(1 Cor. 6:11.)** *So, what makes me weep?*

I am thankful for the mercy shown me by a loving Father. I know who I was and what I still foolishly struggle against. I understand that I did not earn, do not merit, and cannot keep the least of His favors. But He chooses to love me – and I weep for the mercy that is mine. *Jesus loves me, this I know. For the Bible tells me so.*

I want a heart that is tender toward the condition of others. I want it to be more than just an emotional response from an old man with a heart condition! I want to show His mercy to others. I believe this; **(Romans 2:4)** ... *that the goodness of God leads you to repentance.* I want desperately to be no one's judge.

I would be, "One beggar showing another beggar where to find bread." Weep with me!

JUNE 22

Cookies on the Lower Shelf

LUKE 18:15-17

And they brought unto Him also infants, that He would touch them: but when His disciples saw it, they rebuked them. But Jesus called them unto him, and said, suffer little children to come unto Me, and forbid them not: for of such is the kingdom of God. Verily I say unto you, whosoever shall not receive the kingdom of God as a little child shall in no wise enter therein.

How busy are you? I look at daily life in ministry as a juggling act. You have 24 things (hours) in the air every day of your life. They are not all the same, in fact, some of them are pretty heavy (*how did that bowling ball get in the mix?*) Every time you add something, you must take something out. You make decisions about what you are juggling before you add and remove, or the decision gets made for you.

The disciples were trying to manage Jesus' "career" and determine what was the best use of his time. Jesus overrules their opinion. (I took note this was a sidebar and not a public rebuke – really important for a leader to NOT humiliate those he leads!)

Jesus says that people are important and that children are very important in the Kingdom! The child like ability to accept and trust is essential to be part of His Kingdom. One of those things that I must remember is to never "talk down" or "talk over" people. In other words, humiliate people because they don't get the Greek or understand the Biblical sequence of events.

My responsibility as a shepherd is to know what this "particular sheep" can digest and lead them gently into greener pastures. I am sure you understand the process of sanctification, but some in the flock can only handle, "Jesus loves me, and wants me to follow Him."

The Holy Spirit enabled many someone(s) to speak into your heart, at the right time. Someone took the time to tell you and the Holy Spirit helped you to understand.

Ask for His help to keep everything on the right shelf.

JUNE 23

Chosen?

JOHN 6:70-71

Jesus answered them, have not I chosen you twelve, and one of you is a devil? He spoke of Judas Iscariot the son of Simon: for he it was that should betray Him, being one of the twelve.

I enjoy the editorial comments that John makes in his storytelling. Each one of them helps keep us on topic and reminds us of his theme; Jesus is God, and as God, He is sovereign. Every remark that is recorded and every conflict reveals that Jesus is not a victim to a lost and dying world. He is the Eternal Son of God, and He will purposefully die for our sins, that we may have life through Him.

Peter has just made the statement that Jesus is different from everyone else. You would think Jesus would say, 'You got that right!" But He brings us up short by saying, "I chose you twelve, and one of you will serve the enemy."

Why would the Son of God choose a loser? And why, "tip your hand," if you know what the enemy will do? If we were building a team that is to transform the world, why select a ne'er-do-well? How often have we thought, "If I knew then, what I know now, I'd have…."

John explains the meaning behind Jesus' remark. This traitor fulfills the prophecy about this fellow: **(Ps. 41:9)** *Yes, my own familiar friend, in whom I trusted, which did eat of my bread, has lifted up his heel against me.* Because God told about this betrayal, it must happen. This also provides Jesus with the opportunity to teach us what it means to "know and obey" **(John 6:38.)**

There is nothing random about the plan of God. You are part of that plan. We are not automatons, but God's purposes will not be altered. **(Prov. 16:33)** *The lot (dice) is cast into the lap; but the whole disposing thereof is of the LORD.*

Trust what God has chosen. He doesn't make mistakes.

JUNE 24

Beware of Doeg

1 SAMUEL 22:21-23

And Abiathar showed David that Saul had slain the LORD'S priests. And David said unto Abiathar, I knew it that day, when Doeg the Edomite was there, that he would surely tell Saul: I have occasioned the death of all the persons of your father's house. Abide with me, fear not: for he that seeks my life seeks your life: but with me you shall be in safeguard.

You cannot prepare for every difficulty. That is why we must live by faith. You are not responsible for the actions or reactions of others. You are accountable for your response to the turmoil they cause.

I hope you never have a Doeg in your life or ministry. He is an amoral individual. He is loyal to those in power. We might call him a tale-bearer but he is just responding to the circumstances. He is only mentioned in two chapters (1 Samuel 21 & 22) but he carries out the murder of innocent people (**1 Samuel 22:18**) *… And Doeg the Edomite turned, and he fell upon the priests, and slew on that day eighty-five people that wore a linen ephod.*

We might want to say that his background influenced him to kill. He was *an Edomite, that means he was of* the people of Esau. He isn't part of Israel. He is just a hired hand.

"I can't believe I would ever come across a church member like him!" I have seen people do very wicked things to get rid of the pastor. The end justifies the means and they think they are doing God's work. Are they saved? I don't know.

But let's look at David's response to this genocide. David knew Doeg and what motivated him. David's circumstances are the cause for this tragedy, but David didn't make Saul murder anyone. What happens to you affects those that care for you. You are not God and cannot control what happens or how they respond. David could have sought to kill Doeg, but he knew that his responsibility was to the living.

Vengeance belongs to God. May God forbid, but if you ever cross paths with a "Doeg," leave him in God's hands.

JUNE 25

A Kiss or with a Rod?

1 CORINTHIANS 4:19-21

But I will come to you shortly, if the Lord will, and will know, not the speech of them which are puffed up, but the power. For the kingdom of God is not in word, but in power. What do you want? Shall I come unto you with a rod, or in love, and in the spirit of meekness?

I can remember my mother repeat this to me, "Are you coming with a kiss or with a rod." The Corinthian church was not a model assembly. There were a lot of problems. Paul was presenting an authority statement. I would say to my children, "You can do what I told you to do, or be spanked, and do what I told you to do."

Discipline in the body of Christ is basically nonexistent. You have studied and taught the Matthew 18 passage. It is a great pattern. Very few ever accomplish the first step. If they did, there would possibly never be a need for the next two. It would be with the kiss: a word of instruction or correction to someone off course and the Holy Spirit, using the Word of God and your prayerful support, would begin the process of correction.

No one would claim to be a fool. But we know many foolish people who will not accept the correction from others of good will **(Galatians 6:1.)** The truth is that we are afraid to love, to be involved in someone's life that might bring us to having "our noses bit off." We forget that all of us are to be people of good will. **(Galatians 6:2)** *Bear one another's burdens, and so fulfil the law of Christ.*

Do not say that you love someone if you are not willing to be led by the Holy Spirit to get down into the dirt to pick them up. Show the care and be corrected. **(Prov. 9:8)** *Reprove not a scorner, lest he hate you: rebuke a wise man, and he will love you.*

You must try! Problems avoided do not disappear. They come back as bigger problems.

JUNE 26

Confession of Faith

ACTS 8:36-37

And as they went on their way, they came unto a certain water: and the eunuch said, See, here is water; what hinders me from being baptized? And Philip said, If you believe with all your heart, you may. And he answered and said, I believe that Jesus Christ is the Son of God.

ROMANS 10:9-10

That if you shall confess with your mouth the Lord Jesus and shall believe in your heart that God has raised Him from the dead, you shall be saved. For with the heart, man believes unto righteousness; and with the mouth, confession is made unto salvation.

Philip's encounter is a thrilling and informative story. The Holy Spirit plans and performs a Gospel transformation and uses Philip to touch a life that will touch millions. Philip takes the Word of God (Isaiah 53) and presents Jesus as the Savior. The sincere response is "an outward and visible symbol of an inward and spiritual grace." As a proselyte to Judaism, the eunuch understood the testimony of baptism, but Philip makes it plain that salvation is not in a symbol but the heart's acceptance of who Jesus is and what He did upon the Cross.

Salvation is not through an "ordinance of the church" but in the full trust of the sacrifice made upon Calvary. The eunuch understood that baptism was mere testimony or identification with the finished work of Christ. It is as Paul says in **(Titus 3:5)** *Not by works of righteousness which we have done, but according to his mercy he saved us, by the washing of regeneration (New Birth), and renewing of the Holy Spirit.*

Our privilege is as Philip's, to be so aware of the Holy Spirit's leading that we recognize the opportunities we have both in the mundane and supernatural, to point others to simple faith in the finished work of Christ.

JUNE 27

But I Always Thought ...

JOHN 9:1-3

And as Jesus passed by, he saw a man which was blind from his birth. And his disciples asked him, saying, Master, who did sin, this man, or his parents, that he was born blind? Jesus answered, neither has this man sinned, nor his parents: but that the works of God should be made manifest in him.

All sickness is because of original sin. **(Rom. 5:12)** *Wherefore, as by one man sin entered into the world, and death by sin; and so, death passed upon all men, for that all have sinned.* But not all sickness is because of personal sin. The teaching of the day led the Disciples to believe that sickness was a punishment for your disobedience to God. Jesus makes it very clear that this assumption was wrong. What a wonderful lesson to learn!

Harry Ironside often said this, *"A lie is half-way around the world before truth has a chance to put her boots on."* Those that reject God will always twist the truth. As those commissioned to speak the truth in love, we must be sure that we do not perpetuate half truths about the King, no matter how innocuous it may seem. The lie about sin and sickness placed shame on those afflicted and separated them from the help and comfort that should have been extended to them.

As a boy, I believed that anyone who smoked or drank liquor could not be a Christian. A life of temperance is to be admired, but it is not a litmus test for redemption. Divorce may be willful disobedience, but it does not mean that those affected are outside of forgiveness. Every heart may be healed. All are valued by the King and may be part of His Kingdom. Jesus is filling up Heaven with sinners, washed in His blood.

Yes, there are always the consequences of sinful behavior, but we have the Christian's bar of soap **(1 John 1:9.)** Every one of us should cling to this promise. It is for all, or none. May the love of Christ constrain us.

JUNE 28

Ask Your Father

JOHN 16:23-24

And in that day you shall ask Me nothing. Verily, verily, I say unto you, whatsoever you shall ask the Father in My name, He will give it you. Hitherto have you asked nothing in My name: ask, and you shall receive, that your joy may be full.

This is part of the Upper Room Discourse. It is one of my favorite portions of Scripture. This part instructs us in our communication with our Heavenly Father.

Paul makes this loving relationship clear. **(Gal. 3:26)** *For you are all the children of God by faith in Christ Jesus.* Jesus instructs us to ask our Father in His name. Because of who Jesus is, and His finished work, we have an instant access before the God of the Universe. The assurance is that we will receive what we ask.

This is not *cart blanche but* is directly connected to our service for the King. As His child I can ask anything, but our Father is good and only gives that which is best for us. John gives us this understanding in **(1 John 5:14-15)** *And this is the confidence that we have in Him, that, if we ask any thing **according to His will**, He hears us: And if we know that He hears us, whatsoever we ask, we know that we have the petitions that we desired of Him.*

If we are seeking the will of our Father, we will not ask for things that dishonor Him or are harmful to ourselves and others. He will not grant these things, Praise God!

All of us have felt inadequate for our assignment. We must ask help from our Loving Father who called us into His service. Trust the process. It takes time and Father does not use magic wands. You quoted this, now believe it for yourself: "*God does not call the equipped; He equips the called.*"

Ask that your joy may be full!

JUNE 29

My Zeal for the Lord

2 KINGS 10:16
And he said, come with me, and see my zeal for the LORD. So, they made him ride in his chariot.

What is this about? For two chapters in 2 Kings, we read about Jehu fulfilling the word of God about the family of Ahaz. He wipes them out! The words in our text are spoken by Jehu to a fellow warrior who joins forces with him to wipe out Baal worship. All of this is with God's approval! But what about the heart of this new King of Israel? **(2 Kings 10:31a)** *But Jehu took no heed to walk in the law of the LORD God of Israel with all his heart.* He chose to have no heart relationship with God. If the King asks you to serve in an established work, you may meet "Jehu."

Usually, he appears as a salty trustee, perhaps a deacon. How did he get into a position of leadership?

- In this assembly, election of officers is a popularity contest, and this guy is very likeable!
- No one else was willing to serve, so he was constrained to take the position. He has been there so long; he is now a fixture.
- He likes being in charge. He gets the bills paid and "the everyday," is taken care of, so those who are spiritual tolerate him. Besides they don't want to upset anyone! Usually, he does not try to affect things outside of his "wheelhouse."
- No one has ever really "cared for his soul." No friendship with the Pastor because previous pastors saw him as a problem or in competition for power.

What do you do? Pray. Ask Father for a way into this man's heart. The rough exterior can hide a heart that can be tender. He might think his efforts are making room for him in glory. Remember, it is the goodness of God that leads to repentance. You won't regret it.

JUNE 30

What Do You Do?

1 CORINTHIANS 12:28-30

And God has set some in the church, first apostles, secondarily prophets, thirdly teachers, after those miracles, then gifts of healings, helps, governments, diversities of tongues. Are all apostles? Are all prophets? Are all teachers? Are all workers of miracles? Have all the gifts of healing? Do all speak with tongues? Do all interpret?

I ask questions to get to know others. Their job or occupation might provide insight about those that I want to learn to love. But I rarely ask questions about their giftedness. It would help if I knew about the things that reveal the spark in their heart.

It is never too late to start a good habit. If I ask the right questions, it might help develop a disciple, not just a follower. If this thought stirs you, perhaps the following questions can help you get started:

- What do you feel is the greatest need our church family has at this moment?
- When we come together for worship, what is the one thing you really enjoy?
- Do you like to give to help others? What way of giving provides you the greatest enjoyment?
- Do you wish that someone would ask for your help?
- What kind of tasks do you like to do?
- Is making music something you enjoy?
- How do you define serving others? What does it look like?
- Do you enjoy working with others to complete a task?
- Which do you enjoy more: working with your mind or your hands?
- Do you pray for others when they are in need?
- Do you like sharing information about things you have learned?

I hope this was helpful.

JULY 1

The Witness of God

ACTS 14:17
Nevertheless He left not Himself without witness, in that He did good, and gave us rain from heaven, and fruitful seasons, filling our hearts with food and gladness.

PSALMS 19:1
The heavens declare the glory of God; and the firmament shows His handywork.

I am not an outdoorsman. I enjoy my yard, planting a garden, tending to flowers but my idea of camping is Holiday Inn. Through the encouragement of my wife, we have purchased several tents over the years (she was a highly decorated Girl Scout.) I spent one night in a tent, in our backyard. The two oldest (9 and 7 at the time) wanted to sleep out. After a night of rocks in my back and the youngest flipping out about the bugs on the outside of the tent – that was it.

My closeness to nature comes from PBS. I appreciate the effort that these brave people made to bring creation into my living room. But where so many want to see a cosmic mistake, we know it to be the labor of the Master Designer. Reason does not support the accidental interconnection of trillions of variables over millions of years. We know that the present existence of thousands of species that totally depend on symbiotic relationships could not have developed over a millennia, for they are absolutely dependent on the other species to function as they do. A unique design by an infinite designer is the only answer. (**Rom. 1:20**) *For the invisible things of Him from the creation of the world are clearly seen, being understood by the things that are made, even His eternal power and Godhead; so that they are without excuse.*

It is not reasonable, scientific, logical, or even charitable to support ignorance. Our loving Creator made all we see. At one time it was *Very Good*, until man spoiled it. But the Creator has promised that He will make all things new.

JULY 2

The Need for Boundaries

PROVERBS 29:15
*The rod and reproof give wisdom: but a child left to
himself brings his mother to shame.*

I have often said that the very least that parents can do for a child is to help them learn to be socially acceptable. Perhaps there may be a number of things to define in that statement, but its meaning is drawn from Solomon's brief thought.

Children come into this world with a need to know the boundaries of life and where they are found. Every parent has the responsibility to follow, demonstrate, define, and direct their child's entire experience within those boundaries. Kids may not enjoy the limitations, but they crave the comfort and security they bring.

As an adult, when you enter anything new to you, you want to know and understand where the "fences" are placed. When you are invited into something as simple as a game, you want to know what are the rules, what do I do, how are the rules applied, what is the ultimate purpose of the game?

The terms *rod and reproof* – put off some because they think it means physical punishment. It can be applied in that way, but these terms help us realize that all people need to understand and experience the limits and consequences that life with others bring. If we do not, we will never be able to navigate with wisdom, which brings peace and success.

If left to ourselves, we will screw-up, because we are not in charge of the process. God makes the standards and will enforce them with consequences that will not be escaped **(Ecc. 8:13.)**

Helping your people know and understand the limits and the responsibilities of discipleship is your job. It is not something that they will get by osmosis.

They will not seek; they must be sought.
They will not come; they must be brought.
They will not learn; they must be taught.

JULY 3

The Day of His Wrath

PSALMS 110:5-7

The Lord at Your right hand shall strike through kings in the day of His wrath. He shall judge among the heathen; He shall fill the places with the dead bodies; He shall wound the heads over many countries. He shall drink of the brook in the way; therefore, shall He lift up the head.

Our text is the closing of a key Messianic Psalm. It is the song that Jesus used to shut the mouths of His enemies **(See Matthew 22: 41-46.)** They were speechless because He is the fulfillment of this powerful promise. The Savior of all is also the Judge of all. **(John 5:22)** *For the Father judges no man, but has committed all judgment unto the Son.*

We consider the active role that The Son of Man, The Lord of Hosts, will take in the judgment of the kings and Kingdoms of this world. **(Psalms 2:9)** *You shall break them with a rod of iron; You shall dash them in pieces like a potter's vessel.* There is no passive connection with those that oppose the King of the Universe. Their destruction will be swift and complete. It is stated poetically, but there is nothing imaginary about His judgments or the result for those who have rebelled against Him. **(Psalms 9:17)** *The wicked shall be turned into hell, and all the nations that forget God.*

Verse 7 seems far from conflict and the word picture a bit fuzzy for us. This verse is meant to assure us that the coming victory of our great King will not be in doubt or in haste. To *drink of the brook* – is a refreshing pause that *lifts the head or* enables the strength for victory. **(Revelation 19:15)** *... and he treads the winepress of the fierceness and wrath of Almighty God.*

It is a fearful thing to fall into the hands of the living God. You must remember that the Lord is a Warrior and He lives to keep you safe.

JULY 4

My Life's Verse

1 CORINTHIANS 15:58

Therefore, my beloved brethren, be steadfast, unmovable, always abounding in the work of the Lord, forasmuch as you know that your labor is not in vain in the Lord.

I was growing in Christ. I had the desire to be more like Jesus. This thought was more than just a good "Sunday School" response to life, it was becoming very important to me. I would hear the personal testimonies of people that I knew that were living for Christ. I kept hearing about my "life's verse." The verse seemed to fit that person. I knew enough that I couldn't borrow someone else's story and if I was going to have a verse, it had to fit me. I went a long time without one.

Looking back, I am not sure when this became my theme. It probably came to me after I had been in the pulpit for a few years. When you start to wear off the shine of ministry and get down to the day to day experience, you begin to wonder, "Am I doing the right thing? Is what I am doing making a difference?"

This is why this verse is mine. I am loved of God. I am loved and accepted by His family. I have learned by yielding to the Holy Spirit that I must stick to the task. I can look to Jesus and be unmovable about the truth. I must not use the Word of God or my responsibility as a weapon but as a way to show the love of Christ.

Jesus loves people and I am supposed to love what Jesus loves. I will work to feed and lead the sheep He gives me. He called me to build lives, and He gave me the ability and desire to do this. When I trust the Holy Spirit and present the Word of God, it is never a wasted effort. He said so in Isaiah, and Paul says the same thing here. Jesus says He appreciates me and what I do for Him. That is what gets me up in the morning and keeps me going. This is a promise worth claiming!

JULY 5

T. M. I.

ECCLESIASTES 5:3
For a dream comes through the multitude of business; ***and a fool's voice is known by multitude of words.***

JAMES 5:12
But above all things, my brethren, swear not, neither by heaven, neither by the earth, neither by any other oath: but ***let your yes be yes; and your no, no; lest you fall into condemnation.***

I had exceeded the speed limit. Not by much, but I was being stopped. As the young trooper approached my car, I decided that this was a teaching moment for my eldest (and soon to be driver.) I looked at him and said, "*Only answer what you are asked. Do not provide more information.*" I turned to the officer and dealt with him with the respect due his position. I provided what he required and answered what was asked. He asked Joel a question and he replied in a simple but polite manner. I agreed with the trooper that I had set a bad example – I received just a warning. After the officer left, I added this addendum; "The more information you offer, the more you complicate the situation and add to how they will respond. ALWAYS, keep it simple."

I did not lie or stretch the truth. I did not hide anything. I only answered the question. As you deal with the world, I encourage you to think about what you share with others, especially those who believe they have some kind of influence or responsibility in the King's business. Provide things honest in the sight of all men, but don't show them "your hand."

When dealing with those who seem to oppose your leadership, be careful what you share. We would like to believe that everyone is working together for the good of the Kingdom – but *"Even a child is known by his doings"* (**Prov.20:11.**) Don't give them ammunition.

At an airport security check point, my second son made a joke about one of the items prohibited in carry-on luggage. He was strip searched. **T. M. I.**

JULY 6

One Reference? Be Careful

1 CORINTHIANS 15:29
Else what shall they do which are baptized for the dead, if the dead rise not at all? Why are they then baptized for the dead?

Now, that is certainly not a verse you would expect for a devotional, but it does stir the thoughts! This is the only time this matter appears in Scripture and the only explanation of this practice comes from the cult of Mormons. They believe that baptism is necessary for salvation, so they are giving the dead more options! This certainly doesn't line up with the teaching of (**Hebrews 9:27**) *And as it is appointed unto men once to die, but after this the judgment.*

Baptism doesn't save. There is no salvation opportunity after death. NONE. God's Word is our authority for faith and practice, we should follow its directions.

(**2 Corinthians 13:1**) ... *In the mouth of two or three witnesses shall every word be established.* For any ordinance or practice of the church, there needs to be at least two witnesses of Scripture. It might be a practice that supports the Gospel, but without at least two scriptural witnesses and the command or directive to do so, it is not a requirement of our obedience to Christ.

This does not prohibit things we would consider extra-scriptural. The birth of Christ is prophesied and recorded in Scripture but no where are we commanded to celebrate it. But to celebrate birth is recorded in God's Word. I celebrate Christmas in remembrance of God's love. We must ask the question God asked those who returned after captivity. (**Zechariah 7:5**) ...*When you fasted and mourned in the fifth and seventh month, even those seventy years,* **did you at all fast unto me, even to me?**

Is it witnessed in Scripture? Is it commanded? Is it all about Jesus? Line up the Scriptural evidence, then decide!

JULY 7

No Wicked Thing

PSALMS 101:3

I will set no wicked thing before my eyes: I hate the work of them that turn aside; it shall not cleave to me.

I am a visual learner. This is the direct root to my understanding. I love maps and charts. I have learned to listen and comprehend, but I would rather read it for myself. In the past twenty years of preaching, I have taken to PowerPoint like "a duck to water."

But the visual thing is also the way to lead me into disobedience. The internet is a wonderful tool. I am always getting extra background or illustrations to help me communicate. It is also a way to lead me to sin.

I don't know what David was thinking about when he wrote this powerful warning. It makes me wonder about the timing of this song. Was it before or after Bathsheba? There are at least two different lessons to be derived from the timing. Though I consider Bathsheba complicit in their sin, I know David should have been occupied somewhere else, with something else. That is the key for dealing with the modern snare to our eyes.

(**Proverbs 27:20**) - *Hell and destruction are never full. So, the eyes of man are never satisfied.* We must focus our ocular attention on things that will fill our mind with good images. It is not the source of the visual input; it is the heart of the receiver. What is the occupation of our eyes? Allow me to paraphrase a passage. (**Ps. 119:9**) *How shall a young man **filter what he sees?** By **filling his vision with things connected** to Your word.*

The more we are visually exposed to anything, the more we want. The example of violence in media and entertainment is proof enough. I wish this could be a "pink elephant" thing, but sin never is. Without the intention of our hearts and the help of The Holy Spirit, this is a losing battle. But Jesus died so that sin would not have dominion over us. He is mighty to save!

JULY 8

Much Ado About Nothing

2 SAMUEL 19:41-43

And, behold, all the men of Israel came to the king, and said unto the king, why have our brethren the men of Judah stolen you away, and have brought the king, and his household, and all David's men with him, over Jordan? And all the men of Judah answered the men of Israel, Because the king is near of kin to us: wherefore are you angry for this matter? Have we eaten at all of the king's cost? Or has he given us any gift? And the men of Israel answered the men of Judah, and said, we have ten parts in the king, and we have also more right in David than you: why then did you despise us, that our advice should not be first had in bringing back our king? And the words of the men of Judah were fiercer than the words of the men of Israel.

Politics! This argument follows the defeat of Absalom and the attempt to restore order and David's rule. It is great to hear that everyone wants David back on the throne, but to complain about "I didn't get an invitation to the party," sounds foolish!

The resentment does testify to God's judgment for David's sin. **(2 Samuel 12:10a)** *Now therefore the sword shall never depart from your house.* From your own experience, this sounds like groups in your church arguing over the color of the carpet. It is not about the carpet color! Someone is going to make a choice, but you are getting insight as to your next sermon series!

Every church has leadership issues. You must continually present the Lordship of Christ in every matter. If there is disagreement, there must be prayer, and lots of it *(Acts 6!)*

This disagreement must end with your words. Words about what is important: the proclaiming of the Gospel and the making of disciples. Make each stain and hole in the carpet about spreading the Gospel to the uttermost and raising up servants who yield to the Master. May it be a prayer meeting on how much to give, not on how it is spent.

JULY 9

It is Too Hard

NUMBERS 17: 12-13

... Behold, we die, we perish, we all perish. Whosoever comes anywhere near unto the tabernacle of the LORD shall die: shall we be consumed with dying?

There had been an attempted coup led by Korah. God settled that difference of opinion in a dramatic way, and the general congregation did not like the answer and blamed Moses and Aaron. That didn't turn out so well. **(Numbers 16:49)** *Now they that died in the plague were 14,700, beside them that died about the matter of Korah.*

Their reaction is perhaps natural but by no means a testimony to a repentant heart. God is fulfilling his word about faithless people dying in the wilderness. It is still a difficult road for Moses and Aaron, so God makes a final demonstration of whom He chose to lead, by a blooming rod. Wow! Don't you wish that you had a rod like that when people question your leadership?

I have said before, "Not everyone belongs on the bus." You need to remember that the bus does not belong to you. You are not driving the bus; you are just the tour guide. It is always hard to bear when someone attacks your character and your ability to follow God's leading – but it does happen. Not everyone that professes, really possesses, and the Holy Spirit is going to work to change hearts or the situation. God did all the "sorting out" for Moses. If you will trust and obey, Father will do the same for you. I wish that meant that the ground opened up and swallowed your adversaries, but it may also mean that you are calling U-Haul. That ground thing was neat, but it was a one-time thing.

What sets you apart will be how you handle the trouble. *"In meekness instructing those that oppose themselves"* - that is a real challenge! Then there will be those that just walk away. They can't handle the truth. They do not understand that God is always right. You will be blamed, but Father is still in control.

JULY 10

I Will Sing

PSALMS 104:33
*I will sing unto the LORD as long as I live: I will sing
praise to my God while I have my being.*

I came upon this verse when I took a trip with my parents to England. I was born in Newark, NJ. This was my first time to the land of my family. A wonderful experience! While there, my father had the opportunity to preach at the Pillar of Fire compound where we were graciously staying. Dad asked me to sing. I agreed and The Spirit led me to this verse. I was glad for the opportunity but a bit afraid. This passage gave me comfort and encouragement. The song I chose was, "Take My Life, And Let It Be."

Take my life and let it be,
Consecrated Lord, to thee.
Take my voice and let me sing,
Always, only, for my King,
Always, only, for my King,

Since that time, I have never turned down an opportunity to raise my voice in song to my wonderful Savior. But this is just a way to segway to your life. Whether you sing or need a bucket to carry the tune, you will find the sacrifice of praise to God to be no sacrifice at all, if you know His love. God is gracious and He gives to every humble heart a way to bring Him praise.

John Delgross taught me this and I shall ever be grateful. John had a "tin ear," but he wanted to sing at the camp talent show. At first, we privately scoffed at the idea, then when John continued in earnest, we tried to talk him out of the humiliation. It is we who were humbled by his response, "I love the Lord Jesus and I may not be able to sing as well as you, but I can make a joyful noise unto Him." In shame we agreed. John did sing "joyfully" and everyone in the audience stood giving thanks to God for the worship He had offered.

Little is much when God is in It.

JULY 11

He Puts on His Pants the Same as You

2 SAMUEL 9:13
So Mephibosheth dwelt in Jerusalem: for he did eat continually at the king's table; ***and was lame on both his feet.***

My Uncle Geoffrey had a great job during World War 2. He drove a staff car for officers in the British Secret Service. He dropped this on me one time, that on several occasions he was at a group dinner with Winston Churchill. I was in awe, but he looked at me and said, *"John, he puts his pants on the same way you do!"*

What makes a man different from others? Is it intelligence, talent, or opportunity? Solomon says that in some things, we are all alike. **(Ecclesiastes 9:2)** *All things come alike to all.* Death comes to all. Looking at this "from under the sun," this is a real equalizer. My uncle was right.

But I have a "bum knee," and it dictates how I put my pants on, literally! It started me thinking, that though we might be alike, at times our limitations make us different. Mephibosheth was a cripple until mercy was extended by King David. His heritage was preserved, and he was accepted at the King's table as he was.

As a servant of the King, you may have limitations that make your way in serving your church difficult. You feel that you are not as gifted as others. May you find God's mercy sufficient if the previous pastor could, "do it all!" He was prophet (Bible expositor, teacher, evangelist), priest (compassionate, prayerful, understanding), and king (decisive, visionary, inspirational) and you are really only good at one of those responsibilities. You feel crippled.

Father did not make a mistake in choosing you, but has given you the honor to sit at His table. He is not done with you. Do what He has gifted you to do and ask Him for others to help. Be a true leader. Help others succeed.

JULY 12

Have You Beaten Your Ass?

NUMBERS 22: 31-33

Then the LORD opened the eyes of Balaam, and he saw the angel of the LORD standing in the way, and his sword drawn in his hand: and he bowed down his head and fell flat on his face. And the angel of the LORD said unto him, why have you smitten your ass these three times? Behold, I went out to withstand you, because your way is perverse before me: And the ass saw me and turned from me these three times: unless she had turned from me, surely now also I had slain you and saved her alive.

Here is a fantastic account. Every part of it is teachable. I am suggesting something that some might find troubling or offensive. There are fellow servants that know the Savior, understand their giftedness, and use it for selfish gain. I remember friends telling me of advice they had received about the Gospel ministry. They were told that there are three P's you should be concerned about in approaching ministry. "People – will they follow you? Pay – what is the salary package you are being offered? Pension – What will the church give you for retirement."

This is bad advice for someone who is learning to be a servant. Paul warns us about this type of thinking. **(1 Timothy 6:5)** *Perverse disputing of men of corrupt minds, and destitute of the truth, supposing that gain is godliness: from such withdraw yourself.*

If you are a faithful servant, Father will keep you from the evil. Does money control you *(1 Tim. 6: 9-10?)* It is easy to buy into viewing ministry from the "bottom line." If we think this way, Father has to get our attention through voices we may tend to ignore or even abuse (like your mate.) If you have sunk that low, it may be the Angel of Death will be soon standing in your way. Just because you "Know," doesn't mean you are motivated by godly purposes. **(James 1:22)** *But be doers of the word, and not hearers only, deceiving your own selves.*

Who was the real ass in this story?

JULY 13

What a Question

EZEKIEL 33:11
Say unto them, As I live, saith the Lord GOD, I have no pleasure in the death of the wicked; but that the wicked turn from his way and live: turn you, turn you from your evil ways; **for why will you die***, O house of Israel?*

The poetry of the Old Testament can be challenging to Western minds, but our text needs little explanation. What needs to be understood is the compassion of God and the urgency of the circumstances.

Say unto them – God is the one who seeks. He continually and clearly uses people like us to connect with the lost. *As I live* – Here is a simple and profound declaration. God is the source of all life. As the giver of life, He does not rejoice in the death of anyone. But as *the Lord GOD* – He is the judge of all. He defines right and wrong. Those that reject Him are wicked. All that He does is just and right.

The wicked turn from his way and live – The God of the Universe declares that all have the ability to choose, and that they must choose His way or die. All that is apart from God is evil. To die is to be separated from life. This means to be separated from God. Separation does not mean annihilation, for the Word of God states just the opposite. **(Matthew 25:46)** *And these shall go away into everlasting punishment: but the righteous into life eternal.* The same word is used to define life and punishment. It means, beyond the vanishing point.

When you have Jesus, you have Eternal Life. Because of Jesus, the answer to the question is simple. But yet, there are so many that will choose death. **(Matthew 7:13)** *Enter in at the strait gate: for wide is the gate, and broad is the way, that leads to destruction,* ***and many there be which go in that way.***

And still we ask, "Why will you die?" Let's make it hard for people to go to hell from where you are.

JULY 14

The Way of God

ECCLESIASTES 11:5-6

As you do not know what is the way of the spirit, nor how the bones do grow in the womb of her that is with child: even so you do not know the works of God who makes all. In the morning sow your seed, and in the evening withhold not your hand: for you do not know what shall prosper, either this or that, or whether they both shall be alike good.

My wife has at least one kidney that is seated the opposite way. So, I asked her doctor if this can happen with all the internal organs? He said yes, "But they still function normally – usually."

What is my point? If all the connections are correct, God makes it work. If He changes things, He has a reason and is not obligated to explain it. You are to trust Him and do good!

Solomon uses this as a principle for serving the King. The Word of God is the seed we should sow at all times, even in places where is seems impossible to grow or harvest anything. But methods change with the circumstances. Turning over the soil every planting is no longer done! Weed control, fertilizing, and watering are viewed differently today. Yet, in the end, only God can make a seed germinate and bear fruit.

Through the years I have sought to plant the seed of the Word of God in the hearts of men, but the fruit was always out of my hands. I just read a short story about a man called "Greasy." The seed sown in his life was a New Testament he took from two men he had helped to rob and kill. He and the entire robber band were converted by just reading the Word of God. Through his desire to tell others about Jesus and his changed life, hundreds more were won to Christ.

A tract given, the Bible placed on someone's smart phone, A Gideon Bible – we do not know what will bear fruit because this is not up to us. God is still bringing people unto Himself. You are to keep planting!

JULY 15

The Desert of Zin

NUMBERS 20: 1-2

Then came the children of Israel, even the whole congregation, into the desert of Zin ... and Miriam died there and was buried there. And there was no water for the congregation: and they gathered themselves together against Moses and against Aaron.

Zin, it means to prick. Lots of things were piercing the soul of Moses and he makes a costly mistake. Miriam dies. The sister that watched over him and made songs about how God used him is no longer there. The people are again complaining about God's leadership, but Moses and Aaron are the focal point. They were so discouraged they fell on their faces before God.

God is going to supply from the rock again. This rock is a picture of Christ. **(1 Corinthians 10:4)** *And did all drink the same spiritual drink: for they drank of that spiritual Rock that followed them: and that Rock was Christ.* The first time, Moses was told to strike the rock; **(Ex. 17:6)** which compares with the sufferings of the Cross. Now, Moses was to speak to the rock. Jesus died but once. Our blessings come from asking, not His suffering! But Moses was angry and hurting; therefore, he didn't listen and struck the rock twice [v11.]

God provided, but He was not obeyed, so Moses loses his opportunity to finish the job. On top of this, Edom is a bad neighbor/relative and Aaron dies. This is definitely a place of piercing.

You are God's choice for a leader of His sheep. Because you stick your head out of the foxhole, you become a target for those who rebel. Because you are human, you will know loss and feel discouragement. That does not give you a pass on listening, obeying, and glorifying the King.

Yours is not a 9 to 5 job. Things will "pile on" and just because Father is merciful, does not mean you get a "do over." There are days when sadness and trouble show up at the same time. Don't lose out because you hurt and feel crummy **(2 Cor. 4:16-18.)**

JULY 16

The Cycle of Suffering and Comfort

2 CORINTHIANS 1:3-4

Blessed be God, even the Father of our Lord Jesus Christ, the Father of mercies, and the God of all comfort, who comforts us in all our tribulation, that we may be able to comfort them which are in any trouble, by the comfort wherewith we ourselves are comforted of God.

It was a woman dying of cancer that taught me the meaning of this passage. I was starting to teach from 2 Corinthians. She was able to come to church. I focused in on Jesus being the source of all comfort and our opportunity to help others see the goodness of Christ. She understood what Jesus wanted to do for her and through her. She was comforted.

In this chapter, Paul uses words to express the difficulties we face: *Tribulation, trouble, sufferings affliction.* Because of this difficulty we also know, *The Father of mercies, The God of all comfort.* Paul uses the word *comfort* in different forms ten times. The root word in the Greek is *parakaleo -to come near and give comfort.* Jesus calls the Holy Spirit, the Comforter. He is the only one that can turn our trouble into triumph.

(**Hebrews 4:15-16**) tells us that Jesus, through His humanity, understands our need for comfort. It also says because He is our Great High Priest, He is able to more than provide that comfort through the Holy Spirit!

Jesus takes our trouble and teaches us to trust Him. Trusting Him gives us comfort. In Comfort we experience His love and know that He understands and can deliver us. It is in experiencing His comfort that enables us to understand the hurt of others and provide real help.

We empathize with them and are speaking from experience. We have gained new abilities that really make a difference in this world. Our tragedies have become blessings. Your faith has grown because you have experienced the nature of God and proved His Word for yourself. This is process, and it is good.

JULY 17

Praise the Luck

PROVERBS 16:33
The lot (dice) is cast into the lap; but the whole disposing thereof is of the LORD.

Gambling is popular, legal, and (the most important thing to the government) taxable. If I could remove one phrase from the average Christian's speech pattern, it is, *"Good luck to you!"* A friend, who had grown tired of well-meaning but spiritually ignorant expressions of goodwill, yelled out, *"Well, praise the luck! Thanks to the luck! Glory to the luck! Luck has nothing to do with it!"*

You might think him harsh, but I was amused. Do we really believe there is a force outside of the providence of God that can bring about any type of beneficial effect? This cultural expression has its roots in superstition and has absolutely nothing to do with the honoring of our God. He alone is in control of our next breath and the outcome of all of life.

The writer provides a word picture of how "games of chance" were once played. The garments usually worn were robe-like and when you sat, the lap would be a convenient place to throw the dice and not loose them. It seems impossible to predict the outcome of dice, though I believe that "chaos theory" can be applied (yes, that is a real thing.) But how the dice land is not the important matter, for the writer concludes that the ultimate outcome is controlled by God. **(Acts 15:18)** *Known unto God are all his works from the beginning of the world.* **(Ps. 18:30)** *As for God, his way is perfect.*

Yes, we do have choice, for that too is the will of God. Many times, God calls us to choose, and in **(John 3:16)** it is declared that we are responsible to believe. God has determined the outcome, *"Whosoever will, shall not perish."* God declares human responsibility and Divine Sovereignty and they meet in the Cross. We may consider gambling an unknown, but God knows all, and the results are in His gracious will.

JULY 18

Not My Monkey, Not My Circus

PROVERBS 26:17
He that passes by and meddles with strife that does not belong to him, is like one that takes a dog by the ears.

Now, that is quite a word picture! Recently, an insurance company has been airing a series of commercials about young homeowners turning into their parents. They meddle and try to fix everything they believe is wrong or needs attention. I can identify with that. I have been that guy for years! I carry tools in my car and some in my pocket, so I can fix what is loose or broken. I suppose I should seek therapy, but I love it so! That is probably why I am writing this devotional.

The world is full of broken people. Because I love Jesus and I have learned to love what Jesus loves, I want to help bring these broken people to Jesus. **That is the point!**

Bringing them to Jesus does not mean micromanaging their existence. Jesus is the Savior, not John. I understand that real love is using who I am and what I have been given to bless others. But I need to ask, am I blessing or busting their chops? If people do not want my help, I should not force them to listen.

The example in our passage helps us clarify what is "help" and what is "meddling."

- I have no personal connection with those involved.
- I do not have a clear understanding of the problem.
- I am not a party to the disagreement, nor have I been invited to help.

As a pastor, you might feel you have a stake in every household in your church family. DO NOT go there! We are a Kingdom of Priests. You are not the Holy Spirit. If you are asked to help, remember, you have no magic wand – everything is process.

If you try to help, you will be bitten AND you will deserve it. You must pray for them, even if you have no information. The Holy Spirit knows how to use you. Yes, make sure everyone knows you are there to help – BUT this is not your circus.

JULY 19

Look and Live - Volume 2

NUMBERS 21: 4-9

And they journeyed from mount Hor by the way of the Red Sea, to compass the land of Edom: and the soul of the people was much discouraged because of the way. And the people spoke against God, and against Moses, ... And the LORD sent fiery serpents among the people, and they bit the people; and many people of Israel died. Therefore, the people came to Moses, and said, we have sinned, for we have spoken against the LORD, and against you; pray unto the LORD, that he take away the serpents from us. And Moses prayed for the people. And the LORD said unto Moses, make a poisonous serpent, and set it upon a pole: and it shall come to pass, that every one that is bitten, when he looks upon it, shall live. And Moses made a serpent of brass, and put it upon a pole, and it came to pass, that if a serpent had bitten any man, when he beheld the serpent of brass, he lived.

We don't have to try too hard to understand the type that is presented. Jesus clarifies it. **(John 3:14)** *And as Moses lifted up the serpent in the wilderness, even so must the Son of man be lifted up.* Unbelief has a killing effect on the soul. Our rebellion will bite and destroy us. The people realized that only God could deliver them from the consequences of their sin. As Moses had to make a brass snake, Jesus had to suffer and die. He had to be lifted up. **(John 12:32-33)** *And I, if I be lifted up from the earth, will draw all men unto me. This he said, signifying what death he should die.*

Christ must be "lifted up" so all can see Him. God did not take away the snakes. Instead, He made a way to heal those who were bitten. All must be told to, "Look and live." Men must choose to "look" to Jesus if they would live. He is the only way to escape the fiery serpent. Its bite will always cause death. **(Rom. 6:23)** *For the wages of sin is death; but the gift of God is eternal life through Jesus Christ our Lord.*

JULY 20

I Have Sinned

2 SAMUEL 24:10, 14

And David's heart smote him after that he had numbered the people. And David said unto the LORD, I have sinned greatly in that I have done and now, I beseech You, O LORD, take away the iniquity of your servant; for I have done very foolishly. {14} And David said unto Gad, I am in a great strait: let us fall now into the hand of the LORD; for his mercies are great: and let me not fall into the hand of man.

Is this a phrase that is a regular in your prayer life? There was a time when it was a stranger to my lips. Why do we sin? We will disobey when we forget to hide God's Word in our heart **(Ps. 119:11.)** But the Holy Spirit won't let us go! He will convict us. (Not condemn, that is the enemy's work.)

David's sin was trusting in numbers instead of God's protection, provision, and power. The Holy Spirit "smote his heart." We call it conviction. We may look at this numbering as just being practical and prepared, but David (and hopefully you also) realize it is faithlessness. Are you ready to follow the direction of God, or do you have to count the *nickels, noses, and kneelers,* first?

There is a lot to preach in this Chapter! David quickly repents and seeks God's mercy. This is a great pattern. God says there are consequences. There are always consequences (***James 1:13-15.***) Do you think because you are in leadership, you can avoid the consequences of your sin? Listen, the higher you go, the fewer choices you have. Your actions ALWAYS affect your ministry.

David understands his options and casts himself on God's mercy (good choice!) Who will your sin destroy? Good came to my life because of David's transparency. Not everyone needs to know about your sin, but God will use it, if you allow Him, to help others.

Yes, He will.

JULY 21

He Knows Our Frame

PSALMS 103:13-14
Like as a father pities his children, so the LORD pities them that fear him. For he knows our frame; he remembers that we are dust.

My son, Steven, is a big man. The amazing thing is that people still run into him in the store. It is like they can't see him! He is a pastor and a faithful servant of Christ. I am so proud! But there was once a time when he wasn't that big.

My life lesson begins on my return from a trip. My wife and Steven greeted me with hugs and kisses near the place I would park the car. There was the usual conversation about the trip and the visit, then it was time to open the trunk of the car and carry my bag into the house. As I did so, I got the big suitcase out of the trunk, placed it on the ground, and closed the trunk lid. Steven came up beside me, put his two-year-old hand through the bag handle, lifted up his face to me and said, "Me carry, Daddy!"

I could have dismissed this touching offer with a "No." The bag was bigger than he was, therefore, it was foolish to even try. I might have even laughed at the offer, but I let him try. Steve struggled for a few moments and did manage to move it several feet. But then he disappointedly looked up at me and said, "Daddy, too heavy."

Again, I could have said, I know or derided him for a wasted effort, but at that moment Father directed me to say, "Let's do it together." So, I placed my hand around his on the handle and together we carried the bag into the house. Father then said, "I do this for you all the time."

Father knows how He made you. He knows what He has enabled you to do. He understands what is happening in your being and He is a compassionate Daddy.

"I am weak, but He is strong." Thank you, Abba.

JULY 22

Every Promise in the Book is Mine

2 CORINTHIANS 1:20-22

For all the promises of God in Him are yes, and in Him Amen, unto the glory of God by us. Now He which establishes us with you in Christ, and has anointed us, is God. Who has also sealed us and given the earnest of the Spirit in our hearts.

I learned this chorus as a child:

> *Every promise in the Book is mine,*
> *Every chapter, every verse, every line,*
> *Every blessing of His love divine,*
> *Every promise in the Book is mine!*

To me, I wasn't misappropriating blessing; I was learning to trust the heart of my Father. Faithful teachers have instructed me to know that "context is king." Later, I learned this simple line: Not everything is written to me, but everything is written for me." (**1 Cor. 10:6**) *Now these things were our examples, ….*

I am eager to apply the principles of interpretation and remember the direction of Peter. (**2 Peter 1:20**) *Knowing this first, that no prophecy of the scripture is of any private interpretation.* But I also hear what he says in the previous verse, "*You do well to take heed.*" The principles of our unchanging Father are in every word of scripture. Lessons of His faithfulness and undying love toward me are to be found in every sacrifice.

When I read them, it causes me to see my hopelessness without the one perfect sacrifice of Christ. I am no longer under the school master of the law but am called to trust in and live by the Grace of our Lord Jesus Christ. But the lessons of the law are not diminished. They are clearly pictured in the life of Christ and the mercy of the Comforter.

As Paul instructs, so will I rejoice. God will keep His promises to Israel and therefore His promises to me.

(**Romans 11:15**) *For if the casting away of them (Israel) be the reconciling of the world, what shall the receiving of them be, but life from the dead?*

JULY 23

Be A Man!

1 CORINTHIANS 16:13-14
Watch, stand fast in the faith, quit yourselves like men, be strong. Let all your things be done with charity.

"Be a man!" I hope that no one ever said this to you. It usually is heavily laden with feelings of disrespect and contempt. Many times, it comes from someone who doesn't know how to handle emotions of any kind or doesn't want to help the receiver of the insult because they don't know how to handle their own trauma. Its like saying something stupid like, "Big girls don't cry." or "You never finish anything." (That was said to a four-year-old.)

Praise God, Paul is not trying to blame and shame anyone! *Watch* – we must be aware of the dangers and pitfalls that we will meet on the way home. This warning is in the middle of something special: a list of faithful servants that were coming their way. Watch out for the people that can and will help you. You are not alone!

Stand fast in the faith – fix yourself to what you know to be true. Go by what you do know, not by what you don't. Biblical faith rests upon the Character of God and the Content of His Word. Fix yourself to knowing more about Jesus and what He has promised.

Quit yourselves like men, be strong – this has nothing to do with gender and everything with understanding the calling of God upon your life. God made you. In making you he created you to, with the Holy Spirit's help, lead, care, and nurture those He has given you. Being strong is not how much you can carry alone but how much strength you will seek from God. **(Isaiah 40:31a)** *But they that wait upon the LORD shall renew their strength....*

All done with charity – Charity does not mean a "hand out" but love in action. It is using who you are and what you have been given to help others and glorify God. These words speak to us of process. Just do it.

JULY 24

A Double Portion

2 KINGS 2:9
And it came to pass, when they were gone over, that Elijah said unto Elisha, ask what I shall do for you, before I be taken away from you. And Elisha said, I pray thee, let a double portion of your spirit be upon me.

JOHN 3:34
For He whom God has sent speaks the words of God: for God did not give the Spirit by measure unto Him.

You are chosen by God through your predecessor, to continue this work to a rebellious people. Elijah was an extraordinary servant. His faith and courage inspire us to a greater faith in God. To be granted one last request is an amazing gift!

"Where is the God of Elijah?" ***(2 Kings 2:14)*** God grants Elisha's request, and every wonder that Elijah had done, Elisha does two times! But what about you?

Perhaps Father has blessed you with this kind of a spiritual mentor. I have had several influential servants speak into my life; some are still nurturing me. We know we are to look to Jesus (***Hebrews 12:1-3.***) But I seek to make my point about His example and our need. Please, consider this dynamic information from John:

- Jesus was sent, so are you.
- Your opinion about anything does not change eternity, but Jesus spoke the Word of God. Your message must be God's Word.
- Jesus did everything He did by the power of the Holy Spirit.

Philippians 2 says that Jesus humbled Himself and took the role of a servant. You must allow the Holy Spirit the tools He so skillfully uses to form Christ in you. It is more than a prayer of surrender; it is submission to process. We grow in grace and the knowledge of Christ.

Truly, it is a "double portion," for the Holy Spirit is in us, transforming us (**Galatians 2:20.**) This is God's gift of a Double Portion; Christ and The Holy Spirit.

JULY 25

A Covenant of Salt

NUMBERS 18:19
All the heave offerings ... have I given you and your sons and your daughters with you by a statute forever: it is a covenant of salt forever before the LORD unto you and to your seed with you.

1 CORINTHIANS 9:13
Do you not know that they which minister about holy things live of the things of the temple? And they which wait at the altar are partakers with the altar?

The term, "a covenant of salt" is found only three times in scripture. Salt was considered unchangeable, the substance that preserves and endures. It was vital to any society. We are told that part of the pay for a Roman soldier was salt. The phrase "worth his salt," meant that a person earned his pay, did his job. God is making an unchangeable promise to Aaron and his descendants that God would meet their needs forever as they continued in their responsibilities.

Paul uses this same truth in 1 Corinthians to talk about you. When God calls you to ministry, He will provide for you. Just as God provided for Levi from the sacrifices of the people, so God will provide for you from the support of God's people.

No matter what the people of God are able to provide (I realize many of you are bi-vocational,) do not rob them of God's blessing by turning down their support. I am serious about this – you may think you are a noble "tent maker," but you are hamstringing God's people by removing their opportunity to give in faith. Yes, the reality of this moment may direct for you to work two jobs *(I am sure you have prayed about this to the Boss, right?)* But the opportunity for you to be transparent and for your people and you to "walk by faith," is very important.

Has God called you or are you doing this for your ego? Who really provides for you? Is it not "the giver of every good and perfect gift?" Please, disagree with me if you must, but do it in obedient faith. Trust the Covenant.

JULY 26

As Iron Sharpens Iron

PROVERBS 27:17
Iron sharpens iron; so, a man sharpens the countenance of his friend.

I am a man who works with wood. If you use a dull blade, you burn the wood, can splinter the cut, or bind the blade in the cut. There are no positives there! Because of this, I have a man skilled at sharpening all kinds of blades and cutters. He does it for a living. He knows what He can sharpen and what I must throw out.

The text is a great word picture. There is friction between two different kinds of metal. When they come into contact, the purpose is to refine and repair, not destroy. One part of this combination is prepared or purposed to change the other. Pieces of metal are knocked off. Edges are sharpened to do work. Brass does not sharpen steel, for brass is too soft and will break; therefore, the steel will not be sharpened. It takes a sharp edge to create things of beauty and purpose.

To be sharp takes friendship. **(Proverbs 17:17)** *A friend loves at all times, and a brother is born for adversity.* Friendship to me, is a commitment to love. Jesus defined it this way. **(John 15:13)** *Greater love has no man than this, that a man lay down his life for his friends.* Jesus did this and more!

To find a man to fit the description in our text is more than being friendly to others; it is a Holy Spirit thing. This fellow is committed to sharpen you. Sparks must fly. Tough things must be tackled. Not every good man is suited for this intense contact. This guy may be hard to find. If you want this kind of connection, you must seek your best friend, Jesus, and ask for His choice. Jesus knows who you need.

While you wait for your "sharpening" friend, let Jesus harden you to be this kind of tool in His hands, so you can sharpen others as well.

JULY 27

A Big Time Loss

1 CORINTHIANS 16:22
If any man love not the Lord Jesus Christ, let him be Anathema Maranatha.

I understand the words. I hear the warning. I am mystified at the context! I realize that Paul had a challenging relationship with the Corinthians. He spent a lot of time with them, over 18 months. That was a sizeable investment by Paul.

Even though the book is filled with correction, it was written to believers. This statement is similar to an earlier one. **(1 Corinthians 12:3)** *Wherefore I give you to understand, that no man speaking by the Spirit of God* **calls Jesus accursed**: *and that no man can say that Jesus is the Lord, but by the Holy Spirit.* There is only one response from the heart and life of a true believer; Jesus is right and without Him I am wrong!

What does it mean to Love the Lord Jesus Christ? Jesus took the guess work out of that question. **(John 14:15)** *If you love me, keep my commandments.*

(Matthew 7:21-23) *Not every one that says unto me, Lord, Lord, shall enter into the kingdom of heaven; but he that does the will of my Father which is in heaven. Many will say to me in that day, Lord, Lord, have we not prophesied in Your name? and in Your name have cast out devils? and in Your name done many wonderful works? And then will I profess unto them, I never knew you:* **depart from me, you that work iniquity.**

So, Paul is saying, if they will not obey Him, they do not love Him, and those who choose to disobey are excluded from the blessing of His Kingdom. *Anathema Maranatha* – means cursed from the return of Christ. Obedience is not an option. It is works that testify to a genuine faith **(James 2:20.)**

To be removed from His return means you never were part of the family. What a sad thing to say. There are many who have substituted activity for true spirituality. "Trust and Obey, there's no other way."

JULY 28

I Will Pass On This Assignment

EZEKIEL 24:15-18

Also, the word of the LORD came unto me, saying, Son of man, behold, I take away from you the desire of your eyes with one stroke: but you shall not mourn or weep, neither shall your tears run down. Forbear to cry, make no mourning for the dead, keep your hat on your head and put on your shoes upon your feet, and do not put a covering upon your lips, and eat not the bread of men. So, I spoke unto the people in the morning: and in the evening my wife died; and I did in the morning as I was commanded.

How can we assume to understand this? My calling is not Ezekiel's; I have not been asked to illustrate God's judgments with counter-cultural behavior. I do not have any interest in asking for or experiencing the grace necessary to deal with the pain of losing - *"the desire of my eyes."*

My wife and I are now in our 50th year together. To quote a contemporary poet/song writer, *"life with you is half as hard and twice as good."* Father has chosen to use our blessing for His glory. We hold no expectation of loss.

As I read, it tugged at my heart. I recognize the supernatural commitment that God had created in Ezekiel. Father worked a process in Ezekiel to accept this loss for His divine purpose. God said that his tragedy would teach. When it happens to these people, then, *"they shall know that I am the Lord* [v 27.]"

There is a "bit of crazy" that thinks, "If I am really spiritual, I should volunteer for duty like this." That is pride talking, not humble obedience. Yes, I am willing to do whatever my King commands, but I have faith in a loving Sovereign who prepares His servants for the task He assigns. **(Psalms 25:12)** *What man is he that fears the LORD? He shall teach him in the way that He shall choose.* Let us say it again, "Whom God calls, He also equips." Ezekiel was not, "Next Man Up." God prepared him for His glory. He is doing this in you also.

JULY 29

The Lust of the Flesh - Personal

MATTHEW 4:2-4

And when He had fasted forty days and forty nights, He was hungry. And when the tempter came to Him, he said, If you are the Son of God, command that these stones be made bread. But He answered and said, It is written, Man shall not live by bread alone, but by every word that proceeds out of the mouth of God.

Your enemy understands your personal physical limitations, all the things you don't want to admit! [v2] From the physical standpoint, Jesus is at His weakest. Jesus' example again shouts to us about our daily conflict. **(Galatians 5:16-17)** *This I say then, Walk in the Spirit, and you shall not fulfil the lust of the flesh. For the flesh lusts against the Spirit, and the Spirit against the flesh: and these are contrary the one to the other: so that you cannot do the things that you would.*

[v3] There is nothing wrong with being hungry, especially after 40 days and no food. There is no sin in bread (unless you are on a low carb diet!) To do as Satan suggests would deny the purpose of becoming a man. **(Hebrews 4:15)** *For we do not have a High Priest which cannot be touched with the feeling of our infirmities; but was in all points tempted like as we are, yet without sin.* Jesus as our Leader, teaches us to depend upon our Father (**Heb. 2:10-11.**)

[v4] Jesus responds with **(Deuteronomy 8:3)** *And He humbled you, and suffered you to hunger, and fed you with manna, which you did not know, neither did your fathers; that He might make you know that man does not live by bread only, but by every word that proceeds out of the mouth of the LORD does man live.*

In each situation Jesus used related Scripture to respond to temptation. If Jesus is your great example, what does that say about the way you respond to temptation and trial? In the Deuteronomy quote, Jesus was saying that to obey God is more important than the need. The Giver is more important than the gift.

JULY 30

The Lust of the Eyes

MATTHEW 4:8-11

Again, the devil took Him up into an exceeding high mountain, and showed Him all the kingdoms of the world, and the glory of them; and said unto Him, All these things will I give You if You will fall down and worship me. Then said Jesus unto him, Get away Satan: for it is written, You shall worship the Lord your God, and Him only shall you serve. Then the devil left him, and behold, angels came and ministered unto him.

We often feel like Job, that our troubles come in waves. That is one of Satan's tactics. Perhaps he tried this on Jesus. [v8] The location is not the point; the test is. [v9] Satan offers a shortcut to Jesus' purpose – the Kingdom without the cross. Yet, we must remember that Satan is a liar **(John 8:44.)**

What right or power does a usurper have to give anything. There are no shortcuts to greatness.

> No pain, *No Palm*.
> No gall, *No Glory*.
> No cross, *No Crown*.

[v9] Satan asked, *"Just bend your knee"* Just take the short route. One little act, who could it hurt? It would hurt everyone. Worship is always the lesser acknowledging the greater. Jesus took no shortcuts to glory **(see Phil. 2:5-11.)**

How can I take the high road when temptation comes? Make the decision before the decision needs to be made. If you don't, the decision will be made for you. When you are prepared to do the right, you will just be managing the decision. *How do you do that?* [v10] Like Jesus did. Resist with the Word. **(James 4:7), (Psalms 119:11)** If you don't, you are a victim **(Ps. 119:130.)**

Even in the weakest of times, the Holy Spirit will aid you. Accept no substitutes!

> *The arm of flesh will fail you,*
> *You dare not trust your own.*

JULY 31

The Pride of Life – National

MATTHEW 4:5-7

Then the devil took Him up into the holy city, and set Him on a pinnacle of the temple, and said unto him, If you be the Son of God, cast Yourself down: for it is written, He shall give his angels charge concerning You: and in their hands they shall bear You up, lest at any time You dash Your foot against a stone. Jesus said unto him, It is written again, You shall not tempt the Lord your God.

[v5] Why the trip to the top of the Temple? Stanley Toussaint in his commentary on the book, says – *"A Rabbinical saying – In the hour when the King Messiah comes, He will stand on the roof of the Sanctuary."* Perhaps this is why the enemies of Jesus were always asking for a sign **(Matt. 16:1.)**

Note the little word "if" in [verses 3 and 6] The Greek means- *forasmuch as*. Satan does not doubt Jesus' Deity; he is challenging it. *"Since you are."* All this trouble comes after John's Baptism. When you step out to do something for God, that is when the enemy takes a swing at you!

Satan changes his tactics and misquotes the scripture. What we observe are two things:

1. Presumption – *Jump off the Temple and the angels will catch you.* This act would serve no Godly purpose and would test God, which is an act of unbelief. Testing God is not trusting.
2. Perversion – **(Ps.91:11-12)** - Satan leaves out –*In all thy ways.* This is classic Satan, *"Hath God said."* Jesus' response is with the Word **(Deut.6:16-17.)**

Jesus is setting the standard for Spiritual Warfare. (**James4:7**), (**1 John4:4**), (**Rom. 10:17**), (**1 John5:4**)

You do the same.

AUGUST 1

Speak No More of This

DEUTERONOMY 3:25-26

I pray You, let me go over, and see the good land that is beyond Jordan, that goodly mountain, and Lebanon. But the LORD was angry with me for your sakes and would not hear me: and the LORD said unto me, Let it alone; speak no more unto me of this matter.

Except for the Lord Jesus, there was no greater servant than Moses. Hebrews calls him faithful. The end of Deuteronomy declares that he knew God face to face. He spent so much time in the presence of God that his face glowed from the experience and Moses had to put a veil over his face so people could talk with him. But his friend said, "No."

Is this what we expect from our Father? We can tolerate, "wait," or "later," but not a "No!" This can't be a Biblical answer! We were told "No good thing will He withhold!" We have "faith," so we can wear God down and He will finally give us what we want! After all, we developed these prayer (nagging) skills as children!

Ok, enough of the humor. Moses' no, was because his disobedience at the rock did damage to the type that was being presented, **(1 Corinthians 10:4)** ... *and that Rock was Christ.* He did not obey as he was commanded; his disobedience came from his frustration with whiny people and was in unbelief. That certainly doesn't fit your experience with Father, does it?

How do you know when Father says no to you? Paul has an answer. *(2 Cor. 12:7-10) My grace is what you need. I can make this the best because you are weak, and I am strong. But the answer is still, no.*

So, what will you do? Jab a little, like Moses, at those who messed things up? God is still in control. Or do you develop an attitude like Paul, who joyfully accepted his limitation. How are you going to react when Jesus tells you that the work He started with you will be continued under someone else's leadership? No whining allowed.

AUGUST 2

The Spirit of Man

PROVERBS 20:27
The spirit of man is the candle of the LORD, searching all the inward parts of the belly.

JEREMIAH 17:9-10
The heart is deceitful above all things, and desperately wicked: who can know it? I the LORD search the heart, I try the reins, even to give every man according to his ways, and according to the fruit of his doings.

My Creator is my Redeemer. My Redeemer is my Creator. Hebrews 4, tells us that nothing is hidden from our Loving Father. He not only knows us, but His Word reveals our deepest thoughts. For each of us, this can be comforting and frightening, depending on whom we are seeking.

Proverbs tells us that our spirit is the tool God uses to reveal what happens in our heads. Jeremiah informs us that our nature is deceitful, but that Father clearly understands us, knows how to use the reins of our being, and that the consequences of our actions are all determined by our Creator God.

My wife has the spiritual gift of discernment. She has never used this in a negative way, but it has helped me to know the hidden agenda of others. Not everyone has this gift, but in Christ, we all have access to the wisdom of God through the Holy Spirit.

Follow Paul's advice: be wise as a serpent and harmless as a dove. As a leader in the family, seek the Holy Spirit's early warning detection. You do not have to be deceived, as the leaders of Israel were by the Gibeonites.

(**Joshua 9:14**) *And the men took guidance from their supplies and asked not counsel at the mouth of the LORD.*

We would all like to believe that everyone who claims relationship with Christ is a person of "Good Will," but time will show us this is not the case. Jesus warned about deceivers, so it must be true. You can depend upon the Holy Spirit. Do just that.

AUGUST 3

I Have Your Nose!

PROVERBS 30:32-33
If you have done foolishly in lifting up yourself, or if you have thought evil, lay your hand upon your mouth. Surely the churning of milk brings forth butter, and the wringing of the nose brings forth blood: so the forcing of wrath brings forth strife.

"I stuck my nose in where it didn't belong." "I got my nose bit off!" As a servant of the King, do you know when to be quiet? The older I get, the more I have to pull on the reins and not try to solve everyone's problems. If I have a problem with this, you must have it as well! **(Proverbs 15:1)** *A soft answer turns away wrath: but grievous words stir up anger.*

We value honesty, especially when we are on the transmitting side of the truth. Sure, we have the Holy Spirit within, and with His help we see the bigger picture. Our whole ministry is geared to problem solving, shining the light, and helping wandering souls stay on the path. BUT the Holy Spirit does not strive with men. He convicts and does not condemn.

Our greatest tool in rescuing the perishing is to pray! Pray for wisdom. Pray for Holy Spirit control. Pray for those distressed and ignorant of the problems they cause themselves, that if Father wants to use you in this way, you will be able to give that soft answer. Otherwise, lay your hand upon your mouth – especially with your adult children. (That is a lesson I have had to learn with all six of my kids!)

You are a light in a dark place. Let the light shine through your actions. **(Romans 2:4b)** ... *the goodness of God leads to repentance.*

I still call them as I see them, but only when I am asked. Fellow servant, I found that being available to help is of greater value than telling everyone what their next move should be. I still have my nose, I have not cast my pearls at the wrong people, and others value my wisdom because I let God be in charge.

AUGUST 4

Follow the Pattern

MATTHEW 4:1
Then was Jesus led up of the Spirit into the wilderness to be tempted of the devil.

Jesus is the greatest of leaders. He never asks us to do anything that He has not already done. (**John 6:38**) *For I came down from heaven, not to do mine own will, but the will of Him that sent me.*

Our King pictures for us, how we should be, *"led of the Spirit."* (**Romans 8:14**) *For as many as are led by the Spirit of God, they are the sons of God.* Father is going to use Satan, our great enemy, to testify to the perfection and superiority of His Son. (**Ps. 76:10**) *Surely the wrath of man shall praise You: the remainder of wrath shall You restrain.*

Some have mistakenly considered this a trial, to see if Jesus would pass. This is contrary to the rest of Scripture. From conception, Jesus was sinless (***Luke 1:35.***) Jesus was not a divided personality with tremendous turmoil within. As the Second Adam, He was not touched with the fallen nature as the first Adam, after yielding to temptation (***2 Cor.5:21.***)

How then can I identify with Jesus? Because He did become a man. Man was never meant to be identified by the fall (***Gen.1: 27.***) We are deceived by the enemy to cause us to imagine that our rebellion makes us human! Our sinfulness doesn't make us human; **it makes us dead!** (**Romans 6:23**) *For the wages of sin is death; but the gift of God is eternal life through Jesus Christ our Lord.*

Paul calls Jesus the Second Adam. He is the only one that can represent us before the Holy God. Jesus is without sin (**Heb. 7:26.**) The Anointed One was tempted in the three areas we all are tempted. Every sin you will ever commit falls in one of these three groups; the lust of the flesh, the lust of the eyes, and the pride of life (***1 John 2:15-17.***)

Jesus used the Word of God with every trial. We must do the same. Follow the pattern.

AUGUST 5

Done Suddenly

2 CHRONICLES 29:36
And Hezekiah rejoiced, and all the people, that God had prepared the people: for the thing was done suddenly.

What does it take to move the work of The Kingdom forward? We have been instructed to pray, *"Thy Kingdom come, Thy will be done."* So, it certainly takes a heart eager for Christ to be glorified.

We understand that God chooses to work through people. We get the truth that everything rises and falls on leadership. Our hearts are stirred by the Old and New Testament accounts of God using imperfect people to do His perfect will.

That is the point – God chooses, God uses, God moves hearts to bring glory to His name. It isn't such a big secret. Paul speaks into this wonderful process.

(**Philippians 2:12-13**) *Wherefore, my beloved, as you have always obeyed, not as in my presence only, but now much more in my absence, work out your own salvation with fear and trembling.* **For it is God who works in you both to will and to do of his good pleasure.**

The conforming of our will, our desire, our obedience to a righteous cause is a process. We *work out,* not work for our salvation. The word *salvation* does not speak about the conversion event, but the continual process of our transformation into the reflection of Christ. Paul says: want this, work for this; not because you are required, but because it your new nature.

And who made this supernatural change? The God who sought you and gave His only Son for you is responsible! He works in you to want, and gives you the ability to perform, His perfect plan.

As Hezekiah, we should rejoice to see the miraculous take shape in the lives of saints and seekers. It will never happen because of our brooding or painful planning, but because Father is able to use humble hearts that He has chosen. Yes, *"Ponder the path of your feet,"* but Father has planned it all!

AUGUST 6

How Far Will You Go?

PROVERBS 20:5-6

Counsel in the heart of man is like deep water; but a man of understanding will draw it out. Most men will proclaim everyone his own goodness: but a faithful man who can find?

If you are seeking to build the Kingdom on your own, you are not leading; you are just taking a walk.

Paul taught that leaders prepare leaders. (**2 Tim. 2:2**) *And the things that you have heard of me among many witnesses, commit the same to faithful men, who shall be able to teach others also.* There is really no success without a successor.

I wish I had taken my own advice, but I know how hard it is to keep all those juggled balls of regular ministry in the air at the same time. Adding in the time to find, inspire, and train someone for specific ministry is a process that few have experienced, and most have never seen. We expect professionals, (college, seminary) to prepare "no-assembly-required" leaders. But it is part of your job, and it is worth it.

Our text speaks about the long process of bringing the best out of the people who are in some form of leadership. You may not see any "#1 draft choices," but Jesus didn't have the crème dela crème, and look how that turned out! In every one of the people that Father has given you, there is a deep resource that only the Holy Spirit can draw out.

Everyone who takes on a leadership position, has something that makes them want to lead. It may not be noble, but it is there. Your faithfulness to Jesus and them may be used to develop a faithful servant.

Your commitment to the process of developing Godly leaders is not a litmus test of your ministry, because some will disappoint you, fail to continue on, and even become antagonists. You are a servant of the Living God and He has called you to "make disciples." The results are in His hands. Do your job.

AUGUST 7

Do Not Be Ignorant

2 CORINTHIANS 2:10-11

To whom you forgive anything, I forgive also: for if I forgave anything, to whom I forgave it, for your sakes forgave I it in the person of Christ; Lest Satan should get an advantage of us: for we are not ignorant of his devices.

Don't you wish Paul would give you a check list on things like this, so you don't have to think about it? But he didn't, so we seek to discover by using the rules of interpretation. Context is king, so what was Paul talking about? He is referring to church discipline, correction, and the results of this responsibility if it is done correctly. What is the reason for correction? It is to restore, not to destroy.

Things can get emotional when you deal with sin and the trouble it produces **(*James 1: 13-15.*)** You would like to think that you will "just deal with the facts." That is impossible. You will get emotional, the sinner is emotional, the people who are affected by the sin are emotional – what a mess!

But you are committed to deal with the problem! You are a good servant, an exceptional leader (because most never deal with sin properly) and now, it is all over! No, it is not. Where is the forgiveness? I am not saying that you can't, or you won't forgive. My question is: have you focused on forgiveness as the leader and are you leading your people into this process of forgiveness?

Have you taken the opportunity to teach your people what has been done in discipline and also that they need to be ministers of reconciliation? Restoration is a process that must be experienced by everyone in the church. Why? *Lest Satan should take advantage.*

Bitterness can affect everyone – you, the repentant, the family of God **(*Hebrews 12: 12-15.*)** Answer these questions:

- Is there personal help for the repentant sinner?
- Is there a plan for recovery besides repentance?
- Are we bringing the healing from God's Word?
- Are we all depending upon God's Grace?
- Are we allowing bitterness in anyone's life?

Don't be ignorant.

AUGUST 8

Consider One Another

HEBREWS 10:24-25

And let us consider one another to provoke unto love and to good works: Not forsaking the assembling of ourselves together, as the manner of some is; but exhorting one another: and so much the more, as you see the day approaching.

Paul says to think hard about this. *Consider,* means to observe fully. Does the "family" want to be together? What shall we *consider*? Paul says we should be deeply caring about other believers. Jesus says this is THE testimony to you truly knowing Him *(John 13:34-35.)*

Do you love your church family? I am not asking if they are gifted, etc. Do you want to use who you are and what you have been given to bless them? If you do not, then this is a matter for urgent prayer!

You are expected to *provoke* them. This is not about your "spiritual gift of contention," but the setting of a pattern for all and being willing to sharpen others with how God has made you (compassion, faith, courage, vision, etc.) Your provoking should result in good works (acts complying to the Word of God and the Will of God.)

The habit of man is to hide, like Adam and Eve tried to hide from God after their sin. Christians with unconfessed sin will hide from the family because they don't want the exposure. They begin to focus on other's short comings and complain about the leadership. You are not the Lone Ranger **(Ecclesiastes 4:9.)**

To *exhort* – means to call near. We are required to speak into the lives of those around us in mercy *(Gal.6:1-2.)* The closer we get to the return of Christ, the more vital this is and the greater the challenges to do so. Provide an environment for broken people to help and heal each other. The church is a hospital, not a museum. Love must be our mother tongue. Helping everyone to care about the body is your task.

AUGUST 9

Groaning for Heaven

2 CORINTHIANS 5:1-2

For we know that if our earthly house of this tabernacle were dissolved, we have a building of God, a house not made with hands, eternal in the heavens. For in this we groan, earnestly desiring to be clothed upon with our house which is from heaven:

The older I get, the less I enjoy travel. As a child I loved family vacations. I would ride in the back of the station wagon with the window down and in my own personal space. I had it set up with almost everything I needed. Nowadays, I just miss my bed and want to get home.

My dear friend, Windell Watson would make good natured fun of other believers and their view of life and death. *"They all talk about Heaven and being with Jesus, but they spend lots of money and fight hard not to go home."* Perhaps we do this because we do not either understand God's promises or do not believe them.

I love life and I want to spend as much as I am given, to love others and show the love of my Savior. I have no death wish, BUT I must remember to ask myself, is Jesus Lord of my next breath? **(Ps. 48:14)** *For this God is our God for ever and ever: he will be our guide even unto death.*

Paul says, *we know.* God created us to be tri-part beings. This body, broken as it is, is home to my soul and spirit. This is not a mistake, we were created to have a physical presence. This is the message clearly presented in *1 Cor.15,* and Paul says the same thing here. Christ died to redeem our entire being. If this is not so, then His sacrifice is not a complete work, and the grave does have the victory **(1 Cor. 15:53-54.)**

Jesus did win! We will be whole again when we get home!

AUGUST 10

In Real Earnest

2 CORINTHIANS 1:22
Who (God) has also sealed us and given the earnest of the Spirit in our hearts.

2 CORINTHIANS 5:5
Now He that has wrought us for the selfsame thing is God, who also has given unto us the earnest of the Spirit.

EPHESIANS 1:13-14
In whom you also trusted, after that you heard the word of truth, the gospel of your salvation: in whom also after that you believed, you were sealed with that Holy Spirit of promise, Which is the earnest of our inheritance until the redemption of the purchased possession, unto the praise of His glory.

ROMANS 8:16
The Spirit itself bears witness with our spirit, that we are the children of God:

Oh, what a wonderful and complete redemption is ours! Jesus has truly paid it all! The proof of this complete payment for our entire being (soul, spirit, body) is the presence of the Holy Spirit. He is our promise of a complete redemption. The grave has no victory because of the earnest of the Holy Spirit.

When you buy a home, the bank requires a downpayment. This is testimony to everyone that you not only have the means to purchase the property in full, but you sincerely intend to do exactly that. This downpayment is called earnest. It is so wonderful that the earnest is not given to a third party, but He is given to you! You are the one who has been redeemed, *"bought out of the slave market at full price AND set free."*

The Holy Spirit is your earnest. He alone is the Comforter, who will never leave you and will provide the full assurance of faith that God will redeem you completely. The third person of the Trinity is your personal guarantee that you belong to God. The Holy Spirit is proof of your security in Christ. God is in earnest.

AUGUST 11

The Witness of God

ACTS 14:15-17

And saying, Sirs, why do these things? We also are men of like passions with you and preach unto you that you should turn from these vanities unto the living God, which made heaven, and earth, and the sea, and all things that are therein. Who in times past suffered all nations to walk in their own ways. Nevertheless he left not himself without witness, in that he did good, and gave us rain from heaven, and fruitful seasons, filling our hearts with food and gladness.

No Contact, No Impact. The more time we invest in connecting with seekers, the greater the opportunity to be used by the Holy Spirit to present Christ. But then the Holy Spirit gives you that, "Fragrance Moment" **(2 Cor. 2:14-17.)**

This is a fragrance moment for Paul and Barnabas. The people of Lystra are about to do something these missionaries can't seem to control. But Jesus is in control. The words flow from His servants and provide us with insights about how our testimony should be before a confused world.

- [v15] People get the wrong idea about God's servants. Be transparent and demonstrate your humanity.
- [v15] The message of Jesus that changed your life is different from the lies they "know." As you present the truth, expect confusion.
- [v15] God is the giver of life. You must speak about Him in this way. Jesus is the Answer.
- [v16] God is patient and merciful to everyone. You must show this **(Romans 2:4.)**
- [v17] The things God has made and the blessing He gives prove that He is good, all the time. Talk about this as often as you can.

This fragrance brought an attack on Paul, but that wasn't the end. They returned **(14:21-22,)** and The Holy Spirit used their fragrance to bring life out of death. They proclaimed the Gospel, a man was healed, an idol sacrifice was turned into a Gospel testimony, and then a stoning!

Their fragrance went everywhere!

AUGUST 12

"We Don't Need No Stinkin' Badges"

1 CORINTHIANS 4:1-2
*Let a man so account of us, as of the ministers of Christ,
and stewards of the mysteries of God.
Moreover, it is required in stewards, that a man be found faithful.*

If you are a movie buff, you recognize this line from the film, *"The Treasure of the Sierra Madre."* People don't need authority to do what is wrong. That is part of our sin nature **(Romans 3:11.)** You need authority to do what is right. If you do not know where your authority derives, you cannot lead.

All can know right from wrong. The Scripture declares this to be conscience **(Romans 2:14-15.)** The ability to lead others to do right, comes from God, and that ability is given to those that acknowledge Him and follow His wisdom. **(Proverbs 1:7)** *The fear of the LORD is the beginning of knowledge: but fools despise wisdom and instruction.*

You have been called to serve in the Kingdom by the Holy Spirit. You are not better than others, but He has called you to lead the family. His choice of you is your authority. The other portion of that authority is your submission and obedience to the mystery of Grace. You cannot lead by a title, for that is the lowest form of leadership. Your ability flows from the King you serve.

Your leadership is demonstrated in your obedience and proclamation of the truth. You will be an effective leader when you are a faithful servant. Your ability to lead is not found in your character or competency (training). The world determines leadership in this way. Your authority to lead comes from your personal commitment to Christ and the control of the Holy Spirit. You don't need a badge.

AUGUST 13

The Curse Unfounded

PROVERBS 26:2
*As the bird by wandering, as the swallow by flying,
so the curse causeless shall not come.*

ECCLESIASTES 7:21-22
*Also take no heed unto all words that are spoken; in case you
hear your servant curse you: For many times your own heart
knows that you have in the same way cursed others.*

In my belief that I am a righteous man, I have quoted platitudes like: "*I would let none of my words fall to the ground.*" "*You should say what you mean and mean what you say.*" I know that my Father never lies, and that Jesus never spoke a lie to support the truth. BUT then the Holy Spirit reminds me of the last time I was cut off in traffic!

If this is coming too close to home for you, then I guess I don't feel as bad as I did. We all say stupid stuff! We know we shouldn't, but we do, especially behind the wheel of our cars or on Social Media. Is this an excuse? No, but it does speak to us about mercy. (**Luke 6:35-36**) *But love your enemies, and do good, and lend, hoping for nothing again; and your reward shall be great, and you shall be the children of the Highest: for he is kind unto the unthankful and to the evil. Be therefore merciful, as your Father also is merciful.*

As a servant leader, you need to remember that the spiritual foolishness that can come out of your mouth, can and will come out of the mouths of the people you shepherd. They can become mad at God and, since they think that God can't handle their feelings, you are their target. No, this does not excuse abuse or the mistreatment of God's servants, but you are not in charge of retribution.

Perhaps the "curse" they uttered has another explanation? Father knows what is true. He will defend you. How can you teach/reach them to grow up and not throw a fit? Do they know what Father expects from their speech? Can you model this kind of mercy?

AUGUST 14

Boldness to Enter

HEBREWS 10:19-20
Having therefore, brethren, boldness to enter into the holiest by the blood of Jesus, By a new and living way, which he has consecrated for us, through the veil, that is to say, his flesh.

We have, at this present moment, a continual invitation to come before the very presence of the God of the Universe. It is not just for a select few but for all who know the Fatherhood of God through Christ. (**Galatians 3:26**) *For you are all the children of God by faith in Christ Jesus.*

We are family and we may enter without the fear of rejection. Father has no favorites. He is never too busy or so disappointed with us that He can't see us now. The access we need, and hopefully we crave, is because our elder brother has prepared for our welcome and comfort in Father's presence.

This opportunity to commune with our Abba is not through a method that is old, limited, and fearful. The text says it is *new and living;* this means that our way has never existed before. This privilege of instant access did not exist until Jesus paid the penalty for our sin. Before this, fear was the only reality in trying to connect with the Father. (**Hebrews 10:31**) *It is a fearful thing to fall into the hands of the living God.*

Now it is *living;* that is, it is the only way that we can know life. Jesus told us this in (**John 14:6.**) Jesus is life. Life is God's gift and eternal life is only through the sacrifice of Christ. Even when we sin, this new and living way is fully open to us through the Cross.

The veil – refers to the covering that separated God from man. Only the High Priest could go in and only once a year, and not without blood. Jesus' one perfect sacrifice removes the old veil and brings us immediately before the Throne of Grace. When you pray, remember that this instant access cost a great deal!

AUGUST 15

What is That Smell?

2 CORINTHIANS 2:14-16

Now thanks be unto God, which always causes us to triumph in Christ, and makes manifest the savor of his knowledge by us in every place. For we are unto God a sweet savor of Christ, in them that are saved, and in them that perish: To the one we are the savor of death unto death; and to the other the savor of life unto life. And who is sufficient for these things.

I have a sensitive nose. My rule is, if it does not smell good, I am not eating it. I have only a few allergies and I use my nose as an early warning system. Smell is the first and most powerful sense in connection with memory.

Paul uses this powerful picture to present the affect of the Gospel on all people. The context is a victory parade for the Roman legions. As they march in triumph into the city, in the parade are significant members of the defeated. All along the parade route, a special incense, commonly known as the "smell of victory," wafts through the air. Even though you are not close enough to see the procession, you can smell sweet victory! Those defeated smell the incense as well, but it smells like death, for that is what awaits them at the end of the parade.

As we share the Gospel message, we release its sweet odor everywhere we go. We are stirred in memory each time we share the truth, "once I was blind but now, I can see!" Yet we cannot control the reaction of other's olfactory nerves to our sweet message. We are not *sufficient* for this. We are overwhelmed by the idea and certainly cannot control the outcome.

What we can do, is to be very careful how we handle the message. Our prayerful communication of the truth should fill us with concern. We are making eternal connection with all who "smell us." Please, be a sweet, clean fragrance.

AUGUST 16

Use Your Words

ACTS 19:1-6

... Paul ... came to Ephesus: and finding certain disciples, He said unto them, have you received the Holy Spirit since you believed? And they said unto him, we have not so much as heard whether there be any Holy Spirit. And he said unto them, unto what then were you baptized? And they said, Unto John's baptism. Then said Paul, John verily baptized with the baptism of repentance, saying unto the people, that they should believe on him which should come after him, that is, on Christ Jesus. When they heard this, they were baptized in the name of the Lord Jesus. And when Paul had laid his hands upon them, the Holy Spirit came on them; and they spoke in other languages and prophesied.

Have you received the Holy Spirit – Here is a question that you may never have asked! Why does he ask this unusual question? It gets to the heart of the relationship *(Rom. 8:9.)* Mental assent to the Gospel is not the New Birth. Many understand the Gospel, but it is the Holy Spirit that places us in the Body *(1 Cor. 12:3,13.)*

We have not heard - Paul does not discount their belief but informs them that repentance is only half of the process. *(Acts 20:21* – Repentance and Faith.*)*

No one comes to Christ in a vacuum. There is more to this story than we are given, BUT when the Holy Spirit draws, no one resists *(John 6:44.)* Why the laying on of hands? Is this necessary? No, but it establishes the authority of Paul and provides "the sign" needed by Jews *(1 Cor.1:22.)* The Greek text does not say heavenly language.

Here is the point I want to make: this redemptive story doesn't match your experience, but it is genuine. The essentials are present (Repentance and Faith) but the timeline is strange and Paul didn't have them "pray a prayer." They heard and believed. The Holy Spirit gave witness. Look for fruit, not traditional responses. Invest in changed lives, not correctly checked boxes.

AUGUST 17

The Questions You Ask

PROVERBS 13:12
Hope deferred makes the heart sick: but when the desire comes, it is a tree of life.

When you seek to help someone, it is important to ask the right questions. Through questions, the hurting share in their own healing. The Holy Spirit will challenge and change the way they view the hurt. Through this they become open to the help and healing that only Jesus can provide.

Jesus asked questions, but He knew the answers. The hurting needed to face the questions. Here are some questions that might help you get to the real problem for those who come to you. Remember, you don't have to fix everything to help.

- How do you view life?
- What is important to you?
- Why did you seek my help?
- What makes you feel safe?
- Do you feel safe in this relationship?
- What does hope, mean to you?
- What do you want to happen from our time together?
- What makes you believe that I can help you?
- How do you view or think about the world?
- Do you believe you have a problem that needs help?
- Why is this (_____) a problem?
- What have you done to solve your problem?
- Do you know how to fight "fairly?"
- Tell me something positive about ____.

Asking questions helps you get past the symptoms to the cause of the problem. We know that the heart of the problem is a problem with the heart, but most people need to feel heard before they can hear. Listening is not a "checklist" item, it is a way to see people as Jesus sees them, "Sheep without a shepherd."

You cannot fix anyone, just point them to Jesus with your questions.

AUGUST 18

Sealed

2 CORINTHIANS 1:22
Who (God) has also sealed us and given the earnest of the Spirit in our hearts.

EPHESIANS 1:13-14
*In whom you also trusted, after that you heard the word of truth, the gospel of your salvation: in whom also after that you believed, you were **sealed** with that Holy Spirit of promise. Which is the earnest of our inheritance until the redemption of the purchased possession, unto the praise of His glory.*

EPHESIANS 4:30
*And grieve not the Holy Spirit of God, whereby you are **sealed** unto the day of redemption.*

When God does something, it is forever. This is so comforting when it is spoken about your redemption. Paul uses the word "sealed," and every definition of the word provides blessed assurance! This seal is the Holy Spirit. I don't seal myself; God the Holy Spirit does it and His sealing represents four things:

Ownership – He is God's brand upon his own.
(**Romans 8:9a**) *but you are not in the flesh, but in the Spirit, if so be that the Spirit of God dwell in you.*

Authority – I know I am God's child by the witness of the Holy Spirit. (**Romans 8:16**) *The Spirit itself bears witness with our spirit, that we are the children of God:*

Protection – You are God's property. (**John 10:28**) *And I give unto them eternal life; and they shall never perish, neither shall any man pluck them out of my hand.*

Completion - Jesus paid a full price for you, and the Holy Spirit will complete the process in you perfectly (**Philippians 1:6**) *Being confident of this very thing, that he who has begun a good work in you will perform it until the day of Jesus Christ:*

The Holy Spirit's presence in you says this is a "done deal," and nothing will change this.

AUGUST 19

Nehushtan

2 KINGS 18:4-5

He (Hezekiah) ... brake in pieces the brazen serpent that Moses had made: for unto those days the children of Israel did burn incense to it: and he called it Nehushtan. (a piece of brass) He trusted in the LORD God of Israel; so that after him was none like him among all the kings of Judah, nor any that were before him.

We all know the seven last words of the church: *We have always done it this way.* Hezekiah trusted God.

How did this testimony become real? Someone took the time to tell him. The Holy Spirit used someone to teach this man the truth, so he would bring about major reform.

The brass serpent was a miraculous tool, powered by God to make Israel understand their sin and that their only hope was faith in God. But hundreds of years later, this "one-time thing" has become an object of worship instead of creating faith in God! This sounds like people today with their "family" church buildings or their traditions in worship. They worship the creation of blessing and not the Creator of the blessing. Oh, they might have claimed that it helped them focus on Jehovah, but if it were removed, well, there would be hell to pay!

Praise God that Hezekiah had the principle correct. God gave him the power to control the situation, and perseverance to cut up not only a brass snake but destroyed other places that were not places of true devotion but locations of sentimentality, convenience, and disobedience. He could do this because he understood the source of his authority and clearly understood the direction of God's word.

There is no room for therapeutic, humanistic, moralistic, sentimental, superstitious, political deism. Jesus said, *"If you love me, keep my commandments."* Removing tradition and superstitious sentimentality is not easy. If you are not prepared to replace them with instruction in Biblical Faith, all you will be doing is putting down a security deposit on a moving van.

AUGUST 20

Judgment Seat

ROMANS 8:1
There is therefore now no condemnation to them which are in Christ Jesus, who walk not after the flesh, but after the Spirit.

2 CORINTHIANS 5:10
For we must all appear before the judgment seat of Christ; that everyone may receive the things done in his body, according to that he has done, whether it be good or bad.

1 CORINTHIANS 3:13
Every man's work shall be made manifest: for the day shall declare it, because it shall be revealed by fire; and the fire shall try every man's work of what sort it is.

Jesus paid a full penalty for your sin and mine. He did this on the Cross, and He did it "once and for all." There is no condemnation because we are justified in the finished work of Christ.

Yet, we are His servants, and He has promised to reward us according to our works **(See Rev. 22:12.)** Good Works are deeds that line up with the Word of God and the Will of God for your life. The believer does not take part in a comparison type of competition. This journey or race is not a sprint but a marathon.

Faithfulness is the key to a joyous reward. This reward is not given on how you start, but how you finish **(1 Cor. 9:24-27.)** The judgment seat of Christ is a judgment of reward or loss. It is not an "award ceremony." The King will make a perfect examination of our efforts on His behalf. It is a judgment by fire **(See 1 Cor. 3:11-15.)**

I do not know if everyone will see your examination by the King. I do not know if He will examine us one at a time or miraculously all at once. I only know that all will go through it, ready or not. The outcome of this royal examination will affect your eternity. You will always be part of God's forever family. This judgment will give testimony to how your life has honored Jesus.

I want to hear my Savior's "Well Done," so I do not want unconfessed sin or displeasing behavior to rob me **(Revelation 3:11.)** Please, guard your heart.

AUGUST 21

Once For All

HEBREWS 10:12-14

But this man, after He had offered one sacrifice for sins forever, sat down on the right hand of God; From henceforth expecting till His enemies be made His footstool. For by one offering He has perfected forever them that are sanctified.

I love the idea of *"Set it and forget it."* When I do a "DIY," my goal is zero maintenance. If I build something, I look for stress points and over engineer it. I do not want to build a second time!

I have read through Leviticus many times. Every time that I read of all the possible ways to sin, and the sacrifices needed to cover those sins, I recognize how costly is my sin. I think about how many times I would be making sacrifices. I truly weep for the simplicity of the Gospel and must express my gratitude for the sacrifice of Christ. His blood covers every sin the law never covered!

The word pictures of our text are brilliant. *This man* – through this phrase we are reminded of the humanity of our Savior. The book of Hebrews proves this point earlier: *One sacrifice for sins forever.* The efficacy of the blood of Christ is emphasized in this phrase. His offering is not a copy of a system that was worn out and merely covered sins. His finished work removes sin forever!

Sat down – There were no seats in the Levitical Temple. There was no rest, no completed task; for the nature of the offender was never changed by animal sacrifice.

At the Righthand of God – Seated in the place of honor before the God of All. This reveals the equality of Christ with His Father (**Psalms 110:1.**) The complete victory for His glory and the complete defeat of His enemies is all because of this one perfect sacrifice.

By one offering He has perfected forever – This one act of selfless love has made those who believe in His finished work perfected forever. It is a reality of this moment; those who believe the Gospel are now viewed by Divine eyes as without sin. This is the amazing message you get to share!

AUGUST 22

You Do Not Win, Every Time

REVELATION 22:11-13

He that is unjust, let him be unjust still: and he which is filthy, let him be filthy still: and he that is righteous, let him be righteous still: and he that is holy, let him be holy still. And behold, I come quickly; and my reward is with me, to give every man according as his work shall be. I am Alpha and Omega, the beginning and the end, the first and the last.

"*And they lived, happily ever after.*" That was the last line of the fairytale. We understood that all our questions were answered by this convenient phrase. But life is not experienced in this way and ministry problems are not solved with the wave of your "magic wand." *(Those not issued a wand on assignment, please contact me by the 5th of Octember. You will receive some made up excuse and Monopoly money.)*

Jesus provides some challenging information about our ability to choose, or "human responsibility." We do have choice and His words indicate that some choose poorly. If the Son of God declares this about some whom He came to save **(Luke 19:10,)** then we should not be surprised when people we want to help, refuse our help. Get over yourself, you cannot get everyone on the bus! Make the effort, but please, grasp this spiritual truth for your own wellbeing.

Jesus is the Giver of every good and perfect gift **(James 1:17,)** and as the greatest of leaders, He who rewards faithfulness will also reward those who reject Him with the consequences of their choices. His wisdom will use the work done by the individual to be the testimony to the reward. The evidence will be undeniable.

Unlike you, Jesus does not have the hinderance of limited experience. There is nothing that He can learn. We can draw all we need from Him. Do not be discouraged by what you perceive as failure, but trust in Him. He knows the unknowable. Trust, and press on.

AUGUST 23

Keep Your Word

ECCLESIASTES 5:4-7

When you vow a vow unto God, defer not to pay it; for he has no pleasure in fools: pay that which you have vowed. Better is it that you should not vow, than that you should vow and not pay. Do not allow your mouth to cause your flesh to sin; neither say before the angel, that it was an error: wherefore should God be angry at your voice, and destroy the work of your hands? For in the multitude of dreams and many words there are many falsehoods, but you, fear God.

In a moment of deep passion about my call to full-time ministry, I told Father that I would do just that. I would serve Him full-time. I was in a job that paid me a good wage, and I was getting my debt for school paid down.

The next day during my lunch break, I wanted to believe that my promise from the day before had been just a test of my devotion. God did not really want me to give up my job! I had recently asked Alice to marry me and I certainly needed steady employment. I opened to the "My Daily Bread" reading for that day. It was our text for today.

The Holy Spirit hammered me with the truth. "*I keep my word. I expect my children, but more than that, my servants, to keep theirs.*" Had I lied to God? If He was leading in a particular way, would He not also provide what I needed to travel that path?

I am now in 50 years of full-time service, Yes, there were times when I was bi-vocational, but He called me to "*Build lives, not buildings.*" We have raised six children on His abundant provision. At times I have been afraid and have done the "*Abraham Protection Plan*" (doing my own thing to protect my backside.)

But God is good, I have never missed a meal that I didn't want to miss, and my wife developed wonderful creativity in preparing "just potatoes" for a meal.

The lesson to be learned: Be careful about what you promise. God is not a fool. A righteous man seeks to keep his word **(Ps. 15.)**

Be like your Daddy.

AUGUST 24

My Mother-in-law

MICAH 6:8

He has shown you, O man, what is good; and what the LORD requires of you, but to do justly, and to love mercy, and to walk humbly with your God?

I am truly blessed. I had In-laws that were never "Outlaws." My mother-in-law only tried to interfere with our family once. My wife took care of that matter. They were EXTREMELY generous. To our sadness, neither one ever had a relationship with the Lord Jesus that we would call redemptive.

There were times that my mother-in-law would have called herself, at the best, an agnostic. She acknowledged our life calling, never mocked us for it, but never heard me preach. We tried to witness to her, but speaking about spiritual matters was always on her terms. If she asked us a question, when the answer was getting close to home, she cut it off.

One day, as Alice was speaking with her, she said, that she had read the Bible through, at least twice and that her favorite verse was (***Micah 6:8.***) This information floored us! She had a favorite verse? In fact, she quoted it for us from memory.

With such a verse, you might hope the need for Christ would be pressed strongly on her heart. But she used the passage as a moral compass. Doing right, living by a higher standard than just what was "convenient," was important to her. She showed an intentional pattern of mercy. She was an extremely intelligent woman (a Mensa member) but she did not seek to make others feel inferior by a display of her intellect. She was generous and there were never any "strings attached" to her giving.

Those you love (and I did love her), can be moral but still without Christ. Sharing the goodness of God with them is what you are called to do. Loving them is what you get to do. Jesus does the rest, and we must trust Him to do what is right (***Genesis 18:25.***)

AUGUST 25

He is Always There

HEBREWS 7:24-25
But this Man, because He continues forever, has an unchangeable priesthood. Wherefore He is able also to save them to the uttermost that come unto God by Him, seeing He ever lives to make intercession for them.

I have been told that the only people who like to be changed are babies in dirty diapers. I hate to get a new computer because it means my "hot keys" are gone, moved, or need to be reset. You want to feel safe, and change seems to go against that feeling. But things fail and must be replaced.

Paul is speaking about a failing system that never did what we all needed, completely remove our sin, and bring us into a permanent relationship with God. Part of that old system was a priesthood that kept dying. They couldn't help it.

But Jesus has a permanent position and is not hindered by the dying thing anymore. He did the dying for us and now is Eternal Life **(See 1 John 5: 11-12.)**

Because He has conquered death, He alone has the ability to save us from death. There is no one He cannot save. Under the law, the priest could only offer sacrifices for certain sins. This man saves to the uttermost. There is no sin His sacrifice does not cover.

There is no person that He cannot save from their sin. No one will be cut off from God. There is nothing in them, about them, done by them that His blood sacrifice will not pay **(1 John 2:2.)**

For His faithful Priesthood to work for you, you must come to God through His sacrifice. **(Acts 20:21)** *Testifying both to the Jews, and also to the Gentiles, repentance toward God, and faith toward our Lord Jesus Christ.*

But wait, there is more! We will continue to need His work as our High Priest. Now He ministers, not as our Savior but as our Sustainer. He freely serves in a grace filled relationship toward us and He does this 24/7. He never tires of you needing Him!

AUGUST 26

God Remembers

HEBREWS 6:10

For God is not unrighteous to forget your work and labor of love, which you have showed toward His name, in that you have ministered to the saints, and do minister.

People may not remember your deeds, but God does not forget those things that are done in obedience to His Word and according to His will for our lives. What is a *labor of love*? I would define it as a task done to bless others. It is not done from obligation but comes out of deep affection for those it blesses.

Paul further describes these deeds, that they are done in the name of Jesus. The Savior gives us a wonderful promise about these acts of love. **(Mark 9:41)** *For whosoever shall give you a cup of water to drink in my name, because you belong to Christ, verily I say unto you, he shall not lose his reward.*

You have and you do – this says that these acts of service demonstrate a pattern of compassion. This is not a one-time thing. Jesus says that this is a testimony of our relationship to Himself **(John 13:34-35.)**

John Phillips made this memorable quote: *"Love is not only the practical truth of Christianity but also the practical test of Christianity."* Since Love is the Christian's Law, then one's holiness must be measured chiefly by love. Selfishness mars holiness. **(1 Thess. 3:12-13)** *And the Lord make you to increase and abound in love one toward another, and toward all men, even as we do toward you: To the end He may establish your hearts unblameable in holiness before God, even our Father, at the coming of our Lord Jesus Christ with all his saints.*

Through your intentional deeds of compassion and the everyday acts of kindness, Christ is being formed in you. Father will not forget, because you are doing His will and honoring His Son. Pass it on!

AUGUST 27

Deception and Concealment

2 KINGS 10:18-19

And Jehu gathered all the people together, and said unto them, Ahab served Baal a little; but Jehu shall serve him much. Now therefore call unto me all the prophets of Baal, all his servants, and all his priests; let none be wanting: for I have a great sacrifice to do to Baal; whosoever shall be wanting, he shall not live. But Jehu did it in subtlety, to the intent that he might destroy the worshippers of Baal.

Jehu practiced deception of the servants of Baal and the concealment of his purpose to kill them all at one time **(See 2 Kings 10:24-25.)** Since God gave him this mandate, it is difficult to speak against it. Perhaps we should applaud it, but do we do the same thing? Do we think that "the end justifies the means?"

Have you ever operated under this idea: "*Better to ask for forgiveness than permission?*" When we lead the family of God, we must abandon the way of the world. (**2 Corinthians 4:1-2**) *Therefore seeing we have this ministry, as we have received mercy, we faint not; But have renounced the hidden things of dishonesty, not walking in craftiness, nor handling the word of God deceitfully; but by manifestation of the truth commending ourselves to every man's conscience in the sight of God.*

John tells us that "*no lie is of the truth.*" I do not believe that we have the right or the responsibility to reveal confidences, expose our plans to our enemies, or be naive about the evil that can hide in those who "play at church." Jesus told us, (**Matthew 10:16**) *Behold, I send you forth as sheep in the midst of wolves; be therefore wise as serpents, and harmless as doves.*

The caution is, that when we lead the family of God, we must do this with transparency and trust the Holy Spirit to bring about obedience to the King and not subjection to ourselves. Are you often *asking for forgiveness?*

Be wise and transparent.

AUGUST 28

Cast Not Away Your Confidence

HEBREWS 10:35-36

Cast not away therefore your confidence, which has great recompense of reward. For you have need of patience, that, after you have done the will of God, you might receive the promise.

People facing adversity need genuine encouragement. None of us need or want "Participation trophies!" It is not "also ran" that God rewards but faithfulness. Jesus promises to reward your faithfulness!

(**Revelation 22:12**) *And behold, I come quickly; and my reward is with me, to give every man according as his work shall be.* You do not labor in competition with anyone. You must strive to honor the Savior, who gave His all for you.

Why go through the struggle, the transformation, the adversity? Because we are confident that honor is ours because we trust and obey. Patience is a key part of our growth cycle *(**See Romans 5:1-5.**)* Patience only comes through the enduring of tribulation.

Tribulation is not referring to the regular challenges of life. (**Job 5:7**) *Yet man is born unto trouble, as the sparks fly upward.* No, this is life experienced while seeking to do the will of God, or the use of who we are, and what we have been given for His divine purpose. (**Romans 12:1-2**) *I beseech you therefore, brethren, by the mercies of God, that you present your bodies a living sacrifice, holy, acceptable unto God, which is your reasonable service. And be not conformed to this world: but be transformed by the renewing of your mind, that you may prove what is that good, and acceptable, and perfect, will of God.*

We have His mandate to use our resources for His glory. The cup of water given in Jesus' name has a reward. Pour your life into others. Make a difference in just one other person in a sacrificial way. Don't cast away what is almost in your grasp.

AUGUST 29

Are You Constrained?

2 CORINTHIANS 5:14-15

*For the love of Christ constrains us; because we thus judge,
that if One died for all, then were all dead:
And that He died for all, that they which live should not henceforth live
unto themselves, but unto Him which died for them, and rose again.*

Constrain, can give us the wrong idea. It does not equate to constipated. Think about it in this way, *"to be bound to or closely connected by something."* Paul says that what binds us is the love of Christ. *"Does this mean His love for us, or our love for Him?"* The answer is, yes. But order is essential. **(1 John 4:19)** *We love him, because he first loved us.* The more we understand the love that Jesus has for us, the more we will **want** to demonstrate that love to others. There is no greater love than sharing the Good News.

The process is simply presented. We are moved along to demonstrate this love of Christ, because we understand this great sacrifice of Christ for all who will trust Him. The fact of His death for all proves that all were condemned to death. Through His one death, life is presented to all who will trust in His sacrifice. His death purchased our life. It also obligates us to live for Jesus because He also gives us the power of His endless life.

Living for ourselves is opposite to what Christ's love constrains us to do. If we are in love with Jesus, we will love what He loves *(John 13:34-35.)* To be in love with Jesus demands that we care about dead people; those without eternal life in Christ. The only way we can talk to the dead is by the power of the Holy Spirit (**John 16:8.**)

You understand that your "calling" means you are supposed to care about the lost, but do you know the constraint of being in love with Jesus? I can ask this question, because, in the past, I looked at evangelism as a duty and not as an opportunity to love on Jesus. This is a change in heart that only the Holy Spirit can do for you.

AUGUST 30

Are You Being Sifted?

LUKE 22:31-32
And the Lord said, Simon, Simon, behold, Satan has desired to have you, that he may sift you as wheat: But I have prayed for you, that your faith will not fail, and when you are converted, strengthen your brethren.

1 PETER 5:8
Be sober, be vigilant; because your adversary the devil, as a roaring lion, walks about, seeking whom he may devour.

Is it not wonderful that the man who was warned passes on the warning? Sifting is an extremely traumatic event for grain. The ancient method requires a threshing floor located on a hilltop and a wide, flat, high-edged basket call a sieve. The dried grain is beaten from the stalks on to the threshing floor. The loose grain is scooped into the sieve and the sieve is held flat as the grain is smashed against its sides by violent movements, causing the husk to crack off the kernel. The contents of the sieve are then tossed into the air and the wind causes the chaff to blow away and the grain falls back to the sieve. This is hard, intentional work, but it breaks the useless from the essential.

The enemy wants to attack for the purpose of destroying you. He intends to hurt you any way he can, so that you feel helpless, hopeless, and hindered from being of any good to anyone. But your King is your hero (**Hebrews 7:25.**)

Peter went through the adversity, seemingly to fail, but the King prayed and gave him a promise. When his faith was fixed on the risen Christ, everything would change (converted,) and his life would be a blessing.

The enemy will keep on attacking! But you and Peter have the same King! He will make you more precious than gold. All is under His loving control. God will break the useless from your life to bring forth the essential. Follow Peter's advice. (**1 Peter 5:7**) *Casting all your care upon Him; for He cares for you.*

AUGUST 31

A Room of Blessing

LUKE 22:10-12

And he said unto them, Behold, when you are entered into the city, there shall you meet a man, bearing a pitcher of water; follow him into the house where he enters in. And shall say unto the goodman of the house, The Master says unto you, where is the guest chamber, where I shall eat the Passover with My disciples? And he shall show you a large upper room furnished: there make ready.

"*Prayin'? That's women's work!*" Honestly, that is what a male leader said to my father about coming to prayer meeting. This remark left no doubt as to why they wanted my dad out of the pulpit.

The man in our passage was a real stand out because he was doing "women's work." Carrying water to the home was a task that traditionally women did. That is why he was easy to spot with that pitcher on his head! There are times when doing things outside of your comfort zone or area of expertise is vital for the Kingdom. Are we willing to try, for the King?

Then there is the thought about this room. Logic dictates that there had been previous conversation about this room. What is important is that the owner of this chamber knew Jesus as "master." He was prepared to provide for Jesus whatever He wanted. We could make much speculation as to the reason for his generosity, but this one thought touches me: (**1 John 4:19**) *We love him, because he first loved us.*

If we have experienced the mercy of the King in our lives, how could we ever withhold anything from His use? The missionary, C. T. Studd, expressed it this way; "*If Christ be God, and died for me, then no sacrifice I make can be too great.*"

I don't think the owner of the room considered it a sacrifice, and I am sure you do not think that about your giving either. We have proven the truth; what we give to God, we never lose.

SEPTEMBER 1

Two Immutable Things

HEBREWS 6:17-19
Wherein God, willing more abundantly to show unto the heirs of promise the immutability of His counsel, confirmed it by an oath: That by two immutable things, in which it was impossible for God to lie, we might have a strong consolation, who have fled for refuge to lay hold upon the hope set before us: which hope we have as an anchor of the soul, both sure and steadfast, and which enters into that within the veil.

The foundation of Biblical Faith abides on two things: The Character of God and the Content of His Word. The account in Hebrews chapter 6, speaks to the promise God made to Abraham in **(Genesis 12:2-3)** *And I will make of you a great nation, and I will bless you, and make your name great; and you shalt be a blessing: And I will bless them that bless you, and curse him that curse you: and in you shall all families of the earth be blessed.*

Because God chose Abraham, He was more than willing to confirm His unchanging promise with a *blood oath*. We find this amazing demonstration in Genesis chapter 15. While Abraham slept, God passing through the divided animals alone making an unbreakable promise to Abraham. Both these unchangeable things were based upon the character of God and the content of His Word.

Abraham expressed faith God, and through faith God declared him righteous. **(Genesis 15:6)** *And he believed **in the LORD**; and he counted it to him for righteousness.*

It is our wonderful privilege to proclaim this righteousness. With such immutable expressions of faith, may the Holy Spirit inspire your heart and mind to make the Gospel clear to all. **(Romans 4:5)** *But to him that works not, but believes on him that justifies the ungodly, his faith is counted for righteousness.*

SEPTEMBER 2

All Men Are Liars

PSALMS 116:11
I said in my haste, All men are liars.

PSALMS 5:9
For there is no faithfulness in their mouth; their inward part is very wickedness; their throat is an open sepulcher; they flatter with their tongue.

These are not the words of a jilted lover, but someone who has been attacked with lies. If you have not experienced this kind of an attack from those who are professed believers, then thank God for His mercy. David relates this as a chief weapon in the arsenal of his enemies. Lies will be used against you because you are an agent of truth. I didn't declare you an example of sinless perfection, just an agent of truth.

We were all sinners by nature and by choice. In the past, we resorted to lies to supposedly protect ourselves and divert examination. (**Genesis 3:12**) *And the man said, The woman whom You gave to be with me, she gave me of the tree, and I did eat.* Lies are used to shame and blame others.

We know that God never lies. (**Titus 1:2**) *In hope of eternal life, which God, that cannot lie, promised before the world began.* Jesus is the truth (**John 14:6.**) John tells us that lies never support the truth. (**1 John 2:21b**) *… and that no lie is of the truth.* As believers we are to recognize that lying is part of our old nature, and that we are to act against it (**Eph. 4:25.**) If we are "putting on" the new man, lying is not a weapon we use or a cloak that we wear to hide our failures and sinfulness.

Do Christians lie? Yes, when they are not yielded to the Holy Spirit. H.I. Ironside would say, "*A lie is halfway around the world before truth has a chance to get her boots on.*" By well doing, put to silence the ignorance of foolish men. Trust the King. His light will dispel the darkness. He knows the truth about you.

SEPTEMBER 3

A New Creature

2 CORINTHIANS 5:16-17

Wherefore henceforth know we no man after the flesh: yea, though we have known Christ after the flesh, yet now henceforth know we Him no more. Therefore, if any man be in Christ, he is a new creature: old things are passed away; behold, all things are become new.

These words certainly provide great comfort. This hope provides a new path and new purpose and a new promise. They present essential information for the work of sanctification.

Being in love with Jesus demands that everything is changed. It is not "like" a change; it is changed! **(1 John 3:14a)** *We know that we have passed from death unto life, because we love the brethren.* Without Christ we were dead, and now we are alive **(Eph. 2:1.)**

[v16] Our understanding of man and ourselves in the world has been completely changed. Those without Christ as Savior are dead, and we are not. Even if we had accurate knowledge of Jesus, now we know Him as Savior! Everything before this change must be scrapped, for it is worthless! All is understood through the giver of Life and His finished work.

[v17] Being "in" Christ means a totally different process. Before, everything moved toward decay and death; now, everything is for blessing and life! We have become "*a new type of being that has never existed before.*" The infinite God, living in finite man. This is not reformation but transformation.

I am still me *(Gal. 2:20.)* All my spiritual DNA is not being re-sequenced but is replaced. The old way of thinking and doing is being remade by the Holy Spirit through the perfect knowledge of Jesus *(2 Pet. 1:3-4.)* The Holy Spirit brings the Word of God into our hearts, and transformation into the image of Christ continues.

When we see Jesus, it will be completed *(1 John 3:2.)* What a wonderful Savior!

SEPTEMBER 4

I Stole From My Mother!

NUMBERS 32:23
But if you will not do so, behold, you have sinned against the LORD: and be sure your sin will find you out.

I would like to blame the kids in the neighborhood. I was young (1st grade.) I was impressionable. I wanted to be important. But we know the truth. *It was my heart.*

No one told me or encouraged me to do this wicked thing. I had already figured out that money influenced people, and I wanted to be a big deal! I snuck around and found my mom's purse and took $10. You must remember this was the late 50's and $10 was a lot of money! I was successful but I didn't know that the storekeeper (the store was behind my house, on the next street) would call my mom!

I was the big spender! I was buying candy and soft drinks for all my buddies. When the storekeeper asked where I got so much money, I told her, "I found it." I wasn't a practiced liar. She didn't buy it.

I got home and was called into my father's home office. There I was, caught! They didn't give me a chance to lie my way out; they were too smart for that! They confronted me with the truth, and then I had to get down on my knees and pray! No beating, they made me confess to God! I wish they had spanked me! It was awful! I was guilty and I felt guilty! Then they forgave me! That was awful too! How could I have done this? Oh, the tears!

Oh, there were consequences! I was sent to bed every night after dinner for two weeks – BUT I knew how to work my parents! I got one week off for good behavior. *My heart wasn't ready yet.*

SEPTEMBER 5

Above Your Name

PSALMS 138:2

I will worship toward Your holy temple and praise Your name for Your lovingkindness and for Your truth: for You have magnified Your word above all Your name.

What degrees have you earned? I hope you cherish the entire process that God directed you through to gain this honor. But we would all agree there are things to claim for our honor that are far more important to your ministry than the document on your wall.

David got his degree in *worship* while tending the sheepfold and an advanced honor while hiding in the wilderness **(Psalms 23 & Psalms 57.)**

David attended the seminar on moral failure where he was reminded of the "*kheh'sed*" *(mercy)* of God. Through this opportunity, he wrote a paper that recorded the process of recognizing, receiving, and revealing the lovingkindness of God **(Psalms 51.)**

David later published a brief communication on the truth of God's help in a period of great personal and political turmoil. He learned to recognize the truth of God's unfailing love and favor during a time when family and friends had betrayed him. He wrote about the traumatic failure of his power based as it turned against him **(Ps. 3.)** Through all this, David maintained the truth of God's promises.

All of David's education and personal growth were based on the two C's of faith: Character and Content. He learned to clearly communicate the Character of a loving, unchanging God and his abiding confidence in the Content of God's Word. He stated it powerfully: *You have placed the reliability of your Word above the glory of Your Name.*

The God of David is your God. He will continue to educate you in the walk of faith. **(2 Cor. 5:7)** *For we walk by faith, not by sight.* Your trust in His Word is the most important education you shall ever receive.

SEPTEMBER 6

A Three "Part" Lesson

DEUTERONOMY 10:15-17

[15] Only the LORD had a delight in your fathers to love them, and he chose their seed after them, even you above all people, as it is this day. [16] Circumcise therefore the foreskin of your heart and be no more stiff-necked. [17] For the LORD your God is God of gods, and Lord of lords, a great God, a mighty, and a terrible, which regards not persons, nor takes reward:

This is a great passage to share and very cutting (pun intended.) [15] God chose to love you and demonstrated that love through the sacrifice of His Son. The Gospel is costly and bloody, but its ability to redeem is without limit.

[17] There is no one like your God, for there is no other God and therefore no other hope outside of His loving promise, "Whosoever will may come"!

[16] I am fascinated by the word picture presented. God uses three body parts to describe the natural resistance of man's sinful nature. Eight times in the Old Testament, He says this about the people He chose to love. We should not think it to be a Jewish condition, but the truth about all men (**Rom. 3:23.**)

Most of those circumcised do not remember the pain of the event, but it is painful. When dealing with your personal disobedience, it must be removed. I know of no pain killer except the grace of God.

The heart, covered by a foreskin, presents a similarly painful picture. Around the heart is the pericardium. It must be opened to repair damage. The wonders of modern medicine make this a reality. But it is painful and life changing.

Stiff necked means resistant, unmovable. It describes someone unable to perform flexion, extension, or rotation. Their vision is limited. Anyone damaged like this needs professional help. As a servant, I pray that this does not describe your condition. But if it does, seek the Great Physician. He chose you.

SEPTEMBER 7

A Blessed Combination

PSALMS 85:10

Mercy and truth are met together; righteousness and peace have kissed each other.

This reference presents a challenge because it begs for more. The entire song is filled with hope and encouragement! Yet this phrase stirs my heart, it provides solace and direction to those who wish to have the moniker of *"peacemaker."*

Some consider hearing or speaking the truth a difficult experience. It might be said of them that they have one tool in their toolbox. It is a sledgehammer, and they use it on every job! **(Jer. 23:29)** *Is not my word like as a fire? says the LORD; and like a hammer that breaks the rock in pieces?* They consider the truth to be such a tool. If that is your plan in proclaiming "the truth," I would say to you that you might have the facts, but you are not proclaiming the truth.

Paul, whom some consider very harsh, informed us that truth must be delivered in a special way. **(Eph. 4:15)** *But speaking **the truth in love**, may grow up into him in all things, which is the head, even Christ:*

God says He has no pleasure in the death of the wicked. You should never speak the truth to harm. Painful as the correction may be perceived, we are charged to restore and not destroy.

We are just messengers for the King; therefore, we can depend on Him to direct not only what we say but also how we say it. *Righteousness and peace* – James tells us to think of the wisdom of God in a way that blesses. **(James 3:17-18)** *But the wisdom that is from above is first pure, then peaceable, gentle, and easy to be entreated, full of mercy and good fruits, without partiality, and without hypocrisy. And the fruit of righteousness is sown in peace of them that make peace.*

What is your end goal? Truth and righteousness are vital, but do not leave mercy and peace out in the cold.

SEPTEMBER 8

My Way or the Highway

3 JOHN 1:9

I wrote unto the church: but Diotrephes, who loves to have the preeminence among them, receives us not.

I have said this many times: If you are going to stand up in front of people, you have to have an ego. Some do not like this observation, but it is difficult to deny. The ego is not the problem, for that is the way God made you. But who is in control of that "up front" personality is the issue we must face.

I recently had to deal with "Diotrephes." The reality of that matter is that I came to the quick decision that it was not my circus. I am glad to let the Holy Spirit deal with this one. If I got involved, I would have become another Diotrephes and made a mess of it!

Why does this happen in God's family? You know the simple answer is sin, but a detailed answer could find its roots in the foolishness found in the heart of a child. Think of the cheek it took to stand up against "The Beloved Apostle!" Yet to oppose the spiritual leadership of any church (except for immorality) ranks as a dangerous place to stand.

It might be transference. Someone in leadership hurt them, now all leaders are to be opposed. Truth is rarely in the equation. The root cause is perhaps anger with God, hurt feelings, or a fear of being unsafe. *"The Pastor didn't agree with me, and I am never wrong, so he must not be trusted."* Soon, every mistake the preacher makes is another reason to oppose, condemn, and remove him from ministry. *"There is no mercy when it comes to those in ministry."*

John's answer for this behavior? **(3 John 1:11)** *Beloved, follow not that which is evil, but that which is good. He that does good is of God: but he that does evil has not seen God.* Be wise as a serpent and harmless as a dove. Pray, and pray some more. You do not have to be silent. John wasn't (verse10,) but don't lean into it and get sucker punched.

SEPTEMBER 9

Loose Ends

1 KINGS 2:6, 9

[6] Do therefore according to your wisdom and let not his hoary head go down to the grave in peace.
[9] Now therefore hold him not guiltless: for you are a wise man and know what you should do unto him; but his hoary head bring down to the grave with blood.

Whoa! What kind of a devotional is this? Are we plotting murder now? Well, I have tried to warn you: I am a slight bit unconventional, but I have never been charged with murder.

Both these verses have to do with final advice that David provides Solomon. These men were problems that David left for his son to deal with. *"Thanks, Dad!"* I am not going to provide you with the details because both stories are worth your time in re-reading; and you will get some great sermons!

I share them because, if you are new to an established church, no matter how beloved the previous Pastor was, no matter how wise and noble a person – he left you with a "few" problems. I am ready to say that he also didn't have a "fatherly chat" with you! How do you hit the ground running and avoid the guy all primed to trip you up?

"But my start is a church plant! I am not inheriting anyone's problems!" If you believe that, I have a bridge to sell you. Your base is going to look just like David's motley group, **(1 Sam. 22:2)** ... everyone that was, *in distress, in debt, or discontented.*

You know the answer to both these scenarios; Jesus never fails! He chose you to lead, and whom He calls, He equips. It is all good if you are forced to your knees. The people who were the greatest problems became my close friends because I learned to listen and love them. David's terrible trio of troubled men became mighty men of valor because David invested himself into their lives. Yes, not everyone belongs on the bus. Father has your back and will guard your steps. But it is usually, you put your foot into _____.

SEPTEMBER 10

I Didn't Go, I Sent My Wife

MATTHEW 21:28-30
... A certain man had two sons ... And he came to the second, and said likewise. And he answered and said, ***I go, sir: and went not.***

I woke this morning thinking about this ministry moment in my life. I am not proud of it, and I had a great difficulty finding the right text to share my failure. What this truly reveals is the kind of hero I have in my wife.

It was mid-summer, and I was doing something outside that was demanding my attention. I was intense, which means I was frustrated but determined to conquer!

The phone rang and I was closest to the house (so Alice tells me,) so I went to answer it. It was our church pianist. She was very upset, *"Pastor, I believe my husband has hurt himself! Would you come, right away!"* I replied, *"Someone will be there soon."*

I came out the door and Alice asks, "Who was it?" Now I was hot, dirty, obsessed with my task, thinking it would take me a half an hour to get cleaned up and ready to go. I said to my wife. "It was our pianist; something has happened with her husband, and she wants me." "It will take me time to clean up, would you go for me?" She looked at me and said, "Yes." Got the keys, kissed me goodbye, (I want to believe I prayed with her) and off she went. I returned to my obsession. (*I don't remember what it was!*)

Her husband had recently received Christ through one of the Evangelists we had to our church. The man was subject to great depression and was an alcoholic. Alice arrived; our sister being terrified, sent Alice into the garage to find that the husband had committed suicide. The police came; Alice comforted the widow and eventually returned to share the news.

I do not think of that moment often, but when I do, I pause and give thanks for the heroic partner that Father knew I needed. She is still brave in Jesus, but I don't send her "solo" anymore. We all need help.

SEPTEMBER 11

Are You On the List?

1 CHRONICLES 24:1
Now these are the divisions of the sons of Aaron. The sons of Aaron; Nadab, and Abihu, Eleazar, and Ithamar.

At one time I was a leader in a good-sized parachurch group. The teens got this crazy idea that it would be a great thing to read the whole Bible (KJV) out loud and in public. A local church gave us use of their worship center and so began this non-stop reading of God's Word. BUT when it came to the names lists in

1 Chronicles – well, we skipped a few chapters!

I use a personal scripture reading pattern, in which I read a chapter from nine different sections, almost every day. When I get to the lists, I skim, sort of! My English tongue has a difficulty with those multi-syllabic names.

I have a simple question – why did the Holy Spirit do this to us? You are already saying that is the wrong question. What is the Holy Spirit telling us? How would you feel if you or someone you care about was listed in God's Word? That is an eternal honor! I don't think we have to read every name to get the message. God considers who they were and what they did important. Their immortalization is significant to every generation.

What can you do with this? My Grandma Worrall would say, *"Don't give me my flowers when I'm dead."*

It may not need a plaque, but honoring the faithful in your life and the life of your church is not giving into pride but the promotion of love. If you will allow me the application: **(Rom. 13:7)** *Render therefore to all their dues: tribute to whom tribute is due; custom to whom custom; fear to whom fear; honor to whom honor.*

Be a leader who celebrates and encourages loving thoughts and deeds. Your church family needs this and so much more! Just follow what the Holy Spirit is doing!

SEPTEMBER 12

A Wounded Soldier

PROVERBS 4:23
Keep your heart with all diligence; for out of it are the issues of life.

PROVERBS 18:14
The spirit of a man will sustain his infirmity; but a wounded spirit who can bear?

I hesitate to say the obvious, but perhaps you are so sanguine; this possibility has not crossed your mind. You can be wounded so badly that recovery seems impossible. I truly believe that Jesus can heal anyone. Stating this, I present an oxymoron. Both are true. Let me illustrate: **(1 Cor. 9:27)** *But I keep under my body and bring it into subjection: lest that by any means, when I have preached to others, I myself should be a castaway (disqualified from receiving the prize.)*

Paul is saying, be careful! You could lose the reward at the end of the race. Jesus warns this: **(Rev. 3:11)** *Behold, I come quickly: hold that fast which you have, that no man take your crown.*

There is something to be gained. There is a possibility of not getting it. I can do all things through Christ, but I can be hurt by the enemy *(1 Peter 5:8.)* I can hurt myself *(1 Cor.3:15.)*

I believe that both texts in Proverbs warn of the same failure. There is no magic wand to fix this. This is a process. I keep my heart by fixing my attention on Jesus *(Heb. 12:1-4.)* I respond to correction with trust in His love *(Heb. 12:6-7.)*

My spirit is wounded because I set my affection on things, people, or circumstances that cannot sustain anyone. As a soldier/servant I must keep my desire on Christ and what He will provide *(Col. 3:1-4.)*

The enemy will attack you personally. Some of us have thick skin but we all can be hurt. When you are hurt and your heart has been trampled upon, remember that nothing will ever separate you from His love.

Let me touch Him, Let me touch Jesus,
So that others may know and be blessed.

Stuart Hamlin

SEPTEMBER 13

A Painful Team

DEUTERONOMY 22:10
You shall not plow with an ox and an ass together.

I am sure you understand about an unequal yoke. Paull is addresses a union that is demonstrated in marriage or business. **(2 Cor. 6:15)** *And what concord has Christ with Belial? Or what part has he that believes with an infidel?* But let's consider this principle in connection with ministry and leadership. If you are an old school farm child, this illustration is plain as day! You are in the process of a difficult task. You must break up soil for planting that has never been cultivated. You do not want to make this harder by making stupid decisions. So, you need the right instrument, and it must be sharp.

An ox is usually a strong, dependable animal. It can be trained to work long hours at hard work. You want an ox on your farm. An ass (donkey) is also a dependable workmate, but its training is different from the ox. It is always smaller than the ox has a different gate, and will pull at a different strength.

The yoke that fits the shoulders of an ox is not suited for a donkey, even if you designed the yoke to fit both animals, their gait and strength is vastly different. If you were foolish enough to team these two good farm animals together, you would break the yoke and hurt both creatures so that both might be unable to labor.

We have stated the obvious, but do you see what this means in ministry? God does not put square pegs in round holes but are you trying to put a round peg in a square hole? There is nothing wrong with different types of servants in the Kingdom, unless you try to make them all the same. Yes, we all serve the King, but the way we serve and what we can do in service will always be different. There are pairs; *"two are better than one,"* but not everyone pulls the same.

Leaders help others succeed. With the Holy Spirit's help, you will learn (process) how to guide your fellow servants to success.

SEPTEMBER 14

The Sin of Saul?

2 SAMUEL 21:1
Then there was a famine in the days of David three years, year after year; and David inquired of the LORD. And the LORD answered, It is for Saul, and for his bloody house, because he slew the Gibeonites.

JOSHUA 9:19
But all the princes said unto all the congregation (Israel), We have sworn unto them (The Gibeonites) by the LORD God of Israel: now therefore we may not touch them.

This is one of those accounts that makes you scratch your head, and you wonder why it's here! If you don't understand the backstory, you will keep on scratching. This is one of those mistakes you have to live with.

When Israel came into the Promised Land, they had to take it by force. God was miraculously with them and they never lost a man (except at Ai, that is another story!) The Gibeonite cities were very afraid of what God was doing (for good reason) so they forged a plan to deceive Israel into making a peace treaty with them. The deception worked! Israel made a promise based on God and they were obligated to keep their word, no matter what. That is the mark of a righteous man, *(see Psalm 15.)*

The Gibeonites lived in safety but became servants to the people (providing common services for the Tabernacle.) This relationship worked for over 400 years until King Saul did some "ethnic cleansing." Perhaps he thought he was doing what was popular or politically correct, but his actions brought a curse on Israel, and it came up during David's reign.

Why now? Why not now? This act dishonored God because a vow was broken, and punishment was due. David was tender hearted and realized the wrong *(Num. 32:23.)*

God holds us to our word because He keeps His word. If your child does damage, you pay for it, and if you are a good parent, so does your kid! Our Father has not changed. Keep your word *(Ecc. 5:4.)*

SEPTEMBER 15

Withered Away

MATTHEW 21:18-20

Now in the morning as He returned into the city, He was hungry. And when He saw a fig tree in the way, He came to it, and found nothing thereon, but leaves only, and said unto it, Let no fruit grow on you henceforward forever. And presently the fig tree withered away. And when the disciples saw it, they marveled, saying, How soon is the fig tree withered away!

I enjoy that the Holy Spirit often challenges our thinking with some startling images. Jesus seems to be petulant. Our family would call this *"Hangry,"* that is, anger brought on by low blood sugar – hungry!

Some might suggest that poor tree didn't deserve this kind of abuse, or why didn't Jesus just make the tree produce fruit? Since Jesus doesn't make mistakes, this kind of reasoning demonstrates foolishness and not faith.

Verses 21 and 22 give us the life lesson that was intended. It would be proper to expound on this wonderful truth – but I want to take a back alley. Do we truly believe that Jesus is always right? If we base our trust only on our ability to understand, we will soon be traveling far from the Son of God.

(**Prov. 3:5-6**) *Trust in the LORD with all your heart; and lean not unto your own understanding. In all your ways acknowledge Him, and He shall direct your paths.* I call this the default position. Jesus cannot lie. Jesus always does what is right. His will is perfect. Job said, *"Though He slay me, yet will I trust Him."* You might have liked it if Jesus had made the tree fruitful, and He could have; but let us not doubt the Creator and sustainer of all life.

It is the height of hubris to suggest anything but perfection from all that Jesus does. Watch for this humanistic deism that seeps into the thinking of so many! There is nothing wrong with the questions. God can handle questions, but some contain poison that will kill our faith.

For example: "Has God said?"

SEPTEMBER 16

Willingly

1 CHRONICLES 29:3,9

Moreover, because I have set my affection to the house of my God, I have of mine own wealth, of gold and silver, which I have given to the house of my God, over and above all that I have prepared for the holy house, [9] Then the people rejoiced, for that they offered willingly, because with a perfect heart they offered willingly to the LORD: and David the king also rejoiced with great joy.

Everything rises and falls upon leadership. I have observed, examined, and lived out this principle during 50 years of pastoral ministry. Spiritual principles must be taught and also caught. Paul understood this: (**1 Cor. 11:1**) *Be followers of me, even as I also am of Christ.*

David had a burden for a building project. He planned, prepared, and provided for this project, which God said would be built by others. He took the next step in leadership and gave of his own wealth. This inspired others in leadership to do the same, which in turn inspired others to do the same!

Godly leadership requires sacrifice (not martyrdom.) (**2 Cor. 8:13**) *For I mean not that other men be eased, and you burdened.* Others must know that you believe this matter is truly important for the Kingdom. The sacrifice does not specifically mean finances and boasting is not godly. Setting the standard by example is something God will use. It develops the principle of the "perfect heart." Your example teaches a love for God, trust in God's provision, and gives a vision of what God will do when His people give willingly (**2 Cor. 9:7-8.**)

> **We have His mandate to use our resources for His glory.**

SEPTEMBER 17

Who Can Change It?

ISAIAH 14:24, 27
The LORD of hosts has sworn, saying, Surely as I have thought, so shall it come to pass; and as I have purposed, so shall it stand: [27] For the LORD of hosts has purposed, and who shall disannul it? His hand is stretched out, and who shall turn it back?

We all have a desire to know what happens next. I hate those *"To Be Continued"* lines at the end of my favorite drama series! I am sure you have used the phrase in preaching, "I read the back of the Book, and I know who wins!" That is exactly what Father is saying in these two verses, "I Win!"

It is the way He says this that makes it so good! In both verses He declares Himself to be *the LORD of hosts*. This is God saying that I am the Self-Existent God of war or of power. This is my Name, and I am on the move! My purposes will not change or be thwarted. No one, absolutely no one can change my plans or alter what I will do!

We would like to think our planning is without fault, especially when we have studied and prayed over every detail. Yet we know we cannot plan for everything, and we do not possess the power to accomplish anything.

Father can learn nothing! That is what Omniscience means. We would have eliminated Saul, but Jesus turned Saul into Paul. He is the God of abundant mercy. We would have never chosen King Saul, but without a Saul, there would be no David.

Understanding everything that Father does is outside of our pay grade. Obedience, because we trust His character and ability, is on our marching orders.

My Father's way may twist and turn,
My heart may throb and ache,
But in my soul, I'm glad to know,
He maketh no mistake.

(From *"He Maketh No Mistake"* by A.M. Overton)

SEPTEMBER 18

What Happened to the Furniture?

2 CHRONICLES 3:17

And he reared up the pillars before the temple, one on the right hand, and the other on the left; and called the name of that on the right-hand Jachin, and the name of that on the left Boaz.

David had a vision. God gave him permission to plan and prepare but not build the Temple. God chose Solomon to do this, and he did it on an amazing scale! Our text relates only one amazing feature of this beautiful sanctuary, the two pillars in front of the Temple proper.

The splendor of this Temple was meant to humble the individual and display the glory of God. Everything from the original Tabernacle was beautiful, but Solomon's expert craftsmen raised the bar! Ultimately, God blessed the place with His presence. (**2 Chron. 5:14**) ... *for the glory of the LORD had filled the house of God.*

The Ark of the Covenant had been placed in the Holy of Holies. But what was done with all the old furniture, curtains, and tent material? (**2 Chron. 5:5a**) *And they brought up the ark, and the tabernacle of the congregation, and all the holy vessels that were in the tabernacle...*

There is no mention of repurposing. They didn't sell it on eBay. Where is this stuff? Solomon had everything except the Ark, made bigger, better, and more of them. Perhaps these things went into storage. (*Where am I going with this?*)

God accepted the new but the old had been given to Him, or consecrated. They were just "things," but they were "His things." We still do the same; we give things to God and He holds us accountable for how they are used. More than things, how about people and changes in ministry assignment? How do we deal with transitions of leadership and responsibility? People also belong to God. Are we honoring faithfulness?

Good question.

SEPTEMBER 19

True Religion

JAMES 1:27
Pure religion and undefiled before God and the Father is this, To visit the fatherless and widows in their affliction, and to keep himself unspotted from the world.

"Much evil has been done in the name of God and religion." This is true. I am personally disappointed with self-righteous hypocrisy. In my years of ministry, I have heard these excuses expressed by many pseudo-intellectuals. Their understanding of life under the sun is based upon the failure of man and their personal rebellion to Divine accountability. They are quick to condemn in others what they excuse in themselves.

I have developed this reply for those brave enough to "bear the preacher in his den." *"I too, do not believe in man's religion. I put my trust in reality, the reality of a personal relationship with the God of the Universe. His words are true, and everything He does is perfect and loving. His Word tells me that pure and true religion is marked by these two things: Genuine Compassion and Moral Purity."*

By this time, the Holy Spirit has taken the wind out of their sails. They are surprised by my seeming agreement. They are caught by their willful ignorance of what God's Word declares as the reality of a life that demonstrates obedience to truth. Most scoffers have no moral code, and their commitment to compassion is based on what makes them feel good. They have no core values and don't understand the heart of God.

But you have both of these! You have a Father who chose you in love to be His child and servant. This means you have a firm relationship and a growing understanding of the truth and your obedience to it. Because you are part of His forever family, you love what Jesus loves. This means you love the lost and the least. You understand that the goodness of God leads to repentance, and the love of Christ constrains you! This is "true religion."

SEPTEMBER 20

The Failure Paradigm

GENESIS 3:5, 22

(Satan said) For God knows that in the day you eat thereof, then your eyes shall be opened, and you shall be as gods, knowing good and evil. [22] And the LORD God said, Behold, the man is become as one of us, to know good and evil: ....

Let's move right to "the skinny" of this devotional thought. There is a worldly-wise thought pattern that has its origin in the mouth of the Great Liar. It goes like this: *"We can never know beauty without ugliness. We shall never understand truth without the lie. We will not enjoy perfection without failure."*

This paradigm of failure is the basis of humanism. It encourages you to believe that the struggle of human achievement is the highest ideal. Job's friend was correct when he spoke of man's difficulty in life. (**Job 5:7**) *Yet man is born unto trouble, as the sparks fly upward.* Moses told us that it is the hard things in life that make you strong and the bitter things that can make you better *(**Ps. 90:10.**)*

Yet I do not need to know sin to desire righteousness. Disobedience is not the path to obedience. Paul condemned this broken thinking. (**Rom. 3:8**) ... *let us do evil that good may come...* That is what Satan told Eve, the only way you will "truly know" is to disobey. This appeals to our sinful nature, We want to do it our way, no matter the consequences. We are sold the bill of goods that ignoring God is ennobling.

In verse 22, the Godhead provides this testimony to the failure of this paradigm. *"man has become one of us, to know good and evil."* Our first parents brought us the consequence of disobedience - death. Man had lost intimacy with God for the lie that knowledge makes us divine. This knowledge did not elevate or empower. The fall produced the opposite; it diminished and enslaved us. Only the knowledge of Christ reverses this curse.

SEPTEMBER 21

Signs of the Times

MATTHEW 16:2-4

He answered and said unto them, When it is evening, you say, It will be fair weather: for the sky is red. And in the morning, It will be foul weather today: for the sky is red and glowering. O you hypocrites, you can discern the face of the sky; but can you not discern the signs of the times? A wicked and adulterous generation seeks after a sign; and there shall no sign be given unto it, but the sign of the prophet Jonah. And he left them and departed.

Edinboro, Pa. has a man-made lake. During a Bible class I proposed a possible miracle. *"What if we could part the waters of the lake with a prayer and walk through on dry ground? Would that cause people to believe in Christ?"* We spoke of this for a few moments and then concluded, *"No, but they would just try to explain away how we did it!"*

We see the signs of His return and of His judgment against sin every day. Fear is proclaimed with every weather pattern, every cruelty of man against man, every shadow of discomfort or distress. The respect of God has been removed, so something or someone must be blamed. The recognition of authority and responsibility is gone because those in authority do not understand that God is the source of their authority and purpose. Lives are snuffed out and no one is held accountable. God has been pushed out of daily life, so fear must take His place. Men's hearts are failing them for fear. Freedoms are given away to secure safety, and nothing is safe.

The Cross is the only place of safety. The storm will come. Jesus will rule and overrule all. You must keep on sharing the Gospel. **(Isa. 59:19)** *So shall they fear the name of the LORD from the west, and his glory from the rising of the sun. When the enemy shall come in like a flood, the Spirit of the LORD shall lift up a standard against him.*

SEPTEMBER 22

Prone To Wander

DEUTERONOMY 31:29-30

For I know that after my death you will utterly corrupt yourselves and turn aside from the way which I have commanded you; and evil will befall you in the latter days; because you will do evil in the sight of the LORD, to provoke him to anger through the work of your hands. And Moses spoke in the ears of all the congregation of Israel the words of this song, until they were ended.

How is this for the conclusion of a sermon: *"I know you haven't been listening, or just giving lip service to my words. You will ignore what I have told you from God and do your own thing and bring great damage on yourself and others!"* Yes, I don't think they taught that in homiletics. What are we to learn?

- God uses leaders to influence for good. As one in spiritual leadership, I am responsible to speak the truth and lead people in the process of obeying the truth. **(Hebrews 13:17)**
- Without continual repetition of the positive, the old nature will draw believers back into disobedience. **(Gal. 5:17)**
- We need the faithful communication of the truth so the Holy Spirit can do what He alone can do. **(John 16:8-11)**
- The consequences of disobedience are not just possible, they are certain. **(Numbers 32:23)**
- Wrong thinking will always end in sinful behavior. **(1 John 2:15-17)**
- Music writes doctrine on our hearts. **Titus 2:1** *But speak* (**Sing**) *the things which become sound doctrine.*

You must be involved in the process! Trust God and seek the Holy Spirit's help to be as skilled as you can in speaking the truth in love. Use every means available. When necessary, use words!

Leave the product in the hands of God.

SEPTEMBER 23

Not Bad Friends, Just Miserable Comforters

JOB 2:11-13

Now when Job's three friends heard of all this evil that was come upon him, they came every one from his own place; … for they had made an appointment together to come to mourn with him and to comfort him. And when they lifted up their eyes afar off, and knew him not, they lifted up their voice, and wept; and they tore their coats, and sprinkled dust upon their heads toward heaven. So, they sat down with him upon the ground seven days and seven nights, and no one spoke a word unto him: for they saw that his grief was very great.

God says that no one got it right, not even Job. Everyone thought their age, experience, ability to observe life, and extreme personal suffering gave them an insight into the mind of the LORD (**Rom. 11:34.**) God front loads the event by telling us that Job was not being punished for sin. The "why" of Job's experience is not germane to my point.

These four men had been friends for years. They all feared God and had a working understanding of life from the hand of the Almighty. The three visiting friends heard about his troubles and cared. They had to plan a trip and coordinate with each other to mourn with and comfort Job. Their shock at his physical condition is genuine and honored the custom of the day. Their silence was not from stupidity but from observation of his grief. They did not come back at a "better time" but sat down in the dirt with him for SEVEN DAYS! Do not try to tell me these men did not understand friendship!

These fellows did not understand how to comfort. Job says so. (**Job 16:1-2**) *Then Job answered and said, I have heard many such things: miserable comforters are you all.* Your friend (family) may only have one tool in their toolbox and not know how to use it, but that does not make him a bad friend, just ignorant. Friendship is a choice you make, not a course you take. You want mercy? Then show it. Job did *(Job 42:7-10.)*

SEPTEMBER 24

More Things in Heaven and Earth...

JOB 1:6; 2:1

Now there was a day when the sons of God came to present themselves before the LORD, and Satan came also among them. **2:1** *Again there was a day when the sons of God came to present themselves before the LORD, and Satan came also among them to present himself before the LORD.*

"There are more things in heaven and earth, Horatio, than are dreamt of in your philosophy." - Hamlet, by William Shakespeare.

From the earliest writing of God's Word, the curtain is drawn back, and we peek at what we can only imagine. We are presented with the government of Heaven and the requirement to file reports. The Omniscient God does not need any reports, but He demands them. How do we know this? Because the God who reveals the truth, told us the truth. *(Isa. 45:19!)*

The phrase, *sons of God,* relates to us their creation and submission to Father God. They are spirit beings and different from man, who was created in God's image *(Ps. 104:4.)* They are not the same status as the Son of God, the Lord Jesus Christ. (I felt the need to state the obvious **Hebrews 1.**)

We are amazed by Satan being in the number, but this gives us more information about our enemy:

- The name - *Satan,* means enemy.
- He is not confined to Hell, for it is a place of torment.
- He is the Prince of the power of the air *(Eph. 2:2.)*
- He is subservient to God and only what God allows *(Job 2:6.)*

There was a day – Heaven is not regulated by our clocks. The creator of Eternity is the ruler of time. He governs but is not governed by His creation. God is not confused by time, nor is He above what it means to us *(Isa. 46:4.)* Our time is in His hand. As He governs Heaven, so He rules all of the Universe. Trust His ability to make your time count for Him.

SEPTEMBER 25

Keeping the Books

PROVERBS 11:1
A false balance is an abomination to the LORD: but a just weight is his delight.

How are you with finances? You have heard it said that Jesus talked more about money than He did about Heaven. The reason for His multiple illustrations about money is easy. **(Luke 16:10-11)** *He that is faithful in that which is least is faithful also in much: and he that is unjust in the least is unjust also in much. If therefore you have not been faithful in the unrighteous mammon, who will commit to your trust the true riches?*

People consider their wallets personal. When you are not responsible with ministry funds, you make them feel insecure. You may be great in the pulpit, but you need to be Spirit-controlled in the Board Room as well.

"Well, I am not concerned about material things." That is not what Jesus expects. If you are unsure or lack training in the balance sheet, do two things:

1. Seek out people who are good at these things and that trust the King, not just the bottom line.
2. Get some education! Today, you really have no excuse for carelessness in finances when there are so many ministries and material available to help you to grow.

Living by faith means that we *"Ponder the path of our feet and let all our ways be established."* Yes, you are called to live by faith, but that does not mean you play twiddly winks with manhole covers in the middle of the expressway. Being a good leader means you understand your weaknesses and pray and seek for others to come along side and help you.

Jesus knows who you are and still chose you! Since He does not make mistakes, don't make the mistake of thinking you must do it all by yourself. It might take some time to find the right help. After all, Jesus had a thief handling the books, but he eventually got hung up.

SEPTEMBER 26

Intercession

JOB 1:5

And it was so, when the days of their feasting (his children) were gone about, that Job sent and sanctified them, and rose up early in the morning, and offered burnt offerings according to the number of them all: for Job said, It may be that my sons have sinned, and cursed God in their hearts. Thus did Job continually.

"I may not always be right or do it right according to you, but I will always be your dad." I have had the opportunity to say something like this to each of our children. All are adults, and I have made mistakes during the transition time when our relationship was changing. Job seems to have found the key.

I do not consider Job's decision to make sacrifices on their behalf an act of interference. We know that each man is responsible for their own soul. (**Ezekiel 18:20**) *The soul that sins, it shall die. The son shall not bear the iniquity of the father, neither shall the father bear the iniquity of the son: ….*

I understand this for what it is; Job is a man who understands human nature, who recognizes the foolishness of youth and the opportunity and the responsibility to intercede for those we love.

When your children do not walk in the way that you have demonstrated with your life, you can feel that you have failed them. I am no judge as to your successes or failures to live the truth before your family. I consider it a waste of time and spiritual energy to engage in the game, *"If I had only!"* We know that it will not alter the present.

Have a little talk with Jesus and start doing this instead. (**Rom. 2:4b**) *… the goodness of God leads you to repentance.* When we begin to pray for Father's will for these adults and demonstrate unconditional love to them, we make room for the Holy Spirit to help them and heal us. He is a better Father than you.

SEPTEMBER 27

Wisdom's Testimony

JAMES 3:17-18

But the wisdom that is from above is first pure, then peaceable, gentle, and easy to be entreated, full of mercy and good fruits, without partiality, and without hypocrisy. And the fruit of righteousness is sown in peace of them that make peace.

For over twenty years, I had the wonderful opportunity to conduct a weekly Old Testament Bible Study at a state prison. This opportunity taught me so much! I learned to listen to people and began to understand when a fellow was asking a question or just trying to prove what a deep jailhouse theologian I was hosting! Many times, there was a debate on the jail block about a particular matter, and they wanted me to prove that they were right!

Father gave me understanding and a few great inmate clerks that would help me "get to the skinny." (*skinny – what is really going on!*) Our passage provided me with a phrase that helped me direct men's thoughts. *"Let us seek Father for an answer of peace."* Father did, every time.

God's wisdom affirms purity and says it must be practiced. It speaks peace into troubled hearts and calms us to rest in God, Wisdom is never aimless and provides direction. God's wisdom is reachable for all, never cold, or legalistic.

Mercy is God's to give, and He requires that we demonstrate mercy all the time. His wisdom always works to make a life fruitful in Christ. God's wisdom directs us to speak the truth and not just feign agreement to control others.

Wisdom does not lie to speak the truth. Father's wisdom produces a "God view" of men. Others are not here to be controlled by us but helped. Wisdom helps other succeed.

The result of perfect wisdom is a life of blessing sown or given out from a heart of love. This wisdom preserves unity and peace, for Christ is our peace. He will work His peace without, when He reigns within.

SEPTEMBER 28

Whom Do You Trust?

ISAIAH 2:22
Cease from man, whose breath is in his nostrils: for wherein is he to be accounted of?

It sounds very cynical. It is akin to the old Scottish saying, *"Fool me once, shame on you! Fool me twice, shame on me!"* John says something similar about Jesus and popular opinion. **(John 2:24-25)** *But Jesus did not commit himself unto them, because he knew all men, and needed not that any should testify of man: for he knew what was in man.*

So, is looking at people with a "jaundiced eye" the way we should conduct ourselves in ministry? I think my Dad did. He had a big heart, but he also had been hurt many times. He was a lonely man.

No, if we are going to pattern ourselves after the Master, we need to bring people with us in ministry and friendship, just as Jesus did. **(John 15:15)** *Henceforth I do not call you servants; for the servant does not know what his lord does; but I have called you friends; for all things that I have heard of My Father I have made known unto you.*

I am not seeking to be contradictory. Ministry is not a popularity contest. Just because you like people does not mean you are called to ministry. You must be called, and Jesus is the One who called you! People are going to like how you preach, sing, or how you make them feel. All that is "icing on the cake." But all that can change, *"like the breath from their nostrils."*

Be like Jesus. Understand the Master's call on your particular skill set. He didn't make a mistake choosing you. Your mistake is thinking it is all about you feeling good in ministry! Trust in the comfort and encouragement of the Holy Spirit every day. It is nice to hear, *"Good message, Parson!"* But tomorrow you might get a U-Haul discount flyer from the same guy. Take others with you on the journey and listen to Jesus.

SEPTEMBER 29

What is the Root of Bitterness?

HEBREWS 12:14-15
Follow peace with all men, and holiness, without which no man shall see the Lord: looking diligently lest any man fail of the grace of God; lest any root of bitterness springing up trouble you, and thereby many be defiled.

This is a warning that, as my dad would say, *"is meant to jack you up."* For those of you not familiar with English idioms, "This should make you think and challenge your behavior." The question that has always come up in my mind is, *what is the root of bitterness?*

The word *bitterness* means something acrid. The "ph." is off, and it destroys what is growing. Paul points to the root, revealing that this is different from just unpleasant circumstances. When I look to [verse 14], I believe I see a process that should be followed as Father corrects our pattern of sinful behavior.

Follow peace with all men – If Father is in charge, then I must confess that I am not, nor am I a judge of other people's actions. *Holiness* means *maturity*, but I can see it as moral purity. (**James 1:27**) says that purity is one of the two pillars of true religion. Jesus is the only one that makes this possible, and therefore, we have help from a loving Father.

Looking diligently – I must apply myself to peace and holiness, or the unmerited favor of God will not be my help but give testimony to my bitter heart. The wording in this verse is not a qualifier but a clarifier. Is Jesus bitter? Does He not bring joy? Does bitterness define your life? If nothing is sweet to you, then nothing sweet will come from you. You are *"failing of the Grace of God."*

I cannot define what might be bitterness to you, but I am sure that the Holy Spirit will reveal it if you ask. Remember, God works through process. It is not enough to say that there is a problem when Father wants to remove your bitterness and nourish joy.

I don't think I answered my question.
Let's put a pin in this and circle back.

SEPTEMBER 30

Unite My Heart

PSALMS 86:10-11

For You are great and do wondrous things: You are God alone. Teach Me Your way, O LORD; I will walk in Your truth: unite my heart to fear Your name.

The expression of praise to our King is more than the expression of appreciation and admiration for the greatest leader in the universe. It has a transformative effect on my behavior. I must not just state the facts about God; I need to express my commitment to the One who has always been greater than I.

You are God alone – I begin to abdicate my pitiful attempt to govern my own life because everything You do is faultless, and You rule and over-rule everything!

Teach me Your way – I am willing to admit that Your way is the right way, and my way is never right.

I will walk in Your truth – You have made a way for me to move forward in this life and made it so that I can learn this plain way. It is not just "a way" to go; it is the way of truth. The way I used to travel was false, and it only ended in failure. This cannot be a combination of my way and Your way. I must learn to walk in Your path or fall in darkness. (**Ps. 119:105**) *Thy word is a lamp unto my feet, and a light unto my path.*

Unite my heart – So many voices, so much distraction, so many "squirrels" to chase! I cannot focus unless I realize Your greatness, that You are the true ruler of my existence. You want me to know and live the truth, and You can put the pieces together!

To fear Your name – I want to give You the reverence You deserve and keep You in first place in my heart. You alone have the right and the power to rule and over-rule my life.

I need You.

OCTOBER 1

The Secret Things

DEUTERONOMY 29:29

The secret things belong unto the LORD our God: but those things which are revealed belong unto us and to our children forever, that we may do all the words of this law.

Does God keep secrets? Yes. (**Rev. 10:4**)

... and I heard a voice from heaven saying unto me, Seal up those things which the seven thunders uttered, and write them not. God is not obligated to tell us everything. It is very possible that we could not handle the truth.

But God has revealed to us His love in the person of Christ (**1 John 4:10.**) Moses relates a principle that is very important. Specifically, Moses is speaking to Israel about the law. The law cannot give life, but it does direct life. If we could keep the law, we would be blessed by it. But Moses is speaking about more than the written word. (**Ps. 19:1**) *The heavens declare the glory of God; and the firmament shows His handywork.*

Creation is also revelation. Everything we see about us is given so that we might discover what God has revealed. Through this revelation of the known universe, God has given us minds to reason and examine everything that so wonderfully extols His handiwork. Everything that God has revealed is for us to know. Should the exploration of science be under the morality of the law? Absolutely, but the morality of the law guides investigation and does not restrict true science.

Anything man touches can be polluted by him. We have been given the stewardship of creation *(Ps. 8:6,)* but we also know that He will judge those that destroy the earth *(Rev.11:18.)* Discovery without Biblical morality will always result in chaos. Science is noble when directed by the wisdom of the God who wants to be known.

OCTOBER 2

Star Witness, Your Mate

MALACHI 2:14-16

Yet you say, Wherefore? Because the LORD has been a witness between you and the wife of your youth, against whom you have dealt treacherously: yet is she your companion, and the wife of your covenant. And did not He make you one? Yet had He the residue of the spirit. And wherefore one? That He might seek a godly seed. Therefore, take heed to your spirit, and let no one deal treacherously against the wife of his youth. For the LORD, the God of Israel, says that He hates putting away: for one covers violence with his garment, says the LORD of hosts: therefore, take heed to your spirit, that you deal not treacherously.

What did you really think about marriage when you finally decided to take the plunge? I considered it responsibility and unlimited intimacy. Neither was realistic. One thing I did know: this woman loved me. She was a person of good will, who loved Jesus more than she loved me. I also knew this to be true about my commitment to her. As my wife often reminded me, *"Divorce was not an option, but other things are."*

In Malachi's sermon we are presented with a life principle about marriage. God intends it to be a lifelong relationship. We start out thinking we know it all and find out we just enrolled in an intense, life-changing class. God is the teacher, and His means of instruction is our mate. Together, we demonstrate the covenant relationship we have with God.

His desire is a fruitful union on many levels. Godly marriage is not a "cookie cutter" approach to life together, but it does mirror His unwavering commitment to us. He would make us holy, and by it, we would be happy. To be false to one another is to harm ourselves and displease Him.

Yes, failure is real, but Father is not done with you yet. Obedience cures and heals. Jesus heals broken people. You must have the help only the Holy Spirit gives. Be a person of good will. Love your mate.

OCTOBER 3

Rebuke

MATTHEW 16:21-23

From that time forth began Jesus to show unto his disciples, how that He must go unto Jerusalem, and suffer many things of the elders and chief priests and scribes, and be killed, and be raised again the third day. Then Peter took Him, and began to rebuke Him, saying, Be it far from You, Lord: this shall not be unto You. But He turned, and said unto Peter, Get thee behind me, Satan: you are an offence unto Me: for you savor not the things that be of God, but those that be of men.

Without the wisdom of the Holy Spirit, we cannot understand the Word of God or comprehend the Hand of God in the every day. Before the resurrection, the disciples believed in Jesus as The Chosen One, but they did not yet comprehend the Gospel.

In our text, Jesus tells His disciples the Gospel. **(Rom. 4:25)** *Who was delivered for our offences and was raised again for our justification.* All the Gospels relate that Jesus clearly explained the Gospel to them. At this moment they did not understand, accept, or keep this message because it had not yet happened. The Holy Spirit will make it clear at the right time.

What about the rebuke? Peter is only hearing part of the message and it scares him. I have seen this thinking in others. They like, even love Jesus and what He did, but do not understand His suffering or what it means in the life of a Christian. *"Your belief system should benefit you, not ask you to sacrifice or suffer. Victory is the defeat of your enemies, not your personal sacrifice."*

As a leader, you may be rebuked by those who measure success by worldly standards. When these critics are in your leadership team, it will cause you distress. Jesus stuck to the plan. Satan wants you to follow the way of compromise and comfort. Remember, that person is not the enemy, he is just serving him.

OCTOBER 4

On the Receiving End

JOB 2:9-10

Then said his wife unto him, Do you still retain your integrity? curse God, and die. But he said unto her, You speak as one of the foolish women. What? shall we receive good at the hand of God, and shall we not receive evil? In all this did not Job sin with his lips.

We shutter at just the pale image expressed on the page of Job's trauma. Some have shared with Job the depression that comes next in the cycle of loss. The difficulty comes when the attack begins from those close to our heart. What is written gives proof to Job's core values.

Mrs. Job is dismayed. These were her children too! Now her husband's affliction seems to give evidence to the popular opinion that trouble does not come in this way without it being caused by personal failure. She thinks it is God's punishment. Forgive her grief and desperation! She knows of no way to help her husband and wants it all to stop! There are many today who still think as she, but those into "new age" call it bad karma.

His response is that she is thinking like superstitious people. All that comes to us is from God's hand, and we know that hardship is part of life **(Ps. 90:10)** *The days of our years are seventy years; and if by reason of strength they be eighty years, yet is their strength labor and sorrow; for it is soon cut off, and we fly away.* What Job reveals is the depth of his belief in the nature of God. It is the hard things that make us strong, and the bitter things that make us better. God purposes our tragedy for our good and His ultimate glory.

Our text presents his noble statement, but the cycle of grief is just starting. The numbness will pass. He must push through every step. God has provided Job's journey that we might learn by observation.

Note God's last comment; *"In all this did not Job sin with his lips."* This is where your trouble can either be cut down or continued. In times of trouble, who is guarding the door of your mouth?

OCTOBER 5

No Man Cared for My Soul

PSALMS 142:4-5

I looked on my right hand, and beheld, but there was no man that would know me: refuge failed me; **no man cared for my soul.** *I cried unto thee, O LORD: I said, You are my refuge and my portion in the land of the living.*

I hope you take the time to read this entire Psalm. You may not be prone to melancholy. *You "know" that this emotional state has no place for one who is "Called by His Name."* Well, David is in disagreement with you. Ten years of being on the run from Saul, no opportunity to be productive, living off the kindness of others as well as the care of 600 plus people - he felt alone.

When David uses the word *Cry,* this does not mean a few drops down the cheek. No, this kind of cry is the snot running down my face and I can't stop it, kind of cry. This is the back of the cave and leave me alone kind of crying. Now, that is some picture, and David wants you to understand this emotion.

And no man cared for my soul – I am not sure if this was true, but that is what he felt. Notice that I put that in **bold print** because that is the phrase that tears at my heart. Here is my fear. That is another reason why I cherish the family of God. Father tells me that I am not alone.

According to recent calculations, in America over 3,000 people every year die alone. I see the need as a spiritual opportunity to extend a literal loving touch to those who have no one to connect with them. Think about this as you minister to the lost and the least. This might not be "your personal ministry," but it might be what Father wants from someone in your church family.

Ministry like this might be easy in a Senior Care facility but a little harder in a back alley. It certainly won't pay the light bill or look like success on the annual report, but Jesus seems to care about it. **(Matt. 25:40)** ... *Inasmuch as you have done it unto one of the least of these My brethren, you have done it unto Me.*

OCTOBER 6
Keeping the Door of My Lips

PSALMS 141:3-5

Set a watch, O LORD, before my mouth; keep the door of my lips. Incline not my heart to any evil thing, to practice wicked works with men that work iniquity: and let me not eat of their dainties. Let the righteous smite me; it shall be a kindness: and let him reprove me; it shall be an excellent oil, which shall not break my head: for yet my prayer also shall be in their calamities.

It always impressed me. My Mom told me that she would regularly include verse 3 as part of her devotional time. I knew that she wasn't perfect, but I can never remember her misusing God's name or using anything as an expletive except "Bother!"

Some would consider this thought petty or unimportant, but scripture provides no support for your opinion. (Granny B. called that an excuse. She defined an excuse as a reason wrapped up in a lie. Ouch!) (**Col. 4:6**) *Let your speech be always with grace, seasoned with salt, that you may know how you ought to answer every man.* (Also - **James 3:10.**)

David says that your speech is strongly influenced by your company. Paul tells us that evil companionship corrupts good habits. To speak words that bless, challenge, and inspire, we need to be open to loving correction by others who will lift us up and expect more from us.

We understand that reaching the lost means "eating with sinners." We must make contact in order to have impact. But if you do not set a guard via the Holy Spirit at the door of your mouth, there will be no impact for Christ. It is not, "holier than thou," it is "Holiness unto the Lord."

Do you want to fit in, or be a vessel for the Master's use? *Your speech bewrayeth thee*! Would it not be better to hear, "*No man speaks like this man!*" It is the goodness of God that leads men to repentance. Speak the words of grace and practice that habit.

OCTOBER 7

It Could End You

EXODUS 4:24-26
And it came to pass by the way in the inn, that the LORD met him, and sought to kill him. Then Zipporah took a sharp stone, and cut off the foreskin of her son, and cast it at his feet, and said, Surely a bloody husband you are to me. So, he let him go. Then she said, A bloody husband you are, because of the circumcision.

HEBREWS 3:5
And Moses verily was faithful in all his house, as a servant, for a testimony of those things which were to be spoken after.

We all have feet of clay. We know it. The enemy knows it. Certainly, the Holy Spirit knows it. Our mate probably knows what we think we can hide. If it were not for God's mercy and His watch care revealed from your partner, it would have ended you.

This is complicated and probably you are upset because I am brought it up. When you consider what Moses' failure might have cost him and the intercession that his wife made for him – it could have ended badly. But because his wife stepped in, Moses got this wonderful summation of his life recorded in Hebrews!

I never want to neglect my obedience to such a degree that God would want to kill me! But I really don't want to be disobedient in anything. (Wishful thinking – (***Ecc. 7:20.***) Moses almost lost his opportunity and his place in history because he failed to obey God's Covenant sign for his family.

Though it was Moses' responsibility to lead his home in obedience, thank God for women like Zipporah, who understood what God expects and will do it. She is not wrong in shaming her husband. I think it amazing that Moses included the scene for all to know and that the Holy Spirit wants us to consider the event for our own comparison. May you have this kind of support and may you never need this type of rescue. Father knows you and still chose you. May your mate never be this kind of hero to you. But thank God when she is!

As a side thought: they had been married for almost forty years. There is no way of knowing the age of the son in question. Consider that when you are thinking about any lengthy disobedience in your life.

OCTOBER 8

In the Multitude of Counselors

PROVERBS 11:13-14

*A talebearer reveals secrets: but he that is of a faithful spirit conceals the matter.
Where no counsel is, the people fall: but in the multitude of counsellors there is safety.*

Jesus is not looking for "Lone Rangers." Even the Ranger had a sidekick, Tonto! No, Jesus showed us that *"Teamwork makes the Dream Work."* Missions organizations send teams to establish new ministries. Whether this is a church plant or an established work, you need help!

In your leadership circle, is everyone on the same page? *A talebearer* – you don't need them on the bus! Caring for hurting people means protecting them from continued hurt. People who gossip are not into ministry but desire to be the center of attention. People that are vocal about transparency, if you scratch the surface, might show themselves as judgmental or control freaks. They are not leadership material.

If all people want to do is sit on a board and make decisions, their heart is not in the right place. You must patiently retrain them or prayerfully redirect their efforts. Leaders help others succeed. If they don't get this, they can't lead. **(Prov. 22:10)** *Cast out the scorner, and contention shall go out; yes, strife and reproach shall cease.* They always have something negative about every idea. There can be many reasons for this, and you must be wise in how you "cast out" the scorner. Remember, the Apostles did not come "No assembly required." Jesus invested Himself in them.

You need advisors, not just people that will rubber stamp your ideas. No, contention is not a spiritual gift and challenging the challengers without destroying them is a process, but worth the effort. You are making disciples. You need help, not a governing board. Make the vision their vision, and that is half the battle!

OCTOBER 9

In The Middle of Trouble

PSALMS 138:7-8

Though I walk in the midst of trouble, You will revive me: You shall stretch forth Your hand against the wrath of my enemies, and Your right hand shall save me. The LORD will perfect that which concerns me: Your mercy, O LORD, endures forever: forsake not the works of Your own hands.

Some of you attract trouble like fleas to a hound dog! David is not focused on how the trouble came. Today, the news is not occupied with what happened, but who is to blame. Fixing blame is wasted effort. It makes things, "all about us." God is not at fault, and He is the only one that can free us from the middle!

You will revive me – Father provides the strength to continue through the trouble **(1 Cor. 10:13.)** We must not live in the middle!

My enemies – I may not be the agent of cause, but God is greater than the oppressor **(1 John 4:4!)**

What of the "why" of this present moment? *The LORD will perfect that which concerns me.* "Perfect" – to bring us to maturity. This is a restating of **(Rom. 8:28.)** The God of All Comfort will use my adversity to make me more like Jesus, comforting others in similar trouble (just like this Psalm is doing at this moment) and bringing glory to King Jesus!

Your mercy endures – God is not capricious. His mercy is always extended to His children, no matter what our failure. **(Mal. 3:6)** *For I am the LORD, I change not; therefore, you sons of Jacob are not consumed.*

Forsake not the work of Your hands – This is a plea with great emotion! I am His work! **(Eph. 2:10)** *For we are his workmanship, created in Christ Jesus unto good works, which God has before ordained that we should walk in them.* Father is fully committed to your complete success. He has your back!

OCTOBER 10

Fear or Faith?

DEUTERONOMY 28:66-67

And your life shall hang in doubt before you; and you shall fear day and night and shall have no assurance of your life. In the morning you shall say, Would God it were evening! and at evening you shall say, Would God it were morning! for the fear of your heart where in you shall fear, and for the sight of your eyes which you shall see.

God told the Israelites that this is the psychotic thinking that afflicts disobedient, unbelieving people. If you will not seek to believe and obey God's Word, then fear must take its place. If we understand the loving Character of God and believe that His Word is true, there is no room for fear.

(1 John 4:18-19) *There is no fear in love; but perfect love casts out fear: because fear has torment. He that fears is not made perfect in love. We love Him, because He first loved us.*

We know that God loves us because Jesus died for us. We know that God can not and will not lie to us; therefore, He will not bring us to fear. **(2 Timothy 1:7)** *For God has not given us the spirit of fear; but of power, and of love, and of a sound mind.*

Satan always lies because Jesus said so **(John 8:44b.)** Jesus says that He is the truth *(John 14:6.)* If we are afraid, we are either ignorant or willfully ignorant of the truth. Our default position is either faith or fear. When we are confronted with real or imagined danger, we will experience fear. **(Ps. 56:3)** *What time I am afraid; I will trust in You.*

BUT we do not live in fear because we know His love and have hidden His promises in our hearts. This is Biblical faith *(Heb. 11:6.)* We will always be afraid of the unknown until we go through the process of Biblical faith.

Do you recognize the pattern?

OCTOBER 11

Choose Life

DEUTERONOMY 30:14, 19

But the word is very near unto you, in your mouth, and in your heart, that you may do it. [19] I call heaven and earth to record this day against you, that I have set before you life and death, blessing and cursing: therefore, choose life, that both you and your seed may live:

The Gordian Knot of Difficulty. The great debate. Many say it is between Hyper Calvinism and Arminianism. I have come to describe it as the meeting of Divine Sovereignty and Human Responsibility. The scripture reference we share is focused on human responsibility. God declares it a choice. Even the last chapter in Scripture challenges man to a choice presented by the Holy Spirit. **(Rev. 22:17)** *And the Spirit and the bride say, Come. And let him that hears say, Come. And let him that is thirsty come. And whosoever will, let him take the water of life freely.*

That which seems so difficult (it really troubled me as a freshman in college!) meets sweetly in the Cross. **(John 3:16)** *For God so loved the world, that he gave his only begotten Son, that whosoever believes in him should not perish, but have everlasting life.*

Salvation has always been God's plan, driven by God's love. It was declared by God's choice. It was delivered by God's sacrifice. It is made personal for man through God's direct method of belief in the finished work of Christ. The deliverance from eternal loss is made sure by God's unchanging promise. The divine transformation is eternal through the person of the Son of God. **(1 John 5:12)** *He that has the Son has life; and he that has not the Son of God has not life.*

God's plan is to bring rebellious man into eternal life from death. All are invited, but it is still, "whosoever will, may come." **(Rom. 5:8)** *But God commended His love toward us, in that, while we were yet sinners, Christ died for us.* There is no other choice but to choose.

OCTOBER 12

Great Sorrow

JOB 1:20-22

*Then Job arose, and tore his mantle, and shaved his head,
and fell down upon the ground, and worshipped,
And said, Naked came I out of my mother's womb, and naked shall I return. The
LORD gave, and the LORD has taken away; blessed be the name of the LORD.
In all this Job sinned not, nor charged God foolishly.*

I am sure you feel as I do about these first two chapters of Job. I am overwhelmed by the loss. I want to avoid this experience, and at the same time I ask, how would I handle this?

Is there a primer found in Job's response? God said that He didn't react badly. Does that mean I should try to learn this lesson that no one wants to know firsthand? Job's physical response could be considered to be culturally influenced, but it does not get in the way of his spiritual action. He *worshipped*. He took the physical position of humbling himself before God. His response provides answers to the questions: who is in control of what happens and am I ready to acknowledge that control by my submission?

Job's words have been recognized as truth, and in them is the ability to find peace. *I have no power to sustain anything. God is the giver of all that is good and all that He gives still belongs to Him. I give back to Him what He shared with me. He is worthy to be praised.*

These actions express grief. This worship focuses attention. These words express helplessness, loss, and center my thoughts on life not despair. God is the source of all and the giver in every need. My sorrow is not greater than His goodness. He understands my pain and is unchanged by it. I may not understand the "why," but I know whom I have believed. He will not fail.

OCTOBER 13

2 Ears, 1 Mouth

PROVERBS 18:13
He that answers a matter before he hears it, it is folly and shame unto him.

PROVERBS 13:3
He that keeps his mouth keeps his life: but he that opens wide his lips shall have destruction.

"He really stuck his foot in his mouth!" We say this about someone whose words have accidentally done damage to others and hurt their own existence. I read this thought this morning. **(Prov. 17:28)** *Even a fool, when he holds his peace, is counted wise: and he that shuts his lips is esteemed a man of understanding.*

There is a lot of advice about keeping quiet, thinking about what to say, and suggesting you might be better off not speaking! I realize that the "Leadership Person" in you might be screaming that you must provide positive direction, but I would suggest that you *"be still, and know that He is God."*

"Great advice! Did you always take it?" No. I hope my transparency does not discourage you. I am very concerned that I don't sound like "Johnny one note" when it comes to leadership pitfalls. I know that we can be our own worst enemy. We do not have to fix everyone and master every situation. We do have to listen to the Master and speak what He tells us. I am glad that I don't have an Ezekiel ministry and could only speak when God loosened my tongue. Yet, that might make it easier to keep my foot out of my mouth.

If we are going to make this positive instruction, let's consider the clear direction. Hear the whole matter out before you take direct action. Ask questions that discover facts before feelings. Pray for that which Father freely provides: wisdom *(James 1:5.)* Be willing to admit that the problem might be bigger than your understanding or experience. Spiritual leadership does not mean, "know it all." Father has this! Just ask.

OCTOBER 14

My First Bike Ride

PHILIPPIANS 4:9
Those things, which you have both learned, and received, and heard, and seen in me, do: and the God of peace shall be with you.

I was 7 and my parents had bought me a new bike, but I couldn't balance it to ride. Well then, slap on the training wheels! But this bike didn't come with any. It was a 20- incher, and I was a big kid. So, if I wanted to use the bike, I sat with my feet touching the ground and used my toes to push forward. To stop, I stood up! Not very satisfying but I could not get this balance thing! I knew how the bike was supposed to work, but I needed help.

My brother Philip was 16. The mind of a teenager can be difficult to understand. On this day, he decided to tease me for the way I propelled myself on my bike. In a pitiful way I stated my problem of balance, and then he shocked me by saying, "Ok, I will help you."

As I put my feet on the pedals, he steadied the bike, and we began to move forward down the road and down a small hill that led to Main Street. I was doing it! I was actually riding my bike, pedaling it forward! I turned to share my joy and appreciation with my brother, to see him, not by my side but standing at the top of the hill laughing!

My helper was gone! I was approaching a busy intersection and I panicked. "How do I stop?" I yelled. He, still laughing said, "Put on the brakes!" I reverted to my old braking system and stood up, sliding to a stop in the middle of Main Street. I survived.

Do not teach this way. I learned that day to ride my bike but **please** follow Paul's advice:

- Seek to give clear information.
- Make sure it is understood.
- Teach by demonstration.
- Be right alongside to help and encourage.
- Model trust in God!

OCTOBER 15

Destroyed Without a Cause

JOB 2:3-6

And the LORD said unto Satan, Have you considered My servant Job, that there is none like him in the earth, a perfect and an upright man, one that fears God, and eschews evil? and still he holds fast his integrity, although you moved Me against him, to destroy him **without a cause**. *And Satan answered the LORD, and said, Skin for skin, yes, all that a man has will he give for his life. But put forth Your hand now, and touch his bone and his flesh, and he will curse You to Your face. And the LORD said unto Satan, Behold, he is in your hand; but save his life.*

"That is not fair! Life is not fair!" Both statements seem to speak the truth, as long as we look at them as Solomon did, *"From under the sun."* We are helped by this thought; we do not know or understand everything. Because we know that we don't know, it becomes hard for us to understand that there is nothing that God can learn.

I recently read a book that gave interesting information on my favorite movie, "The Princess Bride." I learned to see the film in a different way, so I watched the movie again. It brought a renewed interest in something I knew. God already knows but still delights in what happens to you. (**Zephaniah 3:17**) *The LORD your God in the midst of you is mighty; He will save, He will rejoice over you with joy; He will rest in his love, He will joy over you with singing.*

But why did this happen to Job? What was the reason? I had a gifted friend tragically die. I was young and asked these same questions. My ideas did not provide any resolution. Patiently, I have come to this answer of

(**Ps. 18:30**) *As for God, his way is perfect: the word of the LORD is tried: he is a buckler to all those that trust in him.*

Job's troubles didn't come because of the "usual reasons." God never answers the question of why. His way is perfect.

OCTOBER 16

A Crown of Glory

1 PETER 5:4
And when the chief Shepherd shall appear, you shall receive a crown of glory that fades not away.

I serve Jesus because I love Jesus, but the benefit package He provides is "out of this world." The task you were assigned can be difficult at times. (That should be obvious.) As spiritual leaders we have much to consider and share. The personal cost and the seeming lack of present rewards can be hard to endure. That we are part of developing a long-term process can be difficult when even well meaning people are always talking and thinking about "product," and Jesus tells you your task is about "process."

The crown Peter mentions is called the Elder's Crown, but I believe that it would be better described as the Teacher's Crown. If thought of in this way, everyone could earn this reward. We may not have a formal teaching situation but our willingness to help others understand spiritual realities gives us opportunity to be rewarded by our King.

So, Peter tells us in verses 1-4, what we should remember:

- You are not alone.
- Your life is a witness to the sufferings of Christ.
- Glory awaits faithful service.
- Spiritual feeding is your job.
- Leadership is your duty, do it in love.
- You will not get rich from this assignment.
- You are not the Boss.
- You are a living example.
- You are accountable to only One.
- The reward He will give you never fades.

OCTOBER 17

Yet Trouble Came

JOB 3:25-26

For the thing which I greatly feared is come upon me, and that which I was afraid of is come unto me. I was not in safety, neither had I rest, nor was I quiet; yet trouble came.

I have heard (perhaps it was from me,) *"I am waiting for the other shoe to drop.* or *"if you say it, you will make it come true."* An even greater superstition among Christians, *"Don't tell God that you don't want to do (blank), because that is what He will make you do!"* We pick these sayings up so easily because, in times of difficulty, we can confuse cause with affect.

Here is another spiritually superstitious saying: *"Things have been going so well, trouble must be around the bend."* Where, in all of God's Word does it tell us that God is capricious? Does He have a "Wheel of Misfortune," that He brings out and spins just to afflict you? If my life is intended to be like Jesus, then I must be governed by **(Rom. 8:29)** *For whom He did foreknow, He also did predestinate to be conformed to the image of His Son, that He might be the firstborn among many brethren.* Why should my speech express that I think my life is like a crap shoot?

Let us get a handle on Job's experience. His children are dead, his family and friends agree with the traditional theology that says he has sinned, and he is very sick! I believe that his thinking is troubled, and he is speaking from pain! Why God brings adversity is not always clear but that He allows it and wills it is very clear.

We can struggle with Job's speeches and his friends' failure *(though they were still his friends,)* but I see some thoughts that are potentially comforting:

1. If you do not let your pain out, it will destroy you.
2. God can handle your pain and your whining.
3. You don't have to be right for God to hear you.
4. Someone else will be helped by your complaint when Father takes it in hand.

OCTOBER 18

Without Being Desired

2 CHRONICLES 21:6, 20

And Jehoram (King of Judah) walked in the way of the kings of Israel, like as did the house of Ahab: for he had the daughter of Ahab to wife: and he worked that which was evil in the eyes of the LORD. [20] He was Thirty-two years old when he began to reign, and he reigned in Jerusalem eight years, and departed without being desired.

Service to the King of the Universe is not about being popular, but if you are a shepherd like Jesus, then you are always ready to give your life for the sheep. That means building loving relationships. You minister by this truth: *"People don't care how much you know, till they know how much you care."*

Jehoram was a failure as a leader. Yes, he wasn't obedient to God like his father Jehoshaphat, but more importantly, he failed at the following:

1. He did not understand his source of authority. Kings rule because God places them there to care for His people. To lead by title is the lowest form of leadership. He killed his brothers because he considered them a threat. You are not the only servant/leader. You are not good at everything. Help others succeed and you will too.
2. He rejected the wisdom of God and replaced it with failed human reasoning. What is the basis for your decisions? You may have great ideas, but a shepherd leads; he does not drive the sheep. If people are not following you, you are not leading but just taking a walk. Be patient. James says it is a perfect work.
3. Jehoram mismanaged the nation's past successes by rejecting God's leadership. If it is not broken, don't fix it. Understanding the history of a ministry is invaluable in determining the direction for the future. If you cut something down, be ready to plant something better in its place. Without wisdom from Father, your intentioned success will be a failure because of forced change. The sheep will resent it, and you will be renting a U-Haul.

OCTOBER 19

Why I Do Not Drink

PROVERBS 31:4-5
It is not for kings, O Lemuel, it is not for kings to drink wine; nor for princes strong drink: Lest they drink, and forget the law, and pervert the judgment of any of the afflicted.

I was born into a temperance home. My parents were active in full-time Gospel ministry. My mother was a State officer in The Women's Christian Temperance Union of New York State. I have never had a drink of any alcoholic beverage. I was very active in the Youth ministry of the W.C.T.U.

I also use to be a real pharisee about alcohol when it came to Christians and spiritual ministry. But I came to understand that temperance was not a requirement for eternal life. (That was big of me, wasn't it!) I had to admit that the Bible does not say that a Christian cannot drink. (But don't bring what Jesus drank into this – that is an "apples vs. oranges" matter and an ignorant example.)

So, if it doesn't keep me out of Heaven and is not prohibited in Scripture, why don't I drink? Because I am always a servant of the King. The advice given to Lemuel is good advice with those who have to speak into troubled lives and always speak the truth. I will never have to apologize for what I said or did under the influence of … I will never have to say, I can't help you because I didn't control myself last night and am still under the influence.

In the Prison Ministry that God graciously gave me for over 20 years, I heard the stories of crimes committed, murder, accidents resulting in the death of others, all because of too much to drink. I personally do not have the self-control to say I will always be able to limit my consumption of a substance that takes away my ability to reason. My wife told me (she did not come from a temperance background) that if I drank, I would be a lush. So many homes destroyed, so many ministries ruined because *"the drink took the man."*

I am always a bondslave to Christ. I do not want another master.

OCTOBER 20
What God has Given

2 TIMOTHY 1:7
For God has not given us the spirit of fear; but of power, and of love, and of a sound mind.

ROMANS 8:15
For you have not received the spirit of bondage again to fear; but you have received the Spirit of adoption, whereby we cry, Abba, Father.

1 JOHN 4:18-19
There is no fear in love; but perfect love casts out fear: because fear has torment. He that fears is not made perfect in love. We love him, because he first loved us.

What wonderful promises! Our world is full of fear. Fear is sold with almost every drug commercial and national weather forecast! God does not sell fear. Biblical faith destroys fear. We trust the character of our Father. We rely upon what His promises say to us. Even when judgment is due, the grace and mercy of God is available through the presence of the Holy Spirit.

We have power through the presence and love of Christ. He makes it possible for us to see things clearly. It may be dark, but Jesus is our light. Biblical faith gives us a sound (clear) mind. We are no longer in chains and under the sentence of death. We have become, through the finished work of Christ, the children of the God of the Universe.

The love of God, through the Word of God, throws out Mr. Fear. Fear torments through the unknown. But we already know our future because Jesus paid it all! We are safe in the arms of Jesus. We did not have to convince Him to love us. He loved us first!

What God has given is powerful. We may experience fear from time to time, but because of what Jesus did, we do not live there.

OCTOBER 21

We Shall Overcome

ROMANS 12:18-21

If it be possible, as much as lies in you, live peaceably with all men. Dearly beloved, avenge not yourselves, but rather give place unto wrath: for it is written, Vengeance is mine; I will repay, saith the Lord. Therefore, if your enemy hunger, feed him; if he thirst, give him drink: for in so doing you shall heap coals of fire on his head. Be not overcome of evil but overcome evil with good.

We do well to follow this passage. I make no excuse for repeating myself. Vengeance is not part of your job description. You are human and are prone to want to control all that touches you. I think of this self-will to be a connection to the Divine. We were made in His image. We get great satisfaction (as God does also) out of our creation, but we have neither the right nor the ability to control anything.

What falls into our purview is to accept people as they are. It may seem trite, but it is true: "love the sinner and hate the sin." **(Jude 1:22-23)** *And of some have compassion, making a difference. And others save with fear, pulling them out of the fire; hating even the garment spotted by the flesh.*

We are commanded to express the love of Christ to everyone, and God says that it begins with compassion for others. **(Isa. 58:6-7)** *Is not this the fast that I have chosen? To lose the bands of wickedness, to undo the heavy burdens, and to let the oppressed go free, and that you break every yoke? Is it not to deal your bread to the hungry, and that you bring the poor that are cast out to your house? When you see the naked, that you cover him; and that you hide not yourself from your own flesh (family)?*

The "social gospel" is vital in sharing the Saving Gospel. When Jesus sent His followers out, He gave them power to help and to heal. Our caring must not start at the "Romans Road."

OCTOBER 22

Though He Slay Me

JOB 13:15
Though He slay me, yet will I trust in Him: but I will maintain mine own ways before Him.

Some read these stirring words and think that Job is rebellious. They believe he has "dug in his heels." This is not the case.

Though He slay me – Father controls life and death. (**Ps. 104:29-30**) *You hide Your face, they are troubled: You take away their breath, they die, and return to their dust. You send forth Your spirit, they are created: and You renew the face of the earth.* The ability to give life and cause death is in the hands of a loving Savior. (**Rev. 1:18**) *I am He that lives, and was dead; and behold, I am alive for evermore, Amen; and have the keys of hell and of death.* He has no equal. God can "end you" and will do it at the right moment.

Yet will I trust Him – There is more to the God of the Universe than knowing the day of our death. He is the only one we can truly trust. Abraham said this about His Character. (**Gen. 18:25**) *... Shall not the Judge of all the earth do right?*

Paul would describe Abraham's relationship with God with this phrase – (**Rom. 4:21**) *And being fully persuaded that, what He had promised, He was able also to perform.* God always keeps His word. God's faithfulness to Abraham proved that we should claim this promise as well.

The Scriptures define death as our greatest enemy, but Job, despite all of his present trauma, would trust the One that no one can control. *I will maintain mine own ways before Him.* Because Father is always the same we are safe.

There is nothing hidden from God's sight (**Heb. 4:13.**) Job's assurance is not in control or subterfuge but trust and transparency. Job hurts and is confused, but he does not forsake the truth. God is God. God is not capricious. He does right, His Word is true. He will deal with me as I am.

OCTOBER 23

The Righteousness of Saints

REVELATION 19:8
*And to her (the Bride of Christ) was granted that she should be arrayed in fine linen, clean and white: **for the fine linen is the righteousness of saints.***

REVELATION 3:5
He that overcomes, the same shall be clothed in white raiment ....

REVELATION 4:4
And round about the throne were 24 seats: and upon the seats I saw 24 elders sitting, clothed in white raiment; and they had on their heads crowns of gold.

REVELATION 6:11
And white robes were given unto every one of them....

REVELATION 19:14
And the armies which were in heaven followed Him upon white horses, clothed in fine linen, white and clean.

Is this covering symbolic or is it to be taken literally? Yes. It represents what Jesus has given them and how they must be covered in the presence of the King.

(**Matthew 22:12**) *And he said unto him, Friend, how do you come in without having a wedding garment? And he was speechless.*

The texts literally mean that the saints are covered in the righteousness of Christ. All our righteousness is as filthy rags. (**Isa. 64:6**)

There is absolutely nothing we can provide to remove our sinfulness nor cover our nakedness but the righteousness of Christ. What a blessed covering is this spotless garment that will never fade or be destroyed!

For all eternity, we will never be out of fashion or have need of something to replace what Jesus has provided us. We will never grow tired of this perfect wardrobe, nor will it need to be mended, altered, or replaced. Your longing to make yourself beautiful, in style, accepted, or fit in, will no longer drive you, for you are perfect in the righteousness of Christ!

OCTOBER 24

The Process of Redemption

TITUS 3:4-7

But after that the kindness and love of God our Savior toward man appeared. Not by works of righteousness which we have done, but according to His mercy he saved us, by the washing of regeneration, and renewing of the Holy Spirit; which He shed on us abundantly through Jesus Christ our Savior; that being justified by His grace, we should be made heirs according to the hope of eternal life.

As humans, we can become fixated on dates. Birthdays, Anniversaries, etc. - the event becomes greater than the life or the relationship. Don't misunderstand me, I want to celebrate my birthday and rejoice with others in milestones. I believe we should celebrate more, not less!

Your redemption is more than a date (mine is July 4.) Your study has taught you that redemption is a life-long process; you are being saved. There is no doubt about the outcome. **(Phil. 1:6)** *Being confident of this very thing, that He who has begun a good work in you will perform it until the day of Jesus Christ.*

I just wanted to remind you of the process and encourage you to celebrate this as well!

- (v4) Father chose to love us. It is His plan.
- (v5) Redemption is nothing to do with human endeavor. It is all about God's mercy.
- (v5) God saved us by the washing of His Word. **(Eph. 5:26)** *That He might sanctify and cleanse it (the Church) with the washing of water by the word.*
- (v5) The Holy Spirit uses the Word to convict of sin, convince of the need for Christ, and convey us into the Kingdom of God.
- (v6) The Holy Spirit gives us abundant life because of Jesus' finished work on Calvary.
- (v7) We have the hope (eager expectation) of all that the life of Christ promises.

So, Celebrate!

OCTOBER 25

The Mind of Christ

1 CORINTHIANS 2:14-16

But the natural man receives not the things of the Spirit of God: for they are foolishness unto him: neither can he know them, because they are spiritually discerned. But he that is spiritual judges all things, yet he himself is judged of no man. For who has known the mind of the Lord, that he may instruct him? But we have the mind of Christ.

It is truly a wonderful explanation that Paul provides about the real differences between the Natural and the Spiritual Man. The Natural man is without Christ. He does not have the Holy Spirit dwelling within. **(Rom. 8:9)** *But you are not in the flesh, but in the Spirit, if so be that the Spirit of God dwell in you. Now if any man have not the Spirit of Christ, he is none of His.*

Paul continues the definition of the Spiritual Man by a contrast with the Natural. The Natural will not receive what God shares. He perceives it as foolishness, and it does not fit in his paradigm because the Holy Spirit is not in him.

The Spiritual Man is able to examine all things because he has the light of God, yet the ungodly have no authority to condemn the spiritual man, flawed as he may be. The world has no part of the wisdom of God, since it is God alone who gives wisdom. God's wisdom is not found in the assimilation of information but in the inspiration of the Holy Spirit. To have the mind of Christ does not imply perfect knowledge, but it does mean we have access to all wisdom. We share in the nature of God, and therefore, have opportunity to understand all things. **(1 Cor. 1:30)** *But of Him are you in Christ Jesus, who of God is made unto us wisdom, and righteousness, and sanctification, and redemption.*

Take comfort in this: the only way anything in this world succeeds to any degree is when Biblical principles are applied. As a servant of the God of the Universe you have all you need in Christ. Trust the process.

OCTOBER 26
The Good LORD

2 CHRONICLES 30:18-20

For a multitude of the people, … had not cleansed themselves, yet did they eat the Passover otherwise than it was written. But Hezekiah prayed for them, saying, The good LORD pardon everyone that prepared his heart to seek God, the LORD God of his fathers, though he is not cleansed according to the purification of the sanctuary. And the LORD hearkened to Hezekiah and healed the people.

I enjoy a well-crafted ceremonial service/event. I have worked diligently to develop services that stir emotion but have a firm foundation in Biblical truth. I hold to the principle that Jesus gave about our worship. **(John 4:24)** *God is a Spirit: and they that worship him must worship him in spirit and in truth.*

Worship is not a spectator sport. To truly worship, it requires intentional participation. Worship is always an action, and Jesus says it must be with our entire being (spirit) and as God directs (in truth.)

Our text records a special keeping of the Passover. It is special for several reasons: Passover was a family activity, not a nationally celebrated event planned by the King and his leaders. This Passover was not at the time the law directed because the Priests were not ceremonially cleansed. The people of Israel were specially invited to join in Judah's celebration.

But many of the people were not cleansed. This was an important, personal preparation. Perhaps the reasons were many, but it also meant that they couldn't or shouldn't partake in the Seder. Hezekiah intercedes with a humble prayer that asks God to look on their prepared hearts and nothing else. God does just that.

This is what Father does, and He does it every day. As His chosen leader, you do not have to lower standards but connect with humble hearts. Be like Hezekiah; share the truth in ways that prepare hearts to reach out to our merciful Father.

OCTOBER 27
The Blessings of Divine Leadership
ISAIAH 35:10
And the ransomed of the LORD shall return and come to Zion with songs and everlasting joy upon their heads: they shall obtain joy and gladness, and sorrow and sighing shall flee away.

The Church is a perfect organism populated with broken and imperfect people. The purpose is glorious, the provision is greater than its need, but the performance is flawed. Your joy as part of it will be affected by where you place your attention. If it starts and ends with Jesus, then no degree of imperfection will change your commitment to the blessing of His Body. As you move in obedience to the Head, you will love what Jesus loves **(Eph. 5:27.)**

I see Isaiah 35 as a Camelot kind of passage. In its application for the church, I would insist that by obedience to the King's leadership, this kind of blessing can be known.

- [v1-2] It blooms where it is planted. If Jesus is lifted up, He will do the rest *(John 12:32.)* Success is not measured by "nickels, noses, and kneelers" but the Glory of the LORD.
- [v3] The weak are cared for and made strong.
- [v4] Limitations are not magnified, but the power of God is proclaimed.
- [v5-6] The Holy Spirit is allowed to heal the broken because He will make them whole.
- [v7] The church nourishes and comforts believers and does not drain their lives.
- [v8] The church becomes a highway of opportunity to holiness for the least and the lost.
- [v9] The leaders of the church provide protection from those that would harm its members.
- [v10] The church develops a culture of praise to God that rejoices in each other.

Once more, I insist; when Jesus is your focus, you cannot help but love what He loves.

OCTOBER 28

Stupid Is, As Stupid Does

2 CHRONICLES 25:16

And it came to pass, as he talked with him, that King Amaziah said unto him, Are you made of the king's counsel? Shut up; why should you be killed? Then the prophet stopped, and said, I know that God has determined to destroy you, because you have done this, and have not hearkened unto my counsel.

Amaziah does not seem to be the brightest bulb on the tree. God provides insight on his spiritual condition.

(2 Chron. 25:2) *And he did that which was right in the sight of the LORD, but not with a perfect heart.* He practiced conformity to ceremony, but he wasn't seeking God. God gave him a victory over the Edomites, and it went to his head. He liked their "shiny stuff" and started worshiping it.

God is good, even to fools. He sends a prophet to warn Amaziah, but our text shows that he rejected the warning. God was behind the rejection.

I have suggested this before, and I am not shy about saying it again. Not everyone belongs on the bus. In fact, some of the people in whom you invest a great deal of time and effort into really don't want your help. They do not want to change; they just like the attention – until they find some "shiny thing" and start worshipping that.

I am not sure if there is some kind of litmus test that you could use to discover who is sweet and who is sour. You may have to ask some hard questions about their personal relationship with Christ. Since most people enjoy talking about themselves, you can soon find out if they have a "perfect heart;" in other words, who is the most important, them or Jesus?

Jesus died for everyone, but it is still directed by this absolute: "*whosoever believes in Him.*" Amaziah was a fool because he gave up the real treasure for the shiny imitation. Warn all. Share the love of Christ with all. Don't be surprised that "*many are called, but few are chosen.*"

OCTOBER 29

Sound Doctrine

TITUS 2:1
But you must speak the things which become sound doctrine:

For the Biblically illiterate, the term *sound doctrine* has a very negative meaning. We understand it means healthy instruction. The focus for everything must be on the person of Christ. Peter informs us that all that we need is found in Jesus. (**2 Peter 1:3**) *According as His divine power has given unto us all things that pertain unto life and godliness, through the knowledge of Him that has called us to glory and virtue.*

To speak as a servant of the King means we use our words carefully. We encourage faith in the Character of God and the Content of His Word. (**Rom. 10:17**) *So then faith comes by hearing, and hearing by the word of God.*

My communication with those I have been given to lead and feed must never be based on popular opinion or anecdotal account. Even my own opinion has no place in the presentation of the truth. You, and therefore your people, must understand what is shared is the Word of God. *"Thus, saith the LORD,"* is the foundation that will provide eternal change and guide them to Christ-like behavior.

The latest sermon series can be topical, but if it does not lead believers to surrender and conformity to Christ, then you boarder on humanistic deism. Your sheep need to understand what the Good Shepherd declares are *"green pastures and still waters."* Your responsibility is holiness not happiness. If they learn holiness from your speech, they will be happy.

If we teach our people to look unto Jesus, then they will not be confused by the next "ism" that appears.

Show them the genuine from God's Word, and they will be able to spot the phony. God speaks the truth. We don't need anything else.

OCTOBER 30

Sin at Your Door

GENESIS 4:5-7

But unto Cain and to his offering He did not respect. And Cain was very angry, and his countenance fell. And the LORD said unto Cain, Why are you angry and why is your countenance fallen? If you do well, shall you not be accepted? and if you do not do well, sin lies at the door. And unto you shall be his desire, and you shalt rule over him.

Abel understood the message. In faith he acted in obedience and made a blood sacrifice (**Heb. 11:4.**) Was Cain ignorant of God's requirement? Genesis and Hebrews help us understand that he was not. He chose what he considered important, not what God required.

There is nothing wrong with the fruit of the ground. Farming the land is a noble task. We are all given gifts by a gracious Creator that we can use for the blessing of all and the glory of God. But our abilities, gifts, interests, etc. are not what God requires in worship. He demands obedience.

(**John 4:24**) *God is a Spirit: and they that worship Him must worship Him in spirit and in truth.* Worship must be in the way (truth) that God has declared. Approach to God is never left to personal choice. Yet what we see is Cain choosing to do things his own way. We can choose to disobey, but the consequences *"lie at our door."*

In this exchange with God, (amazing account!) God knows Cain's heart but still reaches out to him. God does not provide him a way to hide but reveals his heart. He gives Cain the opportunity to correct or repent but he turns from this. Why? John explains it. (**1 John 3:12**) *Not as Cain, who was of that wicked one, and slew his brother. And wherefore slew he him? Because his own works were evil, and his brother's righteous.*

Your way is not God's. To form God in our image is idolatry. With the Word of God tear down, root up, and throw out therapeutic, humanistic, moralistic, sentimental, superstitious, political deism. In its place plant holiness unto the Lord.

OCTOBER 31

Shipwrecked

1 TIMOTHY 1:19-20

Holding faith, and a good conscience; which some having put away concerning faith have made shipwreck: Of whom is Hymenaeus and Alexander; whom I have delivered unto Satan, that they may learn not to blaspheme.

Paul speaks about one of the difficult parts of leadership, public discipline. I think I would be safe to say that you have never done what Paul declares nor do you know any church leader than has!

Holding faith and a good conscience – This speaks about fully trusting in the truth and living it out in the life. I call it your default position. When things are difficult and confusing, you must go by what you do know, not by what you don't know.

But Paul tells us that these people have *put away faith and are shipwrecked.* One reason people abandon the place of blessed assurance is that they are determined to live in sin. Because of this choice, they suppress the truth. The result is a life filled with brokenness. **(Jer. 2:13)** *For my people have committed two evils; they have forsaken me the fountain of living waters, and hewed them out cisterns, broken cisterns, that can hold no water.*

[v20] To make sure Timothy understands, Paul reminds him of two troublesome men. One of them keeps on stirring the pot and is mentioned again in *(2* **Tim. 2:17.)**

Delivered to Satan – This sounds weird. I am not sure how that is done but we know that Satan can only do what God allows – remember Job!

Learn not to blaspheme - The purpose is discipline with the idea of correction not destruction. There are several examples of this in the book of Acts and in Corinth.

The challenge for you is to recognize the problem. Is the problem hardship or is there temptation in someone's life leading them to shipwreck? Prevention is best, but if people won't or can't share their confusion and seek help it will make you the instrument of discipline.

That will put you on your knees. In the multitude of counselors there is safety, so seek help for yourself!

NOVEMBER 1

Where's My Mud, Jesus?

JOHN 9:6-7

When He had thus spoken, He spat on the ground, and made clay of the spittle, and He anointed the eyes of the blind man with the clay, and said unto him, Go, wash in the pool of Siloam, (which is by interpretation, Sent.) He went his way therefore, and washed, and came seeing.

Jesus tells us that this blindness is not because of personal sin. The purpose was to reveal the works of God; i.e., to glorify the Lord Jesus. We don't know how long he was blind, but he is called "of age." A question rises in my heart, *"How long have you waited?"*

To be born blind is hard, but to live in a world where you must survive by begging tells us something about this man. People knew him and he had some kind of relationship with others. He must have been brave because he did not live with family. He had a working knowledge of Scripture. He was feisty; hearing the way he talked back to these hateful people!

But I still have my question – *what about my mud*? Perhaps you, or someone close to you, has been "without sight." In those times, when the difficulty has stretched you thin, are you reading this account and wondering, *"When will Jesus pass by me?"* Or do you think He already passed by?

Living by faith is not easy. You know that Jesus can deliver you right now, and He doesn't need clay to do it. **But will He?** Some might be shocked by my question. Our Heavenly Father isn't bothered by this question. I am warning you; if you do not let these kinds of questions out, they will kill you. **(Prov. 18:14)** *The spirit of a man will sustain his infirmity; but a wounded spirit who can bear?* If you won't ask the hard questions of the One who loves you with abandon, then fear is controlling you.

You are living in torment *(**1 John 4:18.**)* Not good!

NOVEMBER 2

When Frustration Takes Over

NUMBERS 22:27

And when the ass saw the angel of the LORD, she fell down under Balaam: and Balaam's anger was kindled, and he smote the ass with a staff.

I am a mature man of 70, with over 50 years of ministry experience. I have been part of many situations having to deal with obstinate people and have helped them to resolve what others could not. I have personal experience with many different challenges and am qualified to lead others and conduct a church through complex problems. But I still get frustrated.

Who was Balaam? Basically, He was a Seer. That means he was a professional connection between you and God for hire. The superstitious view of the day was that God could be manipulated to do what you want – for a price. *(Western spirituality is coming back to this.)* Balaam has his eyes filled with riches and can't see the danger before him, but the ass can. This whole deal with Balak was straight out of the "Seer Handbook." Balaam is frustrated that it isn't happening the way he wants it to go!

But why do I get frustrated? I am not a man like Balaam. I will speak the truth, no matter the personal cost to me. Balaam doesn't seem to fit when we are viewing the true servant of Christ. Well, his story hits too close to home for me! I get frustrated when my experience tells me what to do and then it doesn't work!

What have I done? I did not ask for the Holy Spirit's help and left Jesus out. He is not part of the solution; He is the solution. Whether it is a people problem or fixing a leaky pipe, I need Jesus! My experience can be used for good and perhaps Father will supply by the way of the ravens, but if I don't ask, seek, knock, then it is all about me. Father may make your efforts fail because you are playing the fool. When you do not seek Him, you will find frustration.

Go ahead; tell me I am wrong.

NOVEMBER 3

Unless The LORD

PSALMS 94:17-18

Unless the LORD had been my help, my soul had almost dwelt in silence. When I said, My foot slips; Your mercy, O LORD, held me up.

I awoke this morning and took stock of the things that surrounded me. This has been happening regularly since I had my duty assignment changed. I have had a greater opportunity to see the abundance of blessing that my loving Father has freely given me.

Many of the things I observe bring full memory of how this blessing came into my life. The God, who needs nothing from me, is the one who came alongside to help me in my need, often before I realized my problem.

My soul had almost dwelt in silence – It means I almost died. I am reminded of Divine protection from (**Heb. 1:14**) *Are they not (angels) all ministering spirits, sent forth to minister for them who shall be heirs of salvation?* My wife believes we have sent a few angels into retirement. The enemy wishes to destroy us, but God is always on guard. (**Ps. 37:32-33**) *The wicked watches the righteous and seeks to slay him. The LORD will not leave him in his hand, nor condemn him when he is judged.*

Lest we believe that Father only protects the good, only those that deserve protection, David draws from his personal experience. *My foot slips,* the picture comes of a narrow path along the mountain with the ground is muddy and death is at every curve. Our footing gives way, but Father's provision demonstrates the *"kheh'sed"* we need. This is not sentiment, but provision that fills the soul. *The LORD held me up* – I became dead weight, no strength to even find a new foothold. The All Powerful, All Sufficient One, carried me to a firm place to stand.

How foolish we are to think that Father cannot or will not help us. Thank you, Abba!

NOVEMBER 4

The Tree of Life, Water of Life

GENESIS 3:22, 24
And the LORD God said, Behold, the man is become as one of Us, to know good and evil: and now, lest he put forth his hand, and take also of the tree of life, and eat, and live forever: [24] So He drove out the man; and He placed at the east of the garden of Eden Cherubim, and a flaming sword which turned every way, to keep the way of the tree of life.

REVELATION 2:7
He that has an ear, let him hear what the Spirit says unto the churches; To him that overcomes will I give to eat of the tree of life, which is in the midst of the paradise of God.

REVELATION 22:1-2, 17
And he showed me a pure river of water of life, clear as crystal, proceeding out of the throne of God and of the Lamb. In the midst of the street of it, and on either side of the river, was there the tree of life, which bare twelve manner of fruits, and yielded her fruit every month: and the leaves of the tree were for the healing of the nations. [17] And the Spirit and the bride say, Come. And let him that hears say, Come. And let him that is athirst come. And whosoever will, let him take the water of life freely.

Here is a mystery. Two things, a tree and special water, that God says are givers of life. They are not symbolic of Christ, for He alone is the giver of Eternal Life ***(John 10:28.)***

There is not enough information about these two things except to state that they exist, and they both have the ability to extend physical life. The **Genesis 3** passage brings us to the dreadful conclusion that extending physical life with the curse of sin upon it would be undesirable, to say the least. That God tells us that these things are available for all Overcomers provides a sense of wonder. We will still be tri-part beings that need physical care, but death is no longer in the equation of existence. There is so much to come! May we live in wonder ***(1 Cor. 2:9.)***

NOVEMBER 5

The Believing Wife

1 PETER 3:1-2

Likewise, wives, be in subjection to your own husbands; that, if any obey not the word, they also may without the word be won by the way of living of their wives; While they behold your chaste way of living coupled with fear.

I have experienced this phenomenon: believing wives getting in the way of their husband's conversion. The reasons for this may be manifold, but the stumbling blocks are real. Peter challenges wives at their core belief. *Is Jesus your Lord?*

Jesus said it very simply, (**John 14:15**) *If you love me, keep my commandments.* In the marriage relationship, the basic is this: *Does God ordain and direct marriage or did you create this union?* If God is the author, then follow His commands. God is not ignorant of who you are and what gifts and abilities He placed in you. Submission is not mindless behavior but lovingly using who you are and what you have been given to honor your husband.

Peter's words are about a husband that is not a believer. The wife's spiritual condition does not supersede the covenant relationship of marriage. The fact that it might have been a pagan ritual does not nullify that God made the institution before man "put on the lipstick." A woman's obedience to Christ can be used by the Holy Spirit to bring that man to trust in Jesus. I remind you of this, (**Rom. 2:4b**) *... the goodness of God leads you to repentance.*

When we fear God, we will live in a way of purity. This lifestyle, or "conversation," is something that the Holy Spirit will use to bring conviction to the wickedest of men and protect the being of the woman who trusts her Savior. Peter's statement is not a guarantee of the conversion of her husband, but it is the assurance that this is the only way that redemption will happen. Teach this truth and trust God to be glorified.

NOVEMBER 6

Taught to be Afraid

ISAIAH 29:13

Wherefore the Lord said, Forasmuch as this people draw near Me with their mouth, and with their lips do honor Me, but have removed their heart far from Me, and their fear toward Me is taught by the precept of men:

I have heard this saying many times, *"If ignorance is bliss, I am the happiest person I know."* It may be funny, but it is not safe. We are at that position of human history when men have been told that the truth of God is a lie and are bombarded with the teaching that, in the fear of everything, there is safety.

Information and the communication of facts has been buried under the editorializing of fear. We are taught that facts are not reliable. Doubt is the intelligent approach to everything. With the creation of AI (artificial intelligence) everything we see and hear can be faked. We are cautioned that we cannot believe anything! **(Hosea 4:6)** *My people are destroyed for lack of knowledge ....*

The "woke" world has fulfilled the judgment of God. **(Isa. 5:20)** *Woe unto them that call evil good, and good evil; that put darkness for light, and light for darkness; that put bitter for sweet, and sweet for bitter!* But this does not change our message or our mission! We might buy into the fear of being rejected, misunderstood, irrelevant, or out of date, but the Omniscient God teaches us this:

(**John 12:32**) *And I, if I be lifted up from the earth, will draw all men unto Me.*

(**John 1:12**) *But as many as received Him, to them gave He power to become the sons of God, even to them that believe on His name:*

(**1 Cor.9:16b**) *... yes, woe is unto me, if I preach not the gospel!*

That is something you should fear.

NOVEMBER 7

Sarcasm – Captain Obvious

JOB 12:1-2
And Job answered and said, No doubt but you are the people, and wisdom shall die with you.

If you are familiar with the narrative of Job, you know that Job and his miserable comforter friends are not even halfway in their debate about the guilt of Job. Two things have already become evident; they have not helped Job and he is still miserable.

When someone who is in the throes of difficulty is ready to share (Job did start the conversation,) providing a listening ear is vital. But many people think that, if you are listening, you must have an answer. I have a high school friend who died during his college days from a tragic bicycle accident. He was gifted, super smart, and a wonderful guy. I was overwhelmed by his passing (I will see him again, Praise God,) but in order for me to process this loss, I started to develop reasons why God took him (some of them were pretty weird.) I am so glad I never shared them with his family!

Just because you are in spiritual leadership does not mean that you have to have an answer for every horror that comes at your people. It is OK to say, *"I don't know"* or *"I don't understand."* Father will give you something intelligent to say or do, but it does not have to be "The Answer." I have been the best comfort when I just helped others to look unto Jesus and avoided the platitudes. I prayed when they couldn't.

Job's friends did care about him because they made time and sat with him for seven days in silence. I understand some of us think that when sorrowers speak and it sounds kind of wonky, then our turn for rebuttal is next. Resist the temptation! Do not be Captain Obvious. Yes, everything happens for a reason, but you should not be the one saying things like this. Father will make you a channel for His blessing if you stay open to just being the pipe and not the source.

NOVEMBER 8

Out of Time

ECCLESIASTES 3:1
To everything there is a season, and a time to every purpose under the heaven:

The gift of time. Some seem able to use time as a tool. A few see it as a slave master. Many consider it an irritation. None can control it. One day, Jesus will declare it to be over **(Rev. 10:5-6.)**

It has been helpful to me in ministry to think of time as balls in a juggling routine. With every item I add, I must remove something from the balancing act. Add an opportunity, we must remove perhaps a moment of rest. Do you get the picture?

Every day, we share time with others. To some, this sharing comes at a sacrifice to them of other opportunities they may value or treasure. Their sharing of time is a gift to you that should not be treated capriciously. To steal time from them is an offense. To believe that your stealing is a minor thing and that it is justified because it is for a good cause or "It is for the Lord" is the height of hubris. It is not cool to think that it is easier to ask for forgiveness than to ask for permission. To believe that your agenda has greater value than theirs is a declaration of pride, not spirituality.

You may be in a position of spiritual leadership therefore, you feel that what you do and how you lead should take precedence over the schedules of those you help. This kind of thinking will negatively alter the way people follow you. **(James 3:1)** *My brethren, be not many masters, knowing that we shall receive the greater condemnation.*

Without the Holy Spirit speaking into the hearts and minds of the sheep, they will not follow. If you do not respect their time, you will be taking a walk by yourself. Use their time wisely. Prayerfully invest this gift. Do not let your words fall on deaf ears. *"The mind can retain, what the seat can endure."*

NOVEMBER 9

No Spite!

PROVERBS 24:17-20

Rejoice not when your enemy falls, and do not let your heart be glad when he stumbles: Lest the LORD see it, and it displease him, and he turn away his wrath from him. Do not fret yourself because of evil men, neither be envious at the wicked; for there shall be no reward to the evil man; the candle of the wicked shall be put out.

We have all seen it in action movies: never turn your back on a bad guy that seems to be down. Our minds scream to the good guy, "Finish him off; then kiss the girl!"

What Solomon shares in our passage and what our culture promotes are extreme opposites. When I think about some of the "problems" that Solomon had taken care of at the beginning of his kingdom, I think I hear, "Don't do as I do, do as I say!"

There also seems to be some superstitious statements about God hearing you, like you will jinx it!

But let's consider this warning based on an understanding of God's Sovereignty. **(Deut. 32:35)** *To me belongs vengeance, and recompense; their foot shall slide in due time: for the day of their calamity is at hand, and the things that shall come upon them make haste.*

God is no one's fool. He understands what is happening and how He will deal with sin. **(Gal. 6:7-8)** *Be not deceived; God is not mocked: for whatsoever a man sows, that shall he also reap. For he that sows to his flesh shall of the flesh reap corruption; but he that sows to the Spirit shall of the Spirit reap life everlasting.*

Because Father describes Himself as the God of mercy, we may not be able to comprehend the redemption He has planned, but I am learning that it is wonderful! He will judge righteously. He will protect me from all evil. He forgave me all my wickedness. With His help, I will let Him do what I cannot do: judge the world in righteousness.

NOVEMBER 10

It is Just Not That Easy

2 CHRONICLES 19:2-3

And Jehu the son of Hanani the seer went out to meet him, and said to king Jehoshaphat, Should you help the ungodly, and love them that hate the LORD? Wrath is upon you from before the LORD. Nevertheless, there are good things found in you, in that you have taken away the groves out of the land and have prepared your heart to seek God.

Obedience is still the litmus test for every servant. Jehoshaphat was a good king and loved God, but he let circumstances and "family connections" control the decisions he made. God has killed Ahab (King of Israel) through war. Ahab had led his people into idolatry, and there were no limits to this disobedience. Jehoshaphat was enjoying the peace God had given them, but he wanted to be the skillful politician and play nice with the Northern Kingdom. They were Israelites too, and working together could be profitable! Ahab wanted the land back that Syria had taken, so Ahab appealed to Jehoshaphat "in friendship." This was a mistake that almost ended his life.

There is a leadership lesson in this. God was the one who blessed Judah and provided them peace and safety. King Jehoshaphat had truly sought God's way.

(**2 Chron. 17:6a**) *And his heart was lifted up in the ways of the LORD.* His friendship with an ungodly leader was taking him down the road to disobedience. Even when Micaiah the prophet had warned him of the disastrous outcome, Jehoshaphat continued in a losing venture. He disobeyed and brought shame on himself, death to his people, and future trouble to the Kingdom.

You must make decisions based on the truth and the display of righteousness. It is not a "holier than thou" smugness but your obedience to revealed truth.

"If you do not make the decision, before the decision has to be made, the decision will be made for you."

NOVEMBER 11

He Is Able

JUDE 1:24
Now unto Him that is able to keep you from falling, and to present you faultless before the presence of His glory with exceeding joy,

This passage is such a benediction, such a comfort! To illustrate this blessing, I share an event that some will question. Yet I experienced it, and the fruit of that moment has brought blessing to me and glory to my Savior. I will never doubt I heard His voice.

The man I called Pastor while I was at Bible School, Dr. Charles Ware, was speaking at a church plant on the eastside of Buffalo. I was excited to hear this wonderful communicator once more. The passage he shared that night was (**2 Peter 1:3-4.**) The Holy Spirit used this text to open my eyes and begin my understanding of how truly wonderful the promises of God are to every believer.

I was lifted to the Throne of God by the Holy Spirit's enlightenment. I did not want the service to end and stayed at this old movie theater until they locked the doors. As I drove home that night, I spoke from a heart overflowing with joy and thankfulness. I was given a clearer understanding of God's Word. I spoke this prayer, *"Oh Father, I feel so close to You. I am so thankful for this wonderful insight into your Word! I never want this feeling to end."*

As I guided my car through the night, I heard a voice from the back seat of my Gremlin, *"He is able to keep you from falling, and to present you faultless before the presence of His glory with exceeding joy."*

I turned quickly to see who had spoken and saw no one, but the memory has never faded. I did not even know that I had heard a verse from scripture until a few months later, someone shared it in a conversation at church! I was shocked! God had spoken in my ears, His promise to my heart. He is able! For over 50 years He has made this precious promise to whisper in my being and encourage me when I was weak. I hear Him now.

NOVEMBER 12

From the LORD

PROVERBS 16:1-4

The preparations of the heart in man, and the answer of the tongue, is from the LORD. All the ways of a man are clean in his own eyes; but the LORD weighs the spirits. Commit your works unto the LORD, and your thoughts shall be established. The LORD has made all things for Himself: yes, even the wicked for the day of evil.

I suppose that ignorance of the goodness of God might make some distressed or at least confused by the poet's insights. For those in public ministry, the simple acceptance of these truths should provide great comfort. My gracious King is directly involved in my service for Him. He is not micromanaging but providing Divine inspiration and power to accomplish the work of the Kingdom.

I have often been amazed by the inspiration and understanding that has come out of these lips of clay. Many times, I have stopped and thought, *"Where did that come from? I am not bright enough to figure that out on my own!"* We may have convinced ourselves that our motives are sincere, but in those times of supposed brilliance, the Holy Spirit is there to remind you that success is only found in surrender to the Savior's Sovereignty.

Many times, I have struggled to make sense of a Scripture passage. It was mud to me, so it will be as clear as lead to Superman! I wasn't even sure I was supposed to cover this part of the text! Then I prayed, pleaded for help, and walked into my woodshop to fix something.

The next day, the light came on, the mud was gone! What the Holy Spirit now revealed stirred my heart! I could not wait to share what Father had given.

We would like to avoid trouble and troublesome people. I do not believe that everyone belongs on the bus. Still, I must remember that Father is intimately connected with my ministry, even when hardship presents us with crushing things. Father has got this!

NOVEMBER 13

When Passion Becomes Poison

1 TIMOTHY 3:7
Moreover he must have a good report of those which are without; lest he fall into reproach and the snare of the devil.

Ah, the qualifications for spiritual leadership! It is good for us to look these over every once in a while. The idea of maintaining a good testimony and a good working relationship with unbelievers in your town should never be minimized. Ignorance of the patch of land where we are assigned is dishonoring to our King.

But I was looking for some way to connect your mission with your passion so that it would not turn to poison. This text fit the need. All of us have things that interest us in a powerful way. My Pastor really likes trains. I was a devoted pro football fan (until recent team disappointments. I still follow it but ….)

You need a hobby. You should maintain an activity that separates you from ministry. Jesus said so. (**Mark 6:31**) *And he said unto them, Come apart into a remote place, and rest a while: for there were many coming and going, and they had no leisure so much as to eat.*

So, collect the stamps, build the models, play golf, or basketball. Fish, hunt, join a book club and read for pleasure. I knew of one pastor who bought a boat and called it *"Visitation."* (Think about it!) But – don't let your passion become a poison that Satan uses to distract and entrap you!

True story: A small town had a community croquet field. A pastor decided to use the field as a ministry opportunity. He really enjoyed the game and discovered that he was good at it too. The "skinny" on the story was that this ministry connection became an obsession in his life. He was vindictive in his play, the game consumed his time, and his entire ministry, both pulpit and personal, failed. He lost his testimony and was forced to resign.

"It would never happen to me!" (**1 Cor. 10:12**) *Wherefore let him that thinks he stands take heed lest he fall.* You need the passion, but you do not want the poison!

NOVEMBER 14

Waiting

ISAIAH 40:28-31

Have you not known? have you not heard that the everlasting God, the LORD, the Creator of the ends of the earth, faints not, neither is weary? There is no searching of His understanding. He gives power to the faint; and to them that have no might He increases strength. Even the youths shall faint and be weary, and the young men shall utterly fall: But they that wait upon the LORD shall renew their strength; they shall mount up with wings as eagles; they shall run, and not be weary; and they shall walk, and not faint.

How do we measure strength? A few days ago, my friend and I (both 70) came to pick up a riding mower from my oldest son. We had no ramps, but we would pick it up and put it in the back of the truck! Thank God, my sons were there to actually do the lifting!

I understand the limitations of this precious promise. God will not make it possible for me to run from my home (central PA) to Dallas, Texas, in two minutes. What would that prove? Where is His glory? I know that He is not limited. Our God is the All Powerful, Self Sufficient One! He is never confused and always makes a way for victory, but it is victory as He defines it!

He uses the powerless and provides His strength to succeed. Age or testosterone is not the measure or the limitation of His ability to bring completion to every task He determines is for His glory. But what does it mean to *wait upon the LORD*?

The prime root of the word *wait* means to bind together by twisting. To know His strength, wisdom, and direction, we must bind ourselves to Him. I cannot, I will not move unless He moves. It makes no difference how He moves, His strength will accomplish the flight, provide endurance to the runner, and surefootedness to those who walk into the unknown. I cannot move without Him. He will do the heavy lifting!

NOVEMBER 15

Trust but Verify

PROVERBS 14:15
The simple believes every word: but the prudent man looks well to his going.

PROVERBS 22:3
*A prudent man foresees the evil, and hides himself:
but the simple pass on, and are punished.*

I would say this is kin to the old saying, *"Look before you leap."* Trust is earned. It is very true in ministry. If you only lead by Position or you haven't moved on from Permission, you will soon be packing the U-Haul. Those you lead must learn to trust you. This trust will come through speaking the truth in love and helping them succeed in applying the truth. That is a long process!

But what about the other side of this matter? A pastor friend told me of a church that called him to be the pastor.

The Sunday he had been a candidate, the church had put on a good show. Everything seemed to be as it should. Six months later, all of his Deacons and Sunday School teachers had retired and moved away! That will give you trust issues!

Unfortunately, some of you already have real trust issues that have nothing to do with ministry! You have got to start somewhere – the "Sunday school answer" is trust Jesus, but you must make connection with the sheep to be a real shepherd. The two verses of our text provide a good place to start.

Your people want to please you, but many are very disorganized in their thinking and living. When you seek their help or commitment, start small, don't micromanage but look for ways you can help them track their progress. Have them tell you what they think the task is and why it is important. This is a way you can mold their thinking to see the purpose in the task and the progress being made.

Don't set yourself or them up for failure. Don't assume that believers know how to minister. Try to be aware of trouble: Show them. Do it with them. Watch them do it. They do it. They do it with someone else.

That is developing trust and building relationships.

NOVEMBER 16

The Description of Perfection

EXODUS 34:5-7

And the LORD descended in the cloud, and stood with him there, and proclaimed the name of the LORD. And the LORD passed by before him, and proclaimed, The LORD, The LORD God, merciful and gracious, longsuffering, and abundant in goodness and truth, Keeping mercy for thousands, forgiving iniquity and transgression and sin, and that will by no means clear the guilty, visiting the iniquity of the fathers upon the children, and upon the children's children, unto the third and to the fourth generation.

You have heard this excuse: *"The God of the Old Testament is all about judgment and cursing. I prefer the God of the New Testament. He is a different God; more about love and acceptance."* Obviously, these people have never read this description of perfection.

We know that God is always the same. **(Mal.3:6)** *For I am the LORD, I change not; therefore, you sons of Jacob are not consumed.* God describes Himself as the One who needs no one and needs nothing. He is the Self-existent God. He does not need us. This is why His continued description of His perfection is so wonderful!

He is merciful. He wants us to understand that this is how He deals with everyone. It is not mercy based on our response or attention. He is full of mercy. He continually shows us that we are not getting what we do deserve. His next description is just as transformative, *Gracious* – giving to men what we do not deserve.

Every word, every line, reveals the God of the universe meeting our every need. He provides all that we lack. He declares that He gives us a choice to know and trust Him, but that He controls the consequences of our choices. There is nothing missing. He is perfect.

NOVEMBER 17

The 3 P's

ECCLESIASTES 1:2-3
Vanity of vanities, saith the Preacher, vanity of vanities; all is vanity. What profit has a man of all his labor which he takes under the sun?

I remember the pressure the first time I taught the book of "The Preacher." It changed my value system. I want to thank God that He gave me the focus of my life in (*1 Cor.15:58.*)

We know Solomon is presenting the perspective of "life under the sun." Eternity is secondary in this wisdom literature. He asks the question, "What gives life under the sun meaning?" By relating his personal experiences and his observation of others, he directs us to three things.

1. Purpose – There must be a purpose in what we do. What is the goal? What will be accomplished by taking part or even completing the task? In ministry we tend to say that things are done for the glory of God, but what does that look like? Leaders will find meaning when we determine how this particular matter advances the Great Commission and fulfills the Great Commandment.

2. Progress – Are we moving forward? Those who seek to lead the church like ranching instead of shepherding, lean on this thought. They fixate on "Nickels, Noses, and Kneelers" and can lose sight of the maxim of "growing in grace and in the knowledge of Christ." Both views are necessary to measure progress in the Kingdom. If we use the Great Commission and Great Commandment as our unit of measurement, the Holy Spirit will reveal the Progress.

3. Permanence – Solomon says life means change. How can anything under the sun be permanent? Communicating the message has changed drastically! The Permanence will be found in the answer to these questions: Are others being equipped to "go and tell?"
Are they prepared to "speak the truth in love?"
These two things will last forever. These two absolutes advance the Kingdom and allow Christ to be the center of all that is done.

NOVEMBER 18

Someone Else's Circus

GENESIS 15:16
But in the fourth generation they shall come hither again: for the iniquity of the Amorites is not yet full.

"Are we there yet?" Abraham doesn't ask the question, but God gives Abraham a timeline *(Gen. 15:13-21.)* There is a lot of information in this revelation, and it connects to God's original promise to make his posterity a great nation *(Gen. 12:2.)* Abraham is going to live a long time, but the future sounds difficult and God is only bullet pointing these events for Abraham to reveal to His friend that, "I have a plan."

Our text presents a thought that we do not usually consider; what happens to me affects others that I may not care about or care for. You may believe that as a fully devoted follower of Christ you care about everyone. Since I know you are not God, I am not buying that.

What fascinates me is that God is going to use my life to move some to faith and some to reject Him and I have absolutely no say in this. **(2 Cor. 2:15-16)** *For we are unto God a sweet savor (fragrance) of Christ, in them that are saved, and in them that perish: To the one we are the savor of death unto death; and to the other the savor of life unto life. And who is sufficient for these things?*

God tells Abraham that His land promise is a sure thing, but it is going to take over 400 years for it to happen. The reason it will take that long is that the people groups that your children will evict have not yet messed up their lives enough! What does that tell me about God? **(2 Peter 3:9)** *The Lord ... is longsuffering to us-ward, not willing that any should perish, but that all should come to repentance.*

So, what God is doing with me is not in any way all about me but about how He decides to work in this world. Therefore, it is possible that the things that I may consider failures in my journey are the perfection of His plan. Go figure. *"Not my circus, not my monkeys."*

NOVEMBER 19

Remove the Dross

PROVERBS 22:10
Cast out the scorner, and contention shall go out; yes, strife and reproach shall cease.

PROVERBS 25:4-5
Take away the dross from the silver, and there shall come forth a vessel for the finer. Take away the wicked from before the king, and his throne shall be established in righteousness.

When you take the leadership of a work that Father didn't use you to build, you must understand that you face a specific set of challenges. You have the title, and you are certainly there by permission, but figuring out who are the real leaders takes time.

God didn't make a mistake in placing you in this role, but He does expect you to use your head for more than a hat rack. First of all, admit that you have an ego; that is why you are in leadership. Remember that there is a process that is required to help others work with you for the King. Leadership is not a corner office but a caring heart.

Do you value these people? Then value their past, even when it is full of mistakes. Everyone you deal with wants to look good on the outside, so it will be a while before they really "show up." Take time to listen to their story, and be available for the Holy Spirit to use who you are and what you have been given to heal them and make them stronger in Christ. That is why you are here, right?

There are some people that like to live broken. This doesn't make much sense. Because you represent God in their life, and they are fighting with Him – well, you are their target. Now, you might be the kind of servant that likes controversy, but too much is not good for the family. If some of your sheep won't let you help them, then they need to be removed from influencing the flock negatively. This is easy to say, harder to do. You may be the instrument for this culling, but it is not your decision. That is above your pay grade.

I believe that problems avoided result in greater problems. You must attack this on your knees! Father is not surprised. You are there, *"For such a time as this."*

NOVEMBER 20

Our Eyes Are Upon Thee

2 CHRONICLES 20:12

O our God, will You not judge them? We have no might against this great company that comes against us; neither know we what to do: but our eyes are upon You.

The first Law of Thermodynamics - every action has an equal and opposite reaction. In spiritual matters, Paul defines it this way. **(Gal. 6:7-8)** *Be not deceived; God is not mocked: for whatsoever a man sows, that shall he also reap. For he that sows to his flesh shall of the flesh reap corruption; but he that sows to the Spirit shall of the Spirit reap life everlasting.* The consequences of our actions will come to us. Praise God, that does not mean the condemnation **(Rom. 8:1!)**

Jehoshaphat had made a bad alliance with wicked King Ahab and had brought shame, death, and continuing trouble on Judah. Before this time, God had kept the nation in peace and safety. This reminds us once more that God is actively involved in this world **(See Psalm 2.)**

Now, the terror of four enemy kingdoms comes against Judah. When trouble comes upon people because of their poor choices and disobedience, we do not have to sugarcoat the truth. It is also not our job to say, "I told you so!"

Jehoshaphat knows something that every child of God should know by heart. **(Ex. 34:6)** *And the LORD passed by before him, and proclaimed, The LORD, The LORD God, merciful and gracious, longsuffering, and abundant in goodness and truth.* He believes that God does not lie and immediately leads all of Judah "to seek the Lord" (verse 4.) He claims the Character of God and reminds God of His Promises. He then asks for help! He does not tell God what to do but admits that only God can deliver them. Everyone in the nation is depending upon God!

Let's teach our people that when they are caught in the consequences of their circumstances to do what Jehoshaphat did. It works!

NOVEMBER 21

My Very Next Breath

JOB 12:9-10
Who knows not in all these that the hand of the LORD has wrought this? In whose hand is the soul of every living thing, and the breath of all mankind.

Is there an all-wise creator? Has He truly created all things? Is He infinitely and actively involved with His creation? For me the answer to these questions is, *"Yes, and Amen."* I take comfort in the fact that I am not an accident. I was intentionally and miraculously created. My creator is actively involved in my existence. My very next breath is in His wise hands.

Others seem to take very little comfort in these truths. It makes them feel constricted and manipulated. The idea of an intimate creator directly involved with His creation causes them to want to cast off the supposed chains of this benevolent dictator. They think of themselves in the mind of "Invictus."

They are not far from the truth. You are responsible for your actions. You do have the ability to choose. The intimate creator has declared it so. (**Deut. 30:19**) *I call heaven and earth to record this day against you, that I have set before you life and death, blessing and cursing: therefore, choose life, that both you and your seed may live:*

God says that we have the responsibility to choose. The consequence of those choices are already determined, but the choice is ours. The heart of man rebels against this absolute, but to no avail. (**Ps. 2:3-4**) *Let us break their bands asunder and cast away their cords from us. He that sits in the heavens shall laugh: the Lord shall have them in derision.*

Many have stumbled over the supposed conflict of Divine Sovereignty and Human Responsibility, but the all-wise, Almighty Creator declares that they meet in the Cross of Christ *(John 3:16.)*

As a believer in Christ, I rest in Father's loving control. As a man, I rejoice in God's infinite wisdom. As a being created in the image of God, I breathe.

NOVEMBER 22

I Sat Down Under His Shadow

SONG OF SONGS 2:3B-4

... I sat down under His shadow with great delight, and His fruit was sweet to my taste. He brought me to the banqueting house, and His banner over me was love.

My first exposure to this song was in a regional chorus comprised of over 400 voices. After 55 years, it still lives in my heart. The declaration of intimate love between a husband and wife is thrilling to consider. The application of the love of Christ for us is what we would pursue.

I sat down – I have no need to stir or seek other comfort. Here I am at rest. (**Isa. 26:3**) *You will keep him in perfect peace, whose mind is stayed on You: because he trusts in You.*

Under His shadow – This is not a dark place but one of comfort from the oppression of life. (**Ps. 91:1**) *He that dwells in the secret place of the most High shall abide under the shadow of the Almighty.*

With great delight – There is no oppression in the company of our great King. For those who enjoy His love, it is an existence of joy! (**Ps. 16:11**) *You will show me the path of life: in Your presence is fulness of joy; at Your right hand there are pleasures for evermore.*

His fruit was sweet to my taste – There is no one like our Father that knows how to give us good and knows what we like. (**Matt. 7:11b**) *... how much more shall your Father which is in heaven give good things to them that ask him?*

He brought me to the Banqueting House – A royal pavilion prepared to honor and bless those He loves! (**John 14:3**) *And if I go and prepare a place for you, I will come again, and receive you unto Myself; that where I am, there you may be also.*

His banner over me was love – Not only is His affection for you shown in His personal care, but it is proclaimed for all to see! (**Heb. 2:13b**) *... Behold I and the children which God has given me.*

You are loved. Take comfort, there is more to come!

NOVEMBER 23

He Believed IN the LORD

GENESIS 15:5-6

And he brought him forth abroad, and said, Look now toward heaven, and tell the stars, if you are able to number them: and he said unto him, So shall your seed be. And he believed in the LORD; and he counted it to him for righteousness.

You recognize this as the moment that Abraham became your Father. He was not the first to trust the Self-sufficient, Almighty God, but God declares that he is to be honored with this title: the Father of all that are of faith. *(**See Rom. 4:11**.)*

Abraham has acted in faith and God delivered Lot. God then does what He always does, speak into our lives with more about Himself (15:1.) But Abraham is troubled because of the promise that hasn't happened yet. Once more Father shows that He is not bothered by our questions if we are ready to listen to His reply. Father is specific; and in verse 5 gives an illustration that is so much bigger than the question asked! All this celestial wonder before the eyes of Abraham was created, ordered, and maintained by the God who chose, called, protected, and provided for this one man. With such an overwhelming display of care, Abraham is led to believe.

And what did he believe? He believed IN the LORD. This is the first "C" of Biblical faith, the Character of God. (**Rom. 4:21**) *And being fully persuaded that, what He had promised, He was able also to perform.* This is always the first step. We must be like Abraham, *fully persuaded.* There are no limitations to His ability, and He cannot lie. (**Titus 1:2**) *In hope of eternal life, which God, that cannot lie, promised before the world began;* Therefore, it must follow that whatever He has said, He will do.

In that moment of faith, Abraham received the greatest good. God declared him righteous. We all must come to this same place. *"Like father, like son."*

NOVEMBER 24

Comfort In Death

JOB 6:7-9

The things that my soul refused to touch are as my sorrowful meat. Oh, that I might have my request; and that God would grant me the thing that I long for! Even that it would please God to destroy me; that he would let loose his hand and cut me off!

It is very possible that you have rarely been down in any way. You have learned to hold tight to the promises of God. They are truly more important to you than your necessary food! Stop now and thank Father for giving you such a wonderful Savior and a personality that can see the good. It is a great blessing!

But you are called to help people of every temperament and not all have had your flavor of blessing. Some have shared your view of life, but God has purposed them for greater and harder things. Dark nights, deep waters, and the furnace of affliction has been placed in their path. Will you help bring them a light?

There are others we might call "Eeyore's." A cloud has been with them most of their days. They love Jesus as much as you, trust the Word of God as you do, but their experience of life is challenging for you to understand.

Understand it you must! This is where you begin to grasp your calling to "care for the lambs and feed my sheep." Your success will not be found in the transformation of their personality but in your "bow to serve them." You are their pastor – so be their Pastor!

You must not try; you must yield. The Holy Spirit is forming Christ in you, and He will use who you are and what you have been given to carry them to Jesus. Like Job, their experience may be soul crushing. Do not aid in their death. Pour in the oil and wine. You are not their Savior, but Jesus is, and He will use you. **(1 Thess. 5:24)** *Faithful is He that called you, Who also will do it.*

NOVEMBER 25

Butt Naked for Jesus

ISAIAH 20:2
At the same time the LORD spoke to Isaiah the son of Amoz, saying, Go and loose the sackcloth from off your loins, and put off your shoes from your feet. And he did so, walking naked and barefoot.

How about that for a memory verse? I can't say I ever remember hearing a sermon on this passage. Someone might want to take this as a theme verse for a nudist Bible Camp, but I will not be signing up for this. I try to avoid being ridiculed. I have modified *(1 Pet.4:8.)* I like to read it as, *"Clothing covers a multitude of sins."*

Putting the humor aside, I am so thankful that Father has not, nor can I recall in recent history, asking anyone of His servants to take this lifestyle illustration. But what would you do if asked to make a greater personal sacrifice for the King? **(Mark 10:29-30)** *And Jesus answered and said, Verily I say unto you, There is no man that has left house, or brethren, or sisters, or father, or mother, or wife, or children, or lands, for My sake, and the Gospel's, But he shall receive an hundredfold now in this time, houses, and brethren, and sisters, and mothers, and children, and lands, with persecutions; and in the world to come eternal life.*

If I understand the Master, we cannot out give Him or out serve Him. We will never make a bigger sacrifice than He made for us. We will not find Him a hard Master. **(Heb. 6:10)** *For God is not unrighteous to forget your work and labor of love....*

He will not be ashamed when He gives out our rewards. But I think we might be ashamed that we have ever thought His service harsh or the task He has given us unreasonable. He knows me and my limitations.

 (Ps. 103:14) *For he knows our frame; he remembers that we are dust.*

Oh, Master! If I must travel the hard road, please hold my hand, and help me to fix my eyes upon You.

NOVEMBER 26

A Lesson Not Learned

2 CHRONICLES 20:35-37

And after this did Jehoshaphat king of Judah join himself with Ahaziah king of Israel, who did very wickedly: And he joined himself with him to make ships to go to Tarshish: and they made the ships in Eziongaber. Then Eliezer the son of Dodavah of Mareshah prophesied against Jehoshaphat, saying, Because you have joined yourself with Ahaziah, the LORD has broken your efforts. And the ships were broken that they were not able to go to Tarshish.

What is that definition of insanity? Doing the same thing over and over and expecting different results. Can you hear Jehoshaphat's excuses? *But it was with a different King! Sure, he is just as bad as his father and what I did with Ahab brought us lots of trouble – but this is not for war but money! No one is going to get hurt. And besides, I will give a tithe to the Temple!*

Well, that is an interesting story, but this idea isn't repeated in the New Testament, right? **(2 Cor. 6:14)** *Do not be unequally yoked together with unbelievers: for what fellowship has righteousness with unrighteousness and what communion has light with darkness?*

Whether it be business, marriage, or politics, God's nature and our obedience to His revealed truth must be our first concern. Compromise does not promote the Gospel. Kindness is our calling. Giving ourselves to help those in need is the mandate from our Father, but tying our interests with those who have no interest in pleasing God or obeying the truth is wrong on every level.

Instructing those in your care to make the decision to follow Jesus in everything means you must instruct them. When their emotions or their wallet gets in the way, you fight an uphill battle. But you must fight the battle.

Say it early, say it often. God's way is best, and His provision, guidance, and comfort are greater than what the world can provide.

NOVEMBER 27

A Continuing Revelation

GENESIS 13:14

And the LORD said unto Abram, after that Lot was separated from him, Lift up now your eyes, and look from the place where you are northward, and southward, and eastward, and westward:

Abraham is our Father by faith. His life story is good preaching and provides a great pattern of the steps of faith: God speaks, Man believes, Man obeys, God gives testimony or shows Himself able. Abraham's life story is a story of the process of obedience. Take comfort! He does not display perfect obedience at the first.

God calls him and gives an amazing promise in Ur but was told to leave his family. He goes but takes his Father and nephew. God removes His dad; God gives him more of the promise. Abraham goes further but still takes his nephew. God separates them, gives more of the promise and Abraham moves forward. With each move, Abraham also expresses worship.

This roller coaster ride is over many years. Each time in this lengthy process Abraham's understanding of God and of His promises grows. With every act of obedience there is greater light. His walk of faith is an example for your walk as well.

We may be fully equipped to teach the truth, but faith is our response to the Character of God and the Content of His Word. God has opened His Word to your heart, and you believe it so much that you eagerly proclaim it. But obeying His command and believing His promise and provision is when faith becomes real.

We might be like our Father Abraham, "Not knowing where he was going," but we go! In response to your obedience, Father gives testimony. He reveals more of Himself and the journey. You are being moved in this process from "faith to faith." We see Father's hand, we hear His voice, we proclaim His Truth, and live in obedience – and He starts the process again! What a great job we have!

NOVEMBER 28

At the Right Moment

PROVERBS 25:11-12

A word fitly spoken is like apples of gold in pictures of silver. As an earring of gold, and an ornament of fine gold, so is a wise reprover upon an obedient ear.

I have always been impressed by how the Holy Spirit describes the boy, Samuel. **(1 Sam. 3:19)** *And Samuel grew, and the LORD was with him, and he let none of his words fall to the ground.* I have always wanted this to be said of me! You might think this as an expression of my ego – perhaps it is, but I like to think about it this way: I am commissioned to speak the Word of God; therefore, I must be careful what I say.

Was it always that way? Of course not! When I was in high school, I developed a sarcastic wit. I waited for others to stick their foot in their mouth, and I would force in the other foot! But one day as I was experiencing one of my few spiritual moments, I asked this question of myself: *"If I was in spiritual need and wanted to talk about it with someone, would I come to me?"* The answer I gave was, "No."

Since that time, I have asked the Holy Spirit for help in applying **(Gal. 6:1-2)** *Brethren, if a man be overtaken in a fault, you which are spiritual, restore such a one in the spirit of meekness; considering yourself, lest you also be tempted. Bear one another's burdens, and so fulfil the law of Christ.*

Those who know me know that this is still a work in progress, but now, it is what I want to do! I do not want to hurt others to make myself feel better than them. I want my words to help them and glorify Jesus! It is not a chore to lift others up. I do not have to say nice things to please, but I am eager to speak the truth in love.

What a joy it is when you are quoted in the presentation of the truth. It is so rewarding to hear the truth being shared by those you have lifted from confusion and despair. This is your opportunity!

NOVEMBER 29

A Deal With Death

ISAIAH 28:15,18, 20

Because you have said, We have made a covenant with death, and with hell are we at agreement; when the overflowing scourge shall pass through, it shall not come unto us: for we have made lies our refuge, and under falsehood have we hid ourselves: [18] And your covenant with death shall be disannulled, and your agreement with hell shall not stand; when the overflowing scourge shall pass through, then you shall be trodden down by it. [20] For the bed is shorter than that a man can stretch himself on it: and the covering narrower than that he can wrap himself in it.

This is unusual stuff. It sits (supposedly) outside of our context. It is about those in Judah who rejected the Hope that God would provide and their scheme to replace it with their own plans. Of course, they believe they will escape the consequences of their disobedience.

Where does this foolish thinking arise? They had rejected the truth and replaced it with a spirituality that deceived people into thinking they could control their fate. But you deal with people like this today. They are religious, and believe they control their destiny or that they must bargain with God and turn "luck" their way. They "make deals with the devil" and think God is a fool who only knows what He is told.

God says that their deal with death is off, and what they have sown, they will reap *(Gal. 6:7-8.)* When I look at verse 20, I wonder if the phrase, "You have made your bed, now you must lie in it," had its origin here? The word picture is very "uncomfortable" (pun intended.) As a tall person, I have had a few uncomfortable nights with the bed too short and a blanket that only covers part of me.

You must have an awareness that people have not changed; men continue in short-sighted planning that is intended to leave God out of their utopia, but they have built upon quicksand. God is still on His Throne.

NOVEMBER 30

A Bond Slave

DEUTERONOMY 15:16-17

And it shall be, if he say unto you, I will not go away from you because he loves you and your house, because he is well with you; Then you shalt take an awl, and thrust it through his ear unto the door, and he shall be your servant forever. And also, unto your maidservant you shall do likewise.

The servitude under the Law's description was not the shameful slavery of our Nation's past. The relationship was entered into because of financial difficulty by the servant, not the criminal selling of souls. There was a time limit of seven years, no matter what the financial difficulty, and the "Master" was required to release the servant with financial blessing, a severance package, if you will.

But our passage provides for a bonding of hearts and lives. This was a lifetime commitment. To make it legal, there was a cost to the servant and to the master. You might think that the servant got "the point," but the act marked the master's home with blood, and he had to mark his servant. You may think it easy, but I do not.

This is referred to as becoming a bond slave. The earring is a mark of slavery, but for the Israelite, a mark of love. Paul calls himself a bond slave **(Rom.1:1.)** This is a beautiful picture of our service to Christ. You have been called to serve the King of the Universe. As John says, *"we love Him because He first loved us."*

I love my Master and never wish to leave His service or stop serving His family. I understand His pattern of life and will imitate it. **(Mark 10:45)** *For even the Son of man came not to be ministered unto, but to minister, and to give his life a ransom for many.* I echo the sentiment of a servant of the past, *"If Christ be God, and died for me. No sacrifice I make can be too great."* – C.T. Studd

DECEMBER 1

Entertaining Angels

HEBREWS 13:1-2

Let brotherly love continue. Be not forgetful to entertain strangers:
for thereby some have entertained angels unawares.

It is a glimpse into the supernatural. Because it is outside of the norm, some would discount it as unimportant or even connect it with the superstitious. But to profess their distain for the inclusion of angels in our theology would deny the ministry of Christ. Jesus often referred to the work of angels. He says they do the bidding of our Heavenly Father, care for us, and that they ministered to Him in times of great physical stress.

Our writer leads the thought of intimate contact with angels with the encouragement to demonstrate compassion to all we meet *(Heb. 12:14.)* With a life focused on Jesus and yielded to the discipline of our Father God, kindness to strangers must be our common practice.

The meaning and practice of hospitality has changed over the centuries (more's the pity,) but God's heart and our commitment to be like Jesus should not be changed. It would be a thrill to know that the hitchhiker we pick up or the meal that we provide for a hungry soul is really for a supernatural messenger – but this is not the norm (not that I know for certain!)

We realize that in the Biblical accounts, angels appear to people for specific reasons. Because we have the Bible and the Holy Spirit, we fail to understand the need for angelic visitation. But Hebrews tells us they are active in our lives and ministry. **(Hebrews 1:14)** *Are they not all (angels) ministering spirits, sent forth to minister for them who shall be heirs of salvation?*

There is no Biblical reason to think that we have any influence on angelic labor, except to be their duty assignment. They serve at the pleasure of God for your protection. My wife says we have worn out a few.

DECEMBER 2

Part of the Testimony

2 TIMOTHY 3:11B-12

... what persecutions I endured: but out of them all, the Lord delivered me. Yes, and all that will live godly in Christ Jesus shall suffer persecution.

My oldest son has friends that have hiked the road that Paul would have taken to minister in the cities he notes in this letter of encouragement. It was over 100 miles of difficult travel. As I think about the opposition I have experienced over the past 62 years of knowing Jesus, I am having difficulty coming up with any real hardship stories. I know I have had people reject what I try to tell them, and I did come close to being punched by a homeowner when I was "cold canvassing," but that is about it for me. Perhaps Father used my size as an advantage (6'4" over 300) to protect me, so I could claim that as deliverance – but it makes me wonder.

But I know that my personal experience is not necessary to prove Paul's words to be true. Every day, there are believers in Christ who are giving up their lives for the truth of the Gospel. We had a family friend, V.T. Moody, whose family held a funeral service for him because he had accepted Jesus as his Messiah. The woman who led him to Christ took him in and raised him as her own. I call that God's deliverance.

To *live godly in Christ Jesus* – what does that take? I know it is knowing the love that will not let me go. It is also being controlled by that same love so that bitterness does not take control of your responses. It means that trusting Christ is more than just a change of thinking or change in habits, it is a new heart. You were dead and now you are alive. Why would you even think about going back to being dead? It makes me think of a quote from C.T. Studd: "*If Christ be God, and died for me, then no sacrifice I make can be too great.*"

Keep on living for Jesus. He will take care of you.

DECEMBER 3

Obedience

HEBREWS 13:17

Obey those that have the rule over you and submit yourselves: for they watch for your souls, as they that must give account, that they may do it with joy, and not with grief: for that is unprofitable for you.

We all want to be obeyed but obedience is not demanded or commanded but modeled and instructed.

King Saul lost his blessing and the future of his kingdom because of disobedience. **(1 Sam. 15:22-23)** *And Samuel said, Has the LORD as great delight in burnt offerings and sacrifices, as in obeying the voice of the LORD? Behold, to obey is better than sacrifice, and to hearken than the fat of rams. For rebellion is as the sin of witchcraft, and stubbornness is as iniquity and idolatry. Because you (Saul) have rejected the word of the LORD, he has also rejected you from being king.*

David had the right idea, *"Touch not the LORD's anointed."* God is the one who establishes order. He uses imperfect people (like you) to accomplish His perfect will. Our obedience has nothing to do with our feelings or our evaluation of someone's leadership skills. It is all about trusting and obeying our Father. Our text says to obey and submit. That is a lot for Western Christians to stomach! It also stipulates that God and not you is the one who holds these spiritual leaders accountable. That means that you are not in charge of anyone but yourself.

How do bad or poor leaders get removed or replaced? Not by you. Yes, to privately speak of your concerns with the offender is Biblical, in fact it is demanded if you really love what Jesus loves! Matthew lays out those steps. Prayer and encouragement are the only God-honoring tools anyone has!

As a spiritual leader, if you are not willing to obey and submit to this instruction, I believe another principle is in control: *"whatsoever a person sows, that shall they reap."* **(Gal. 6:7-8)**

DECEMBER 4

Marriage is Honorable

HEBREWS 13:4
Marriage is honorable in all, and the bed undefiled: but whoremongers and adulterers God will judge.

The world is desperately working to destroy what God created to be held in the highest esteem. We know that God created marriage as the first institution. It is the foundation for human government and the Body of Christ. Marriage is the union of a man and a woman spiritually, emotionally, and physically.

Our text says that this relationship is to be honored above all others *(Eph. 5:31-33.)* Within marriage, the sexual relationship between compassionate partners has no limits. Their intimacy is governed by tender loving that will do no harm. The physical relationship should reflect submission to one another in self-sacrificial behavior. The act of love must always be a blessing not a burden.

The opposite of agape love is presented to show that true intimacy does not use their mate to satisfy the lust of the flesh. Real sexual intimacy does exist but will never be expressed in abuse or harm. The marriage bed does not mean *"anything between consenting adults."* The act of love is not just for procreation, for God created us to know and give pleasure, but when we harm, we are not honorable.

The intimacy God created is purposed to be exclusive. Sharing our sexuality with others brings us into judgment. **(Eph. 5:5-6)** *For this you know that no whoremonger, nor unclean person, nor covetous man, who is an idolater, hath any inheritance in the kingdom of Christ and of God. Let no man deceive you with vain words: for because of these things comes the wrath of God upon the children of disobedience.*

The results of sin will come now, to the body and the mind, and later when unconfessed, in loss of honor or reward. Yes, all sin is dealt with through the sacrifice of Christ, but let us avoid the harm we could bring *(James 1:14-15).*

DECEMBER 5

I Know!

JOB 19:23-26

Oh that my words were now written! oh that they were printed in a book! That they were graven with an iron pen and lead in the rock forever! For I know that my redeemer lives and that he shall stand at the latter day upon the earth. And though after my skin, worms destroy this body, yet in my flesh shall I see God:

I call this a Default Position. Others might refer to Job's expression as his Core Values. Reading the context tells us that he is extremely emotional at this point. If you were facing dire circumstances, would you be able to find your focal point?

The poetry of his words presents a vivid picture.

Your words written in stone. Job got his wish. His words have been shared in every language and have transformed countless lives for eternity. Do you believe that your words spoken during times of great stress are worth sharing forever?

Job's default position is the Lord Jesus Christ. He understood that God would provide someone to redeem man. He knew that this Redeemer would come at the right time. **(1 Peter 1:10)** *Of which salvation the prophets have inquired and searched diligently, who prophesied of the grace that should come unto you:*

Paul tells us it was at the right time. **(Gal. 4:4-5)** *But when the fulness of the time was come, God sent forth His Son, made of a woman, made under the law, to redeem them that were under the law, that we might receive the adoption of sons.*

Job also had confidence that even though death would come to him, he would live again in the presence of that Redeemer. His words testify to the truth that the ancients understood. Death is not the end of all things. Eternal life is not more of this same difficulty in the shadow land but a bright existence with God.

In the times when you are greatly stressed, is the assurance of life with Christ your default position?

DECEMBER 6

I Know

2 TIMOTHY 1:12

For the which cause I also suffer these things: nevertheless, I am not ashamed: for I know Whom I have believed and am persuaded that He is able to keep that which I have committed unto Him against that day.

This is the last known letter of Paul. He says that he is aware that his departure from the shadow land is soon. When you take a trip, the journey which directs you to a known or unfamiliar destination requires you to use GPS or a map, perhaps just highway markers to guide your way. Your reasons for leaving the familiar can be varied, just as the importance of the journey will vary.

Hardships may be a calculated part of your trip. You certainly don't begin this undertaking because of the difficulty but for the reward. Paul was imprisoned for the One whom he loved. He knew that Jesus was dependable and that He was more than able to make the destination glorious.

There is no disappointment in Christ. Your service to Him is difficult. Many have experienced great loss for the love of their Savior. But His understanding of our journey and His ability to make our reward greater than any temporary suffering that meets us in our travels makes us fully persuaded that He can do more than what He has promised. **(1 Cor. 2:9)** *But as it is written, Eye has not seen, nor ear heard, neither has entered into the heart of man, the things which God has prepared for them that love Him.*

Against that day – What day? The day that Jesus will take up the throne and reward His faithful servants for their joyful obedience. No one can outgive God, and God never forgets our faithfulness.

Commit your way unto the Lord; He is a good master. His rewards are eternal. The benefit package is out of this world!

DECEMBER 7

Christmas Giver

MATTHEW 1:24-25
*Then Joseph being raised from sleep, did as the angel of the
Lord had bidden him and took unto him his wife:
And knew her not till she had brought forth her firstborn
son: and he called his name JESUS.*

You would be doing well if you had a Joseph as part of your ministry. *(Matt.1:19)* calls him a "just man." I believe that he was Biblically literate; that is, he not only knew the scriptures but understood the promise. Such a man in your fellowship studies the Bible and is moved by the promises of God.

There is no record of him ever speaking a word, but he was one who listened to God. Four times we are told that God spoke to him in a dream ***(1:20; 2:13; 2:19; 2:22.)*** That is a lot of listening. Four courageous moves for a young family. This man is not the normal carpenter. I call him a man of prayer.

Because he listened to God (we would do better in our prayer experience if we listened instead of talked,) we see that he was a man who protected his family. He protected his wife's reputation through marriage. He protected her by patience, waiting to share intimacy with her till after Jesus' birth. Through his listening, the family lived in safety and fulfilled scripture.

Joseph was also a provider. He worked with his hands to care for his family. Carpentry is a job that always has opportunity. He provided Jesus a home by naming Him. Naming is claiming, and Joseph declared his obedience to God and his love for Jesus by this legal expression.

Is Joseph unique? I believe that he was prepared by our loving Heavenly Father for this privileged role. I also want to believe that developing "Josephs" is part of your ministry. Men need to be encouraged to understand God's calling, see the value in what they do, and be equipped to do the work.

DECEMBER 8

Caution! This Will Kill

ROMANS 7:12-13

Wherefore the law is holy, and the commandment holy, and just, and good. Was then that which is good made death unto me? God forbid. But sin, that it might appear sin, working death in me by that which is good; that sin by the commandment might become exceeding sinful.

Many a well-meaning, but nevertheless ignorant teacher has misrepresented the Law of Moses. This misinformation can come in a variety of ways. An extreme is antinomianism – "Sin as I please and still be forgiven." Others are like the Pharisees – Jesus + circumcision + keep the Law = Salvation. Two extremes that are extremely wrong.

But Paul tells us the truth about the Law. *"It is holy, and just, and good,"* but it can't save anyone! (**Rom. 3:20**) *Therefore by the deeds of the law there shall no flesh be justified in His sight: for by the law is the knowledge of sin.*

The mirror isn't evil because it shows you the truth about your questionable dietary choices. But the mirror has no ability to change the results. The Law presents the way of righteous living. (**Gal. 3:12b**) *... the man that does them shall live in them.*

It also declares the consequences of failing to keep the Law. (**Gal. 3:10**) *For as many as are of the works of the law are under the curse: for it is written, Cursed is every one that continues not in all things which are written in the book of the law to do them.*

The Law cannot make anyone righteous. It reflects God's nature and reveals our fallen nature. To make it any more than a teacher or a mirror makes the Law a killer. Guilt does not make us clean. We are sinners by nature and by choice, and the law makes this clear. (**Gal. 3:24**) *Wherefore the law was our schoolmaster to bring us unto Christ, that we might be justified by faith.*

To teach anything else makes it deadly.

DECEMBER 9

Both Ends Against the Middle

PHILIPPIANS 2:12-13

Wherefore, my beloved, as you have always obeyed, not as in my presence only, but now much more in my absence, work out your own salvation with fear and trembling. For it is God who works in you both to will and to do of His good pleasure.

How do you know that God loves you? My response is, "*The Cross of Christ.*" What is God's attitude toward my spiritual condition? (**Rom. 8:29**) *For whom He did foreknow, He also did predestinate to be conformed to the image of His Son, that He might be the firstborn among many brethren.*

Our text encourages us to keep on keeping on in our spiritual development. A truly regenerated soul does not need human accountability. That does not mean that help from others is not needed or discouraged. (**Gal. 6:2**) *Bear one another's burdens, and so fulfil the law of Christ.* That is why you have a job! Spiritual leadership is part of God's plan for our success, but the Holy Spirit has given us a new heart and we want what Jesus wants. (**1 John 4:19**) *We love Him, because He first loved us.*

So, seeking to grow and be like Jesus is now part of our DNA. Paul says, *with fear and trembling* – respect for our Father and understanding of what might be lost in the way of honor and reward should also be strong motivations to keep us on the upward way.

But there is more! Father and His love for us does not sit by and merely observe our course. No, He is actively involved in the Divine mandate of making us like Christ. (**Eph. 2:10**) *For we are His workmanship, created in Christ Jesus unto good works, which God has before ordained that we should walk in them.*

Therefore, God has saved us, given us new natures; our motivation is now loving obedience, Father has made it clear to us of the possible loss and rewards available, and He is active in helping us. Success!

DECEMBER 10

As Long As He Sought The LORD

2 CHRONICLES 26:5

And he (King Uzziah) sought God in the days of Zechariah, who had understanding in the visions of God: and as long as he sought the LORD, God made him to prosper.

I can still see that portion of this verse. It was a business card that contained this encouragement,

"... *And as long as he sought the LORD, God made him to prosper."* 2 Chron. 26:5

My friend had taped it to the door of his auto shop. He was sincere in his desire to seek God. We met once a week for years for an early morning Bible study. (5:30 AM was not easy for me!) Then another friend joined us, then my second son got up early to join in. It was good that it was in my home, but embarrassing if I overslept!

God helped Uzziah defeat enemies, develop the protection of his nation, even helped him become successful with cattle and growing grapes! His army was well equipped, and he became creative in developing military equipment.

But pride got in his way. He was angry when corrected and unrepentant. He tried to do things which were against God's known will, so leprosy took him out. Instead of being blessed and being a blessing, he was isolated and removed from direct leadership.

Though we would never do such a thing, God is still in the business of correcting His children. **(Heb. 12:6)** *For whom the Lord loves he chastens and scourges every son whom he receives.* Seeking the will and blessing of God is the privilege of His chosen. Thinking we can do it all without our obedience to His Word, His Will, and His Watch care is playing the fool.

Pride does go before destruction. Some of you are so gifted that you can do it all. But you cannot. What do you have that you have not been given? If your title is "Pastor," it does not mean, Almighty.

DECEMBER 11

And the Miserable Comforter Award Goes To...

JOB 16:1-2, 5, 21

*Then Job answered and said, I have heard many such
things: miserable comforters are you all.
[5] But I would strengthen you with my mouth, and the
movement of my lips should asswage your grief.
[21]O that one might plead for a man with God, as a man pleads for his neighbor!*

What did your mother tell you? *"If you have nothing good to say, say nothing."* Men want to fix things, or they don't want to talk about it. If men think they have **the answer**, we won't be quiet until we have made our point.

Job's friends did care about him. They made an effort to come to his side and sat with him for seven days *(See Job 2:11-13.)* But when Job opened his mouth, their limited understanding of his horrific story came out of their mouths. The flood gates were open.

Those who pass censures must expect to have them retorted. Angry answers stir up men's passions, but never convince of judgment nor set truth in a clear light. What Job says of his friends is true of everyone. In comparison with God, we shall be made to see and own that we are miserable comforters. Whether under the conviction of sin, terrors of our conscience, or the arrests of death, only the blessed Holy Spirit can comfort effectually. All others, without him, do it miserably and to no purpose.

Whatever our brethren's sorrows are, we ought by sympathy make them our own. Since we do not control anything in life, these troubles may soon be our own. Our responsibility to each other should be a compassionate response to difficulty. Job's response in (v5), is actually a good pattern to follow, unless you want to win the **Miserable Comforter Award: (From Job 16)**

1. Give Strengthen – (v5) How? By getting others to look up. *(Ps. 30:5)*
2. Show Comfort – (v5) *(2 Cor. 1:3-4)*
3. Be Patient – (v6) *(John 11:35)*
4. Be An Intercessor – (v21) *(Eph. 6:18)*

DECEMBER 12

All Tears

REVELATION 21:4-5

And God shall wipe away all tears from their eyes; and there shall be no more death, neither sorrow, nor crying, neither shall there be any more pain: for the former things are passed away. And He that sat upon the throne said, Behold, I make all things new. And He said unto me, Write: for these words are true and faithful.

One of the greatest things about being a servant of the King is bringing comfort to others. As John introduces us to a "lift the curtain and peek" view of eternity, Father helps us glimpse at what He will do for all who trust His Son. You would give yourself a great ministry boost if this passage lived deeply in your heart.

Why do we cry? Whatever the reason, God assures us that in wiping away our tears He will be a greater comfort than the sorrow that wrings our hearts. Death is defeated. That, which consumed our souls with weeping is gone, and physical pain is no longer possible – it will never return, for all of the fullness of eternal life in Christ now possesses us.

Our reality is now directed by a new paradigm. All that could darken our way is gone. The dread night of the soul will never be experienced again, "for the Lamb is the light."

As you prepare your heart with eternal promises, Father will bring the helpless and the hopeless to you. He will call upon you to speak these words, -*for they are true and faithful.* The Holy Spirit will use your confidence in our future to bring poor souls out of despair and make them *"prisoners of hope."*

Your responsibility is to know and believe the faithfulness of your Father. The Holy Spirit will use your preparedness as He sees fit. Burdens may not be lifted immediately but that is not your assignment. You are just a messenger.

DECEMBER 13

A Form of Godliness

2 TIMOTHY 3:1-5

This know also, that in the last days perilous times shall come. For men shall be lovers of their own selves, covetous, boasters, proud, blasphemers, disobedient to parents, unthankful, unholy. Without natural affection, trucebreakers, false accusers, incontinent, fierce, despisers of those that are good. Traitors, heady, high minded, lovers of pleasures more than lovers of God; Having a form of godliness, but denying the power thereof: from such turn away.

Looking for an explanation of "woke" thinking? Look no further! I understand that the term "*last days*" might be difficult to pin down but the description Paul provides and my observations about our culture give me hope and dismay - hope in the soon return of Christ; dismay at seeing the denial of the truth before my eyes.

I should not be surprised, for Jesus said this would happen. (**Luke 18:8b**) ... *Nevertheless, when the Son of man comes, shall he find faith on the earth?*

When Jesus returns, the spiritual condition of the world will be denial of the truth. (*Not very Amillennial of Jesus, is it?*)

Paul's description and the spiritual condition of man has been true in every generation. (**Rom. 3:11-12**) *There is none that understands, there is none that seeks after God. They are all gone out of the way, they are together become unprofitable; there is none that does good, no, not one.*

Does that stop Paul from preaching the Gospel? No. Should it stop us from speaking the truth? No. But listen to Paul's advice. Those who think this way believe they are right and moral. They believe that prohibition and legislation will transform the heart of man. The heart of the problem is the problem of the heart. Do not connect your ministry with their misdirection. "*You must be born again,*" is the only answer.

DECEMBER 14

The Skin of My Teeth

JOB 19:20-21

My bones cleave to my skin and to my flesh, and I am escaped with the skin of my teeth. Have pity upon me, have pity upon me, O you my friends; for the hand of God has touched me.

Only a few of my close friends have known the sweetness of this sentiment from my lips. They have shared a recent challenge and I ask *"Are you bragging or complaining?"* Yes, I am a real sweet guy!

There are some people that look for opportunities to be the center of attention and sympathy. They seek out their "15 minutes of fame" and are the ones that a TV reporter usually finds to comment on the recent "Breaking News." I am the guy that mocks their comments.

How do you respond to hurting people? Hopefully, better than I. Job draws a sorrowful picture of the way his trauma has affected his physical appearance. This is more than weight loss. Do you understand that loss of appetite is a clear sign of deep trouble? Eating disorders should command our attention as a cry for help. The symptom is a process of distress, whether it be over-eating, bulimia, or anorexia. You know that Jesus is the answer, but you might not be qualified to give the help they need. Find someone skilled to help.

God told us Job's backstory, but Job did not know what we know. He asks for pity from his friends. Wendell Kempton defined pity as, "*A leap from the shores of mercy to the plateau of action.*" Words are not enough, especially cruel words. Job declares that God's hand has touched him. Job knows that God has allowed this, but knowing is not enough.

We may not understand, nor can we change the purposes of God in every situation, but we are capable and must be willing to bring a loving touch to hurting people.

Yes, you need to literally touch them.

DECEMBER 15

How'ya Doin'?

1 PETER 3:15-17

But sanctify the Lord God in your hearts: and be ready always to give an answer to every man that asks you a reason of the hope that is in you with meekness and fear: Having a good conscience; that, whereas they speak evil of you, as of evildoers, they may be ashamed that falsely accuse your good conversation in Christ. For it is better, if the will of God be so, that you suffer for well doing, than for evil doing.

How do you respond when someone attacks your way of life? I am sure you are like me and would like to speak the truth all the time, but how can we? Is there sincerity in their inquiry, or is it according to the old sayings, "*Laugh, and the world laughs with you. Cry, and you cry alone.*"

What does it mean to *Sanctify God in our hearts?* I understand that the word sanctify means to "set apart for holy use." So, I am giving God the control of my heart, and by that process, I will be able to speak about how Father gives me hope in times of difficulty, even when those that ask, ask only to use it against me. I want to think that *meekness and fear* present the idea that your response is not to be used as a weapon but as an expression of hope.

I have found that when people attack you verbally, they are looking for a similar response so things will escalate. My wife calls it "feeding their demons." We are told in **(Prov. 15:1)** *A soft answer turns away wrath: but grievous words stir up anger.* We are to speak the truth in love, even to our enemies. Father will protect us; Jesus promised that, and the Holy Spirit will use what He gave us to bring conviction in their hearts.

Though Peter is speaking about antagonistic attacks on the people of God, we can use his direction to help us speak boldly for Jesus at any time. If Jesus is up front in our thoughts, He will be first in our speech.

DECEMBER 16

Hindered Prayer

1 PETER 3:7

Likewise, husbands, dwell with them according to knowledge, giving honor unto the wife, as unto the weaker vessel, and as being heirs together of the grace of life; that your prayers be not hindered.

Perhaps this might be the greatest ministry advice ever written. Peter addressed it to all believing men, but it has such an eternal impact on your calling that I am going to "stand by my guns" in this one.

The example of Sarah, as she learned to respect Abraham, leaves little room for us to consider this trivial advice. We *dwell* - or commit to the success of our wives. We are joined together but we must treat them as divinely special. We must work to gain the knowledge of what makes her thrive. Peter says that this is part of our job, so don't get frustrated because she does not think as you, or you want a "one size fits all" kind of wife. The lifelong study of your wife will make you a better servant of the King.

Giving honor – that does not mean she has to earn it, but putting up with you is worth some kind of a medal! Treat her as a friend. Speak to her with kindness and the respect that you want from others.

The Weaker Vessel – when we were younger, my wife could dead man carry me up a flight of stairs. Peter is not speaking about physical strength specifically. She is not a tow truck. She is not made of tungsten steel. Her physical and emotional make-up is different from yours. Hard words spoken to you may seem like pebbles, but spoken to her heart, they may be like boulders. I do not use a china gravy boat to collect dirty motor oil. Your words have weight. Be careful.

Joint heirs, prayers not hindered – here is the ministry challenge. You were called, but Father gave her to help you. She can help you if you teach her, if you share with her, if you pray with her. The Holy Spirit will make her strong - if you don't shut her out.

DECEMBER 17
Excited & Ignorant

ROMANS 10:2-4
For I bear them (Israel) record that they have a zeal of God, but not according to knowledge. For they being ignorant of God's righteousness, and going about to establish their own righteousness, have not submitted themselves unto the righteousness of God. For Christ is the end of the law for righteousness to everyone that believes.

Paul is in a powerful portion of his epistle that speaks to God's Sovereignty. He uses the zeal of some of his nation to reveal God's marvelous grace. These countrymen of Paul's also represent many religious people of every viewpoint. They show a determined enthusiasm for their belief system; at times we might call them fanatical. They are convinced that human effort or sacrifice will assure their acceptance with the deity they worship. But their belief is not based in the truth. God has declared the way. **(Rom. 4:5)** *But to him that works not, but believes on Him that justifies the ungodly, his faith is counted for righteousness.*

Man, left on his own, will always seek to earn his way into Heaven. I do not need to convince you of this, but the statistics tell us that you have people in your seats that still are asking these questions: *"If I am good enough, will God love me? What more can I do to keep God loving me?"*

How do we find these confused souls? We must learn to ask salvation questions that draw out testimony. Often, these dear souls, when asked about their testimony, will speak about their family background, baptism, communion, membership, or how long they have attended the church. Paul says they are ignorant. They may not be willfully ignorant, but they do not understand the Gospel. They are afraid of not being good enough. The key is to change their focus from, "Am I good enough?" to "Look, how good Jesus is!" (**1 Thess. 1:9b**) *… and how you turned to God from idols to serve the living and true God.*

DECEMBER 18

He Named Them All

GENESIS 2:19-20

And out of the ground the LORD God formed every beast of the field, and every fowl of the air; and brought them unto Adam to see what he would call them: and whatsoever Adam called every living creature, that was the name thereof. And Adam gave names to all cattle, and to the fowl of the air, and to every beast of the field; but for Adam there was not found a help meet for him.

I just started my Bible reading cycle back into Genesis. Isn't it wonderful how the Holy Spirit keeps on showing us new things? This passage struck me. Adam and Eve were given all the knowledge they needed to operate in this world. They were naked but not afraid. God gave Adam the smarts to name everything! They knew how to tend and take care of everything in their world. And it was their world to care for and protect.

(Ps. 8:5-6) *For You have made him a little lower than the angels and have crowned him with glory and honor. You made him to have dominion over the works of Your hands; You have put all things under his feet.* Man is still held responsible for the care of this world and will have to give a final report someday.

It is sad to realize all that we have lost through the fall of man. God gave us all we needed for a healthy existence, but sin has made us stupid. Instead of teaching life, we spend our existence in the fear of death. I am thankful that all we need is found in the second Adam, the Lord Jesus Christ.   **(2 Peter 1:3)** *According as His divine power has given unto us all things that pertain unto* **life and godliness***, through the knowledge of Him that has called us to glory and virtue:*

In the knowledge of the Holy is understanding. Jesus gave us science and medicine. He gave common sense and the understanding we need to be safe and prosper. The "Good Book" is more than a map to glory. It is **Basic Instructions Before Leaving Earth.**

DECEMBER 19

Flee!

1 CORINTHIANS 6:18-20

Flee fornication. Every sin that a man does is without the body; but he that commits fornication sins against his own body. What? know you not that your body is the temple of the Holy Spirit which is in you, which you have of God, and you are not your own? For you are bought with a price: therefore, glorify God in your body, and in your spirit, which are God's.

You may not need a lot of explanation about the text, but you still need the warning. In the Greek world, *"to play the Corinthian,"* was to sell yourself to all kinds of excess and moral corruption.

We know that God's Word tells us that any kind of sexual behavior outside the bonds of marriage (one man and one woman, for life) is sin. The text makes it clear. The lust of the flesh is not the kind of temptation that is likened to passing a moist finger through the flame of a candle. No, it is like passing that finger through the flame of an acetylene torch. It will destroy the digit! The results of fornication may bring physical sickness, but we can be sure that emotional and spiritual death will also come. **(James 1:14-15)** *But every man is tempted, when he is drawn away of his own lust, and enticed. Then when lust has conceived, it brings forth sin: and sin, when it is finished, brings forth death.*

God is jealous of His Temple. Though we may not live as His dwelling place, it is certain that we are His because of the price He paid. *(I believe we have failed in making this clear.)* God has the ownership, and the sooner we agree with Him the better off we will be.

If we focus on bringing glory to Christ and not feeding our lusts, we will put ourselves in the place of blessing. I am imagining the picture of a place being "corner clean," and that is on two levels, spiritual and physical. This is accomplished by fixing our attention on Jesus. It is more than decision, it is a process that only the Holy Spirit can make real.

DECEMBER 20

Essential Information

1 CORINTHIANS 2:2
*For I determined not to know anything among you,
save Jesus Christ, and Him crucified.*

The last two churches I pastored allowed me to get a good handle on the spiritual condition of the leaders. The Chairman of the Pulpit Committee asked that last question: "Pastor, do you have any questions for us?" This was what I asked, *"I love to hear the stories of others. Please, would each of you tell me your story. How did you come to Christ? What does Jesus mean to you?"*

These were people chosen to lead the church at a very important time. Listening to their stories, without critiquing them, was a great opportunity to know the spiritual health of the church and also show interest in each one as a believer. If you will listen to them, it prepares them to listen to you.

Using this same kind of question with everyone who is affected by your leadership will give insight to their spiritual condition, how you can help them, and possibly begin the work of creating witnesses. If you can do this, without pressuring shy people, they will be forced to focus on Jesus and begin to see how you will help them be more for the Kingdom.

I remind you of the three points of a simple testimony:

1. What I was without Christ.
2. How I came to Christ.
3. What trusting in Christ has done for me.

Though not all three are absolutely necessary to share every time, help your people to practice this so they can feel comfortable sharing in any time frame.

They will learn this from you. (**1 Corinthians 11:1**)

Be followers of me, even as I also am of Christ.

DECEMBER 21

Enemies of the Cross

PHILIPPIANS 3:18-19

(For many walk, of whom I have told you often, and now tell you even weeping, that they are the enemies of the cross of Christ. Whose end is destruction, whose God is their belly, and whose glory is in their shame, who mind earthly things.)

When you know that Jesus said the world would hate us and that we are told that to love the world system is to make ourselves the enemy of God, it is hard not to be a conspiracy theorist! But we also know that that is not the heart of God (**John 3:17!**) It is not the idea of "*us vs. the darkness,*" but it is "*the goodness of God that leads you to repentance* (**Rom.2:4b.**)

Why is Paul giving this warning? As this alarm is sounded, he tells us he is crying! People that he had cared for, even invested his life in, had betrayed the Gospel message. He spoke a similar warning to the Ephesians in (**Acts 20:29-31**) *For I know this, that after my departing shall grievous wolves enter in among you, not sparing the flock. Also, of your own selves shall men arise, speaking perverse things, to draw away disciples after them. Therefore watch, and remember, that by the space of three years I ceased not to warn every one night and day* **with tears**.

What are the signs of these enemies:

- Enemies of the Cross – they do not proclaim the Gospel – (**1 Cor.15:3-4**)
- Lost – *end is destruction* – waste, a life based on selfishness – (**Prov.16:25**)
- Self-satisfaction – lust is their theme. There is never any sacrifice for others – (**Eph.2:3**)
- Foolish – *glory is their shame* – they glorify in a lack of restraint, waste, and idleness – (**1 Thess. 4:7**)
- Misguided – *mind earthly things* – no interest in Spiritual life or submission to God – (**1 John 2:15**)

If you are faithful, you will experience this sadness.

DECEMBER 22

Mary, The Example of Obedience

LUKE 1:38

And Mary said, Behold the handmaid of the Lord; be it unto me according to your word. And the angel departed from her.

What makes the Christmas season so wondrous? I believe it is the supernatural – the interaction of God with His creation by means of the miraculous. The virgin birth of Christ is the foundational truth to our eternal destiny!

Mary's obedience and the specifics of the story present the supernatural:
- The Timing *(Gal. 4:4-5.)*
- The Messenger – *"If God became a man, you could expect a special announcement."*
- The Location *(Isa. 9:2.)*
- The Conditions – A virgin espoused *(Isa. 7:14.)*
- The Family – Joseph, but he is the wrong side of the tree *(Jer. 22:28-30; Matt. 1:12!)*
- The Woman – Mary, of the Royal line [*Luke 3.*]
- The Character of Mary – *Highly favored*, "much graced." Grace is God's gift and not earned by Mary. *Lord is with thee* – God's presence is revealed in her life.

How would you feel about this message? Father understood her fear, but she let Him handle it *(2 Tim. 1:7.) Favor with God* – God looks at our hearts. She was a woman who lived her obedience from the inside out. God's purposes for Mary are clear. *Conceive, bear a son* – All these are miracles under normal circumstances, but this is supernatural!

Mary's question is asked in innocence, not in doubt. The reply of the angel claims the power of the Holy Spirit and the promise of God's Word *(Ps. 2:7.)*

In verse 37, The angel presents a life principle *(Jer. 32:27.)* Our text gives us the heart of the matter. God decrees and Mary humbly obeys. She demonstrates a loving trust in her agreement. Her faith is fixed on the promise of God.

DECEMBER 23

Destroyed

HOSEA 4:6
My people are destroyed for lack of knowledge: because you have rejected knowledge, I will also reject you, that you shall not be a priest to Me: seeing you have forgotten the law of your God, I will also forget your children.

These are words spoken as a warning to a people who had intentionally turned their backs on the Law of God, and in doing so, the way to life. The power of this passage for the people to whom we minister must be firmly fixed in your heart.

Ignorance is its own reward. Failure and loss are certain when we throw out the directions and replace them with trial and error. Knowledge comes from instruction and the observation of success. To assume that success is the end result of effort is the definition of stupidity. God is the source of wisdom. **(Prov. 9:10)** *The fear of the LORD is the beginning of wisdom: and the knowledge of the holy is understanding.*

The consequences of rejecting the knowledge of God is the destruction of our society. We should expect more and more loss of life because our culture has rejected the Author of life. Those that say they stand for God but promote their own selfish concept of existence have created a world void of absolutes and no accountability to God. The children are the first to suffer and become sacrifices to the meaningless existence from the rule of the politically correct.

This is the world you live in, but God is still on His Throne. **(Ps. 2:4)** *He that sits in the heavens shall laugh: the Lord shall have them in derision.* Your mission has not changed. Your message is still the same, *"Look and live!"* **(Ps. 126:6)** *He that goes forth and weeping, bearing precious seed, shall doubtless come again with rejoicing, bringing his sheaves with him.*

The Master will make your effort glorious.

DECEMBER 24

Christmas Eve

LUKE 2:10-11

And the angel said unto them, Fear not: for, behold, I bring you good tidings of great joy, which shall be to all people. For unto you is born this day in the city of David a Savior, which is Christ the Lord.

Today is probably one of the busiest days in your calendar. If you are part of a big fellowship, your intention for worship, celebration, and outreach has been going on for days! Some of you are involved in multiple services on this day alone – you are willing, but it is exhausting! The tear-down will wait till days later!

Even the small local church has things at a high level of energy. Tonight, is the big push! Lots of music, lots of people taking part – the "Marthas" are fussing in the church kitchen because all the cookies are not here!

It is easy for everyone to be so wired that "the why" might be lost.

Keeping the "main thing, the main thing" is part of your responsibility! Your opportunity to show the love of Jesus is your task! Encourage, appreciate, compliment, and keep people breathing! Your formal part in this pageantry might be small, but your influence is huge! We know that the dating of this event is traditional, and this celebration is "extra-scriptural." Yes, the world seeks to ignore our text, and money seems to drive the whole madness – BUT, with the Holy Spirit's power, you can make it all about Jesus.

But you should have started last month…

Oh well, Merry Christmas!

DECEMBER 25

Joseph, A Just Man

MATTHEW 1:24
Then Joseph being raised from sleep did as the angel of the Lord had bidden him, and took unto him his wife:

We often look for meaning in the unusual, the spectacular, the dramatic, yet the tremendous worth of a person can be discovered in the ordinary. Such was the life of Joseph. His character and faithfulness to his role made it possible for our eternal celebration.

The narrative of the Christmas story from Joseph's viewpoint reveals our celebration is based in the promise of God and not the tradition of men.

Espoused – the vows were already exchanged – a divorce would be required to break the contract.

Before they came together – before the wedding night.

Found with child – This would mean fornication and the law called for death **(Deut. 22:23-24.)** *Her husband* – this speaks not about legal status but a relationship of deep affection. *A just man* – more than an outward action – he was loving, compassionate, and controlled **(Prov. 16:32.)** We need men like Joseph, reflecting the love of Christ in the everyday. *A public example* – a tripled Greek word meaning to expose to infamy. But he had to do something! *Put her away* – this means a writing of divorce **(Deut. 24:1.)** This would still shame her without the death. God gave him a dream. Calling him *Son of David* – reminded him of the promise to David. Joseph was not ignorant of God's Word. He understood and believed God's promises. *Conceived by the Holy Spirit* – The Angel's announcement shows that the miracle of the virgin birth is explained through promise and the identity of this Son. Before, it didn't sound right, now it makes sense **(Isa. 9:6!)** *Jesus* – Jehovah Saves, and He shall do just that! Joseph's actions speak of his faith in God. His love for Mary gives Him wings, and he acts quickly. Joseph did the ordinary and turned it into the extraordinary through faith.

DECEMBER 26

Boxing Day

PSALMS 68:18-20
You have ascended on high, You have led captivity captive: You have received gifts for men; yes, for the rebellious also, that the LORD God might dwell among them. Blessed be the Lord, who daily loads us with benefits, even the God of our salvation. Selah He that is our God is the God of salvation; and unto GOD the Lord belong the issues from death.

EPHESIANS 4:8
Wherefore He said, When He ascended up on high, He led captivity captive, and gave gifts unto men.

Today is Boxing Day! In England, Christmas Day was traditionally a religious day of celebration. The following day was the day you carried gifts and shared the holiday with extended family and friends. As our children became adults and established their own families and celebrations, Boxing Day became the day they would come to our home, and we would celebrate together. The Christmas story is read from Matthew, and we open one present at a time! It is a delightful day with good food and a loving family. This has never been "a command performance," but we all look forward to this time together.

We give to each other because God is the giver of every good gift. The Psalmist tells us that He gives even to the rebellious that we might live in His love. The Gift of His Son declares boldly that He is our Salvation for He controls death. To be delivered from our enemy is one tremendous gift!

Paul expands the thought in his quote in Ephesians. Our Great Redeemer has also prepared our future: *Ascended on high,* captivated us in His love.

Captivity captive, assuring our eternity, and given us, daily, what we need to live with and serve Him.

Gave gifts to men. The indwelling Holy Spirit has made us accepted in the Beloved.

Father has planned for us to gather in His Home! Every day, in Jesus, is Boxing Day!

DECEMBER 27

How Shall I Come To You?

1 CORINTHIANS 4:18-21

Now some are puffed up, as though I would not come to you. But I will come to you shortly, if the Lord will, and will know, not the speech of them which are puffed up, but the power. For the kingdom of God is not in word, but in power. What will you? shall I come unto you with a rod, or in love, and in the spirit of meekness?

Do you understand your position? If you are new to ministry, this may not be something you have pondered. Most will answer the question with a reference to the title on the search committee job description. Perhaps it is starting to click that I am not focusing on titles. You are a servant of the living God. (**Ps. 37:23-24**) *The steps of a good man are ordered by the LORD: and he delights in his way. Though he fall, he shall not be utterly cast down: for the LORD upholds him with his hand.*

You are placed here by God. You are commissioned with an assignment by the King. You are empowered by the Holy Spirit for this task. That doesn't mean that you know it all. No, there is much to learn, and you are not the master of anyone, but you are intended to be a servant leader.

Not everyone is as spiritually minded as you. Most of the sheep are headstrong and avoid correction. Instruction that challenges "their liberty," is not easy for them to accept. So, they are "puffed up." If you do not understand your position, there is a possibility you will fold and lose your opportunity to bless. Or you may try to force the issue, and the sheep will be frightened and flee. You must learn to use your "rod and staff" so that you can comfort the sheep, not crush them. Your power comes from the One who called you.

He did call you, didn't He?

You are going to make mistakes. Don't let one of them be this, you took your eyes off of Jesus. He did not choose you to make you a failure.

DECEMBER 28

Blessed Hope

TITUS 2:11-13

For the grace of God that brings salvation has appeared to all men, Teaching us that, denying ungodliness and worldly lusts, we should live soberly, righteously, and godly, in this present world; Looking for that blessed hope, and the glorious appearing of the great God and our Savior Jesus Christ.

This was a passage that was easier to memorize than others. The soon return of Christ is my hope. It stirs my heart to see His control in a confusing world, trust His promise, and know that the future is glorious!

The unmerited favor of God has brought eternal life to us. Through the finished work of Christ on Calvary, We begin to understand the heart of God for the lost.

(2 Cor. 5:14) *For the love of Christ constrains us; because we thus judge, that if One died for all, then were all dead:*

The Blessed Hope teaches that God has provided, no, requires us to understand that new life in Christ means that the life we live is really new. We told to refuse to live our lives in ways that deny God's law. We must not continue doing what He hates. We must live with purpose, doing what is right and pleasing before God. We need to do it right now, even if the world is confused by our choices or hates us for them.

Jesus gave us a promise, "I Will return." But it is not just for a visit; He is coming for us ***(John 14:3!)***

He is all we will ever need. He is our Savior and the great promise giver and the great promise keeper. His return will be glorious because Father has had it planned for a long time, and all that He does is perfect!

When the way is weary and you hurt in more ways than one, think about our Blessed Hope. I quote an old spiritual, *"Soon I will be done with the troubles of the world, I'm going to live with God!"*

DECEMBER 29

All Scripture

2 TIMOTHY 3:16-17
All scripture is given by inspiration of God, and is profitable for doctrine, for reproof, for correction, for instruction in righteousness: That the man of God may be perfect, thoroughly furnished unto all good works.

EPHESIANS 2:20
And are built upon the foundation of the apostles and prophets, Jesus Christ himself being the chief corner stone.

2 CORINTHIANS 1:20
For all the promises of God in Him are yes, and in Him Amen, unto the glory of God by us.

This comment has been made several times in my ministry, and it has made a lasting impression. *"You certainly use a lot of Scripture in your sermons!"*

It is the only way I know to preach.

When Paul says, "All Scripture," is he speaking about the New Testament as well? Well, at the time of this letter, the New Testament Cannon had not been created. The four Gospels were in circulation and all of Paul's letters are out there, but not the collection you have and love. So specifically, he is talking about the Law, the Writings, and the Prophets - our Old Testament, but in a different arrangement.

Does that mean the New Testament is not inspired as the Old Testament? No. Consider what Paul says in (**Eph.2:20.**) The Apostles are grammatical equality with the Prophets, and all their writings are based on the person of Christ. The words of the writers of our New Testament (Luke included) are just as inspired as the Old Testament. Our confidence in the inspiration and authority of the New Testament is sure.

As (**2 Cor. 1:20**) encourages us to have confidence in every promise, may you share that confidence with those you teach. To paraphrase this last passage, "Not every promise is written to me, but every promise is written for me!"

DECEMBER 30

Where Is My Purpose?

JOB 17:11-12

My days are past, my purposes are broken off, even the thoughts of my heart. They change the night into day: the light is short because of darkness.

Solomon tells us that, for life under the sun to have meaning, it must manifest three things: Purpose, Progress, and Permanence. Though the works of our hands can be blessed by God, nothing in this life will endure. **(Ps. 90:17)** *And let the beauty of the LORD our God be upon us: and establish thou the work of our hands upon us; yes, the work of our hands establish thou it.*

And there is the main point: where are we looking for purpose? I lived and ministered in Clarence Center, New York for several years. Today, I Google mapped my home/church. Everything is changed! Of course, it has! *But change only affects others; things are not supposed to change for me!*

All the things that Job used as anchors for his life have been destroyed in a few moments. He is saying, I can't even think straight! Night and day are reversed, and the daylight is too short!

When I transitioned into the supporting role of pulpit supply/interim pastor, Father made it easier on me because I wasn't even out of the pulpit for one Sunday. But right now, no one is looking for that help. If it wasn't for a loving Master, I would go crazy because ministry is not a job for me but a calling. Father knows how He wired me. He is teaching me that it is not what I do but whom I serve.

For almost 50 years, serving my King has meant being a pastor. I am learning that serving my King means being a servant. I have proclaimed, "*You must love what Jesus loves.*" I think I am learning how to do this differently. The task of writing these devotionals makes it easier. If I do what the King says, my purpose is not broken, just changed.

DECEMBER 31

With Every End, There is a Beginning

EZRA 1:3

Who is there among you of all His people? His God be with him, and let him go up to Jerusalem, which is in Judah, and build the house of the LORD God of Israel, (He is the God,) which is in Jerusalem.

I am thankful that Ezra follows 2 Chronicles in our English Bibles. The "teaser" at the end of Chronicles makes you want more about the next chapter in God's grace. Even then, Father only provides us enough to keep the hope alive.

My observation of the way God deals with man might seem to some, bleak. What I see is the wisdom of a Loving God. With every responsibility God gives to man, man eventually fails in his opportunity. The amazing thing is that God is not surprised by the failure and has already prepared the next opportunity. Even in our failure, God is glorified. He is not thwarted by our frailty but uses it as an even greater display of His abundant mercy and grace. **(Ps. 76:10)** *Surely the wrath of man shall praise You: the remainder of wrath shall You restrain.*

Because He loves us, He remembers how He made us. **(Ps. 103:13-14)** *Like as a father pities his children, so the LORD pities them that fear Him. For He knows our frame; He remembers that we are dust.*

So, where are we going with this? At this moment, you may feel that you have failed. If your personal sin is part of that failure, you know Father is ready to forgive and restore.

If your heart doesn't condemn you *(1 John 3:19-22,)* and you can't figure out why things are falling apart, your King is still in charge. He orders all the work for His glory and our good. If He was done with you, you would be home – but you are not. **(Philippians 1:21)** *For to me to live is Christ, and to die is gain.*

INDEX OF SCRIPTURE TEXTS	DATE
GENESIS	
2:18-20	12/18
3:5, 22	9/20
3:22,24	11/4
4:5-7	10/30
13:14	11/27
15:5-6	11/23
15:16	11/18
18:25	1/22
EXODUS	
4:24-26	10/7
18:17-18	2/10
34:5-7	11/16
LEVITICUS	
8:30	1/4
10:1-2	5/13
22:31-33	6/10
25:17	5/18
NUMBERS	
11:1	1/9
12:1-2	2/15
13:33	2/2
14:41-42	3/30
15:32-36	6/2
15:38-39	2/29
16:3-4	2/21
16:41,46,48	4/18
17:12-13	7/9
18:19	7/25
20:1-2	7/15
21:4-9	7/19
21:6-9	6/18

22:27	11/2
22:31-33	7/12
27:15-17	6/5
32:23	9/4
DEUTERONOMY	
3:25-26	8/1
10:15-17	9/6
15:7-8	5/28
15:16-17	11/30
19:3-4	5/26
19:15	5/21
21:6-8	5/19
22:10	9/13
28:66-67	10/10
29:29	10/1
30:14,19	10/11
31:29-30	9/22
JOSHUA	
1:5	3/4
7:20-21	2/28
JUDGES	
2:2-3	2/8
1 SAMUEL	
17:45	1/17
22:21-23	6/24
2 SAMUEL	
9:13	7/11
19:41-43	7/8
20:4-5	1/2
20:19	5/12
21:1	9/14
24:10,14	7/20
24:24	3/14

1 KINGS	
1:11	5/22
2:6,9	9/9
13:18	5/3
17:22-24	4/30
18:43-44	5/31
Chp. 19	1/26
19:4	3/18
19:9	3/19
21:29	6/7
2 KINGS	
2:9	7/24
10:16	6/29
10:18-19	8/27
18:4-5	8/19
1 CHRONICLES	
11:18-19	5/27
19:4	5/25
24:1	9/11
29:3-9	9/16
2 CHRONICLES	
3:17	9/18
10:7-8	3/2
11:4	3/5
14:11	3/24
16:7-9	1/5
19:2	6/13
19:2-3	11/10
20:12	6/4
20:12	11/20
20:35-37	11/26
21:6,20	10/18
25:16	10/28

26:5	12/10
29:36	8/5
30:18-20	10/26
EZRA	
1:3	12/31
JOB	
1:5	9/26
1:6	9/24
1:20-22	10/12
2:3-6	10/15
2:9-10	10/4
2:11-13	9/23
3:25-26	10/17
6:7-9	11/24
12:1-2	11/7
12:9-10	11/21
13:15	10/22
16:1-2,5,21	12/11
17:11-12	12/30
19:20-21	12/14
19:23-26	12/5
PSALMS	
39:1-3	2/27
39:4	2/20
39:7-9	2/26
51:1-2	2/3
51:3-6	2/4
51:7-12	2/5
51:13-19	2/6
66:18-19	5/11
76:9-10	3/15
77:1-3	6/20
81:10	4/21

85:10	9/7
86:10-11	9/30
86:18-20	12/26
94:17-18	11/3
101:3	7/7
103:13-14	7/21
103:14	1/11
104:33	7/10
110:5-7	7/3
115:1-3	2/19
116:11	9/2
120:1	4/3
121:1	4/4
122:1	4/5
123:3	4/6
124:4	4/7
125:1	4/8
126:1	4/9
127:1	4/10
128:1	4/11
129:1	4/12
130:1	4/13
131:1	4/14
132:1	4/15
133:1	4/16
134:1	4/17
138:2	9/5
138:7-8	10/9
139:1-6	4/24
139:7-12	4/25
139:13-18	4/26
139:13-18	4/27
139:19-24	4/28

PSALMS	
139:23-24	4/29
141:3-5	10/6
142:4-5	10/5
PROVERBS	
1:8-9	2/12
1:20-21	2/13
3:9-10	3/3
4:23	9/12
6:9-11	3/26
11:1	9/25
11:13-14	10/8
13:12	8/17
14:15	11/15
16:1-4	11/12
16:18	2/1
16:33	7/17
17:17	1/1
18:13	10/13
18:22	1/25
20:5-6	8/6
20:11	1/21
20:27	8/2
22:10	11/19
22:29	1/18
24:17-20	11/9
25:11-12	11/28
26:2	8/13
26:17	7/18
26:18-19	4/2
26:27-28	4/1
27:17	7/26
29:15	7/2

30:32-33	8/3
31:4-5	10/19
ECCLESIASTES	
1:2-3	11/17
3:1	11/8
3:11	2/9
5:1-7	3/6
5:3	7/5
5:4-7	8/23
7:8	5/4
9:11	1/13
11:5-6	7/14
SONG OF SOLOMON	
2:3-4	11/22
ISAIAH	
2:22	9/28
14:24,27	9/17
20:2	11/25
28:15	11/29
29:13	11/6
35:10	10/27
40:28-31	11/14
45:19	1/14
JEREMIAH	
1:10	3/1
EZEKIEL	
24:15-18	7/28
33:11	7/13
40:2	3/31
DANIEL	
7:13-14	1/7
10:19	5/23
HOSEA	

4:6	12/23
13:3-4	1/30
AMOS	
7:14-15	3/28
JONAH	
2:2	5/5
2:8	3/20
3:9-10	5/20
3:10 -4:1	1/28
MICAH	
6:8	8/24
7:8-9	5/7
7:8-9	5/30
7:18-19	5/24
HABAKKUK	
Chp. 1	1/27
MALACHI	
2:14-16	10/2
MATTHEW	
1:24	12/25
1:24-25	12/7
4:1	8/4
4:2-4	7/29
4:5-7	7/31
4:8-11	7/30
16:2-4	9/21
16:18	1/24
16:21-23	10/3
19:29	2/7
21:18-20	9/15
21:28-30	9/10
MARK	
1:37-38	1/20

6:31	5/29
LUKE	
1:38	12/22
2:10-11	12/24
4:17-19	1/8
5:17	2/22
6:19	3/21
7:35	2/24
8:54-55	3/29
9:49-50	3/17
10:2	4/20
10:38-42	5/2
11:13	3/25
11:23	6/16
11:24-26	1/6
16:22-23	6/1
18:1	1/10
18:8	1/19
18:13	6/21
18:15-17	6/22
22:10-12	8/31
22:31-32	8/30
JOHN	
5:14	5/6
6:70-71	6/23
7:5	5/14
8:7-9	2/23
9:1-3	6/27
9:6-7	11/1
13:34-35	2/17
14:3	1/31
16:23-24	6/28
ACTS	

5:20	6/11
8:26,29	6/8
8:36-37	6/26
13:38-39	6/9
14:15-17	8/11
14:17	7/1
15:37-38	5/8
19:1-6	8/16
ROMANS	
2:4	3/16
7:12-13	12/8
8:1	8/20
10:2-4	12/17
12:18-21	10/21
14:22-23	6/12
1 CORINTHIANS	
2:2	12/20
2:14-16	10/25
4:1-2	8/12
4:7	4/23
4:16	5/1
4:18-21	12/27
4:19-21	6/25
6:7-8	3/23
6:11	3/13
6:12	3/8
6:12	3/9
6:18-20	12/19
6:19-20	3/10
8:9-12	3/11
9:16	5/15
10:11-13	6/15
10:20-21	3/12

10:31-32	4/19
1 CORINTHIANS	
12:28-30	6/30
15:3-4	6/3
15:26	6/14
15:29	7/6
15:33-34	3/27
15:58	7/4
16:13-14	7/23
16:22	7/27
2 CORINTHIANS	
1:3-4	7/16
1:20-22	7/22
1:22	8/10
1:22	8/18
2:10-11	5/10
2:10-11	8/7
2:14-16	8/15
5:1-2	8/9
5:4	4/22
5:14-15	8/29
5:16-17	9/3
12:15	2/16
GALATIANS	
4:16	3/22
6:1-2	2/11
EPHESIANS	
2:1	1/3
PHILIPPIANS	
1:18	2/14
2:12-13	12/9
3:18-19	12/21
4:12-13	5/9

4:9	10/14
4:13	1/15
COLOSSIANS	
4:16	1/29
1 TIMOTHY	
1:19-20	10/31
3:7	11/13
2 TIMOTHY	
1:7	10/20
1:12	12/6
2:15	6/17
3:1-5	12/13
3:11-12	12/2
3:16-17	12/29
TITUS	
1:2	5/16
1:12-13	1/16
2:1	10/29
2:11-13	12/28
3:4-7	10/24
3:8	6/6
3:8-9	1/23
PHILEMON	
1:7	1/12
HEBREWS	
4:12-13	6/19
6:10	8/26
6:17-19	9/1
7:24-25	8/25
10:12-14	8/21
10:19-20	8/14
10:24-25	8/8
10:35-36	8/28

12:14-15	2/25
12:14-15	9/29
13:1-2	12/1
13:4	12/4
13:17	12/3
JAMES	
1:27	9/19
3:17-18	9/27
1 PETER	
3:1-2	**11/5**
3:7	12/16
3:15-17	12/15
5:4	10/16
3 JOHN	
1:4	3/17
1:9	9:8
JUDE	
1:24-25	5/17
1:24	11/11
REVELATION	
19:8	10/23
21:4-5	12/12
22:11-12	2/18
22:11-13	8/22